$2 No Return

COMPETING
ON ANALYTICS

COMPETING ON ANALYTICS

THE NEW SCIENCE OF WINNING

UPDATED, WITH A NEW INTRODUCTION

BY THOMAS H. DAVENPORT AND JEANNE G. HARRIS

HARVARD BUSINESS REVIEW PRESS

Boston, Massachusetts

The web addresses referenced in this book were live and correct at the time of the book's publication but may be subject to change.

Library of Congress Cataloging-in-Publication Data

Names: Davenport, Thomas H., 1954- author. | Harris, Jeanne G., author.
Title: Competing on analytics : the new science of winning / by Thomas H. Davenport and Jeanne G. Harris.
Description: Updated, with a new introduction. | Boston, Massachusetts : Harvard Business Review Press, [2017]
Identifiers: LCCN 2017013509 | ISBN 9781633693722 (hardcover : alk. paper)
Subjects: LCSH: Business intelligence. | Data mining. | Competition.
Classification: LCC HD38.7 .D38 2017 | DDC 658.4/013—dc22 LC record available at https://lccn.loc.gov/2017013509

The paper used in this publication meets the requirements of the American National Standard for Permanence of Paper for Publications and Documents in Libraries and Archives Z39.48-1992.

CONTENTS

Foreword   *vii*
   by David Abney, CEO, UPS

Introduction: Four Eras in Ten Years   *1*

Part 1 **The Nature of Analytical Competition**

   One   **The Nature of Analytical Competition**   *21*
          Using Analytics to Build a Distinctive Capability

   Two   **What Makes an Analytical Competitor?**   *45*
          Defining the Common Key Attributes
          of Such Companies

   Three   **Analytics and Business Performance**   *69*
          Transforming the Ability to Compete on Analytics
          into a Lasting Competitive Advantage

   Four   **Competing on Analytics with Internal Processes**   *91*
          Financial, M&A, Operations, R&D, and
          Human Resource Applications

   Five   **Competing on Analytics with External Processes**   *129*
          Customer and Supplier Applications

Part 2 **Building an Analytical Capability**

   Six   **A Road Map to Enhanced Analytical Capabilities**   *157*
          Progressing through the Five
          Stages of Analytical Maturity

Seven   **Managing Analytical People**   *187*
Cultivating the Scarce Ingredient
That Makes Analytics Work

Eight   **The Architecture of Analytics and Big Data**   *217*
Aligning a Robust Technical Environment
with Business Strategies

Nine   **The Future of Analytical Competition**   *249*
Approaches Driven by Technology, Human
Factors, and Business Strategy

Notes   *265*

Index   *279*

Acknowledgments   *293*

About the Authors   *297*

I'M CONVINCED THAT COMPLACENCY POSES ONE OF THE most serious threats to any business. Companies so intent on staying the course that they don't hear the footsteps behind them pay a high price for misguided satisfaction. Photographic film companies didn't fully appreciate the threat created by digital photography, and probably even less that it would come from smartphones. Newspapers dependent on classified ads didn't react proactively to online sites like Craigslist. Movie rental companies didn't react fast enough to streaming companies like Netflix.

The story is almost always the same. Winners become also-rans, and eventually case studies, because it was easier to keep doing the things that made them winners in the first place. The path of least resistance was more comfortable than challenging whether what built success would be enough to sustain it.

The founder of UPS, Jim Casey, knew the dangers of complacency and advocated for what he called "constructive dissatisfaction." Time and again, Casey restructured and reinvented UPS to counter a host of competitive threats. Over time, one of our biggest competitive advantages came from our early adoption of analytics as a means of continuously assessing and improving every facet of our business.

Analytics enabled us to design one of the first handheld devices, which we put in the hands of every one of our drivers in 1990. To truly harness the power of these devices, we had to kludge together what were then largely regional cellular networks into a proprietary network that covered the United States. That enabled us to gather information on the movement of every package in our system, which in turn helped us build one of the largest data warehouses in the world. The insights we gained via analytics enabled us to achieve new levels of efficiency and to share this learning with customers.

Given a taste of what was possible, our hunger for analytics grew. We created a suite of tools built on predictive models we called Package Flow Technologies. Deployed in 2003, these tools reduced 85 million miles annually. And by opening up our predictive engines to customers and giving them the same information we had, they could interact with our operations directly and personalize their delivery experience.

But for us the analytics jackpot is a prescriptive analytics model we named ORION (short for On-Road Integrated Optimization and Navigation), which tells our drivers which route they should follow to make their deliveries using the least amount of time—and fuel. It's not an overstatement to say that ORION has revolutionized our business. In *Competing on Analytics*, the book now in your hands, Tom Davenport and Jeanne Harris call ORION the "granddaddy" of real-time applications and say it "may be the largest commercial analytics project ever undertaken."

Before the digital revolution took hold, our managers laid out our drivers' routes with pushpins on maps inside our package hubs. Then we transferred that information to our drivers' handheld computers. Drivers were taught to follow pretty much the same route every day, delivering our commercial stops first and then their residential stops, because commercial customers were typically more demanding.

But with the e-commerce revolution, residential customers wanted more control over when and where their packages were delivered. Trying to meet the needs of both commercial and residential customers often meant drivers were crossing the same path multiple times, wasting time and fuel.

Our drivers were good at their jobs, and their customers loved them for their reliability and trustworthiness. But we foresaw a day when our drivers could not wring one more second of efficiency out of their routes. When *their* best would be *our* best. Then what would we do? (You have to remember these were the days before IBM's Watson was a *Jeopardy* champion and before we carried the computing power of early mainframes in our pocket.) What's more, some people in our company thought no computer could improve on what experienced UPS drivers already did so well.

Fortunately, our engineers created a thirty-page algorithm that allows us to determine the optimum route for each of our fifty-five thousand drivers to make their deliveries each day. ORION now shortens each driver's daily route by an average of seven to eight miles, which collectively saves us 100 million miles and 10 million gallons of fuel a year. All told, ORION generates more than $400 million in annual cost savings and avoidance for UPS.

In the process, we have realized the data we collect as a package flows through our network is often as valuable to the customer as the package itself. Based on data extracted from our network, customers are improving their business processes and making more informed decisions, which makes UPS a more valuable partner.

For years, our advertising proclaimed UPS as the company that loved logistics. We still love logistics, but we're forever indebted to analytics. And we've since expanded our use of analytics beyond optimizing our physical network, applying it in many other facets of our business.

This revised and expanded version of Tom and Jeanne's earlier work brings the analytics story forward, with new applications, insights, and forecasts. The authors show how analytics continues to transform technology from a supporting tool to a strategic advantage.

In *Competing on Analytics*, the authors not only introduced business leaders to analytics, they also made them analytical competitors, intimately attuned to its business and strategic value. Michael Lewis' book *Moneyball* may have made analytics cool (with a little help from Brad Pitt), but it took Tom Davenport and Jeanne Harris to make it a business imperative.

—David Abney, CEO, UPS
April 2017

COMPETING ON ANALYTICS

FOUR ERAS IN TEN YEARS

A REVOLUTION IN ANALYTICS

THE WORLD OF EXTRACTING INSIGHTS FROM DATA WAS relatively stable for its first thirty years or so. There were certainly technological advances, but the act of creating a bar chart or running a regression analysis didn't change much. An analyst in 1977 submitted the analysis program and the data to a computer on a deck of punched paper cards; the analyst in 2005 submitted it from a keyboard. But the other details were pretty similar.

Since the turn of the millennium, however, the pace of change has accelerated markedly. If we call the way that business intelligence and analytics were practiced before 2007 "Analytics 1.0," we've seen the advent of 2.0, 3.0, and 4.0 in the ten years since then—three massive changes in a decade in how analytics are undertaken within companies.

When we were researching and writing *Competing on Analytics* in 2005 and 2006, we were largely describing that earliest era and the companies that excelled at it (we'll recap the idea of "Analytics 1.0" in a moment). The companies that competed on analytics then were largely making the best of those older approaches to managing data and turning it into something valuable.

There is a lesson here. Extracting value from information is not primarily a matter of how much data you have or what technologies you use to analyze it, though these can help. Instead, it's how aggressively you exploit these resources and how much you use them to create new or better approaches to doing business. The star companies of *Competing on Analytics* didn't always use the latest tools, but they were very good at building their strategies and business models around their analytical capabilities. They were run by executives who believed that facts are the best guide to decisions and actions. They made data and analytics an integral component of their cultures.

That said, if the external world of analytics changes, the best companies will change along with it. We haven't checked to see whether all of the organizations we described in the original version of this book have evolved beyond Analytics 1.0, but we know many of them have. In this introduction, we'll describe the new opportunities for exploiting data and revolutionizing business that have emerged over the last decade. And we'll briefly describe the earlier eras—not for a history lesson, but to examine what we can learn from them.

Analytics 1.0 and Its Implications for Today

In the mid-2000s, when we wrote *Competing on Analytics*, the most sophisticated companies had mastered Analytics 1.0 and were beginning to think about the next stage. But many firms today are still solidly ensconced in a 1.0 environment. And even though there are more advanced analytical technologies and processes available, every organization still needs to do some 1.0 activities. So it's worth understanding this era even if you have generally moved on.

Analytics 1.0 was (or is, if you're still practicing it) heavy on *descriptive analytics*—reports and visuals explaining what happened in the past—and light on using analytics to predict the future (*predictive analytics*) or to make recommendations on how to do a job better (*prescriptive analytics*). While we've spent much of the past decade trying to encourage companies to move beyond descriptive analytics, they are still necessary; you need to know what has happened in your organization in the recent past and how that compares with the more distant past.

Sophisticated companies in 2017 still generate descriptive analytics, but they try to control their volume and they try to get users (rather than analytical professionals) to create them. A new set of tools has emerged to make "self-service analytics" much easier, particularly when creating visual analytics. Of course, many analytics users employed spreadsheets as their primary analytical tool, and that's still the case, despite issues around errors and the ease of creating "multiple versions of the truth" in spreadsheets.

One consistent problem throughout the eras has been data—getting it, cleaning it, putting it into databases for later access, and so on. As data proliferated over the past decades, a solution was needed in Analytics 1.0. The primary data storage solution developed and used during this period was the relational data warehouse. This was a big step forward from previous approaches to data storage, but it also brought substantial challenges. Getting data in through a process called *extract, transform, and load* (ETL) consumed a lot of time and resources. All data had to be structured in the same way (in rows and columns) before it could be stored. Eventually, data warehouses became so big and popular that it was difficult to know what resources were in them. And while the goal of the warehouse was to separate data for analysis from transactional systems, analytics became so important that some warehoused data was used in production applications.

It is not just technology that caused problems in Analytics 1.0. The culture of this era was reactive and slow. One analytical expert who grew up in those days described her role as "order taker." Managers would ask for some analysis on a problem they were facing, and an analyst would come back—often after a month or so of rounding up data and doing some form of quantitative analysis—with an answer. The manager might not understand the analytical methods used, and might not actually use the results in making a decision. But at least he or she looked like a data-driven executive.

One of the terms used to describe analytics during the Analytics 1.0 era was *decision support*. And the word *support* is appropriately weak. Analytics were used only to support internal decisions, and they were often ignored. Managers didn't typically have a close relationship with quantitative analysts, who largely stayed in the back office. As a result, many decisions continued to be made on intuition and gut feel.

Despite these challenges, the companies we found who *were* competing on analytics in the mid-2000s were making the best of a difficult situation. They figured out where analytics could help improve their decision making and performance, and they produced analytics in spades. It may have been slower and more difficult than it should have been, but they were dedicated enough to make analytics work for them. Their efforts were inspiring to us and to a lot of readers and listeners to the "competing on analytics" idea. But out in Silicon Valley, the world was already beginning to change.

Analytics 2.0: Big Data Dawns in the Valley

Ten years or so ago in Silicon Valley, the leading firms in the online industry (Google, eBay, PayPal, LinkedIn, Yahoo!, and so forth) were moving beyond Analytics 1.0. They had adopted a new paradigm for data and analytics, based on the need to make sense of all the customer clickstream data they had engendered. This data was voluminous, fast-moving, and fast-changing, and didn't always come in rows and columns. In short, it was *big data*. The new era of Analytics 2.0 applies mostly to those pioneering firms. We don't recommend that other types of organizations adopt their approaches directly, but there are many lessons that other companies can learn from Analytics 2.0.

In order to store, analyze, and act on all that data, the online firms needed some new technologies to handle it. So in 2006, Doug Cutting and Mike Cafarella created Hadoop, an open-source program for storing large amounts of data across distributed servers. Hadoop doesn't do analytics, but it can do minimal processing of data, and it's an inexpensive and flexible way to store big data.

Hadoop became the core of a collection of oddly named open-source technologies for processing big data. Pig, Hive, Python, Spark, R, and a variety of other tools became the preferred (at least in Silicon Valley) way to store and analyze big data. The analytics that were created were typically not that sophisticated (a data scientist friend referred to this as the "big data equals small math" syndrome), but the flexibility and low cost of the technologies, and the application of analytics to less structured forms of data, were big steps forward. The open-source development and ownership of these technologies began a slow but significant shift that continues today. Proprietary analytics and data management tools are often combined with open-source tools in many applications.

In order to both program in these new tools and do some data analysis as well, a new job category seemed in order. Practitioners of big data analytics began to call themselves *data scientists*. As Tom and his coauthor D. J. Patil (until recently, the chief data scientist at the White House), noted in their article "Data Scientist: The Sexiest Job of the 21st Century," these people were different than the average quantitative analyst.[1]

First of all, they weren't content to remain in the back office. Patil kept telling Tom that they want to be "on the bridge"—next to the CEO or some other senior executive, helping to guide the ship. Patil himself, for example, went from being a data scientist at LinkedIn to working in venture capital to being head of product at a startup, and then to the White House (where he admitted to having an office in the basement, but was at least in the right building).

Secondly, the data scientists we interviewed weren't interested in decision support. One called advising senior executives on decisions "the Dead Zone." They preferred in many cases to work on products, features, demos, and so forth—things that customers would use. LinkedIn developed *data products* like People You May Know, Jobs You May Be Interested In, and Groups You Might Like—and those offerings have been instrumental in that company's rapid growth and acquisition by Microsoft for $26 billion. Practically everything Google does—except, perhaps, for its phones and thermostats—is a product or service derived from data and analytics. Zillow has its Zestimates and several other data products. Facebook has its own version of People You May Know, and also Trending Topics, News Feed, Timeline, Search, and many different approaches to ad targeting.

It's also clear that analytics were core to the strategies of many of these firms. Google, for example, was formed around its PageRank algorithm. These companies competed on analytics perhaps more than any of the others we wrote about in the first version of this book. Such an alternative view of the objective and importance of analytics is a key lesson from Analytics 2.0 practitioners.

There was also a much more impatient, experimental culture to Analytics 2.0. The most common educational background we discovered among data scientists was a PhD in experimental physics. Facebook, a major employer of this new profession, referred to data scientists and developers as "hackers" and had the motto, "Move fast and break things." This is an interesting component of Silicon Valley culture, although it perhaps would not fit well within many large organizations.

Analytics 3.0: Big (and Small) Data Go Mainstream

It became clear to many companies after 2010 or so that the big data topic was not a fad, and that there were important technologies and lessons to be adopted from this movement. However, given the cultural mismatch between Analytics 2.0 and large, established companies, there was a need for a new way of thinking about analytics at this point.

Analytics 3.0 is in many ways a combination of 1.0 and 2.0; it's "big data for big companies," but small data is still important in this era. Companies may want to analyze clickstream data, social media sentiments, sensor data from the Internet of Things, and customer location information—all "big"—but they are also interested in combining it with such "small data" as what customers have bought from them in the past. It's really not big data or small data, but *all* data.

In the 3.0 world, analytics no longer stand alone. They become integrated with production processes and systems—what our friend Bill Franks, the chief analytics officer at the International Institute for Analytics, calls "operational analytics." That means that marketing analytics don't just inform a new marketing campaign; they are integrated into real-time offers on the web. Supply chain optimization doesn't happen in a separate analytics run; instead it is incorporated into a supply chain management system, so that the right number of products is always held in the warehouse.

Companies in the 3.0 era also have a combination of objectives for analytics—both shaping decisions, and shaping new products and services. They still want to influence decisions with data and analysis, but are interested in doing so on a larger scale and scope. There is no better example than UPS's massive ORION project, which is also a great example of operational analytics. ORION, which took about a decade to develop and roll out fully across UPS, is an analytical application for driver routing. Instead of following the same route every day, ORION bases routing on the addresses where packages need to be picked up or dropped off. Today, ORION gives a different route every day; eventually, it will change routings in real time based on factors like weather, a pickup call, or traffic.

The spending on and payoff from ORION have both been impressive—UPS spends several hundreds of millions, and reaps even more annual benefits. UPS has calculated (in typical analytical fashion) that the ORION project will save the company about half a billion dollars a year in labor and fuel costs. That's the kind of scale that analytics can bring in the 3.0 era.

Decisions are important to companies that have moved into the 3.0 era, but these firms realize that analytics and data can stand behind not only decisions, but also products and services. The same data products that online startups offered in the 2.0 period can also be offered by big companies like GE, Monsanto, and United Healthcare. GE has a new "digital industrial" business model powered by sensor data in jet engines, gas turbines, windmills, and MRI machines. The data is used to create new service models based on prediction of need, not regular service intervals. Monsanto has a "prescriptive planting" business called Climate Pro that uses weather, crop, and soil data to tell a farmer the optimal times to plant, water, and harvest. United Healthcare has a business unit called Optum that generates $67 billion in annual revenues from selling data, analytics, and information systems.

Clearly, in the Analytics 3.0 era, data and analytics have become mainstream business resources. They have become critical in many companies' strategies and business models. In short, competing on analytics has become much more accepted as a concept. Of course, that doesn't mean that it's easy to succeed with analytical innovations, or that companies don't need to continue innovating over time.

Analytics 4.0: The Rise of Autonomous Analytics

The first three eras of analytics had one thing in common: the analytics were generated by human analysts or data scientists after they had gathered data, created a hypothesis, and told a computer what to do. But the most recent change in analytics is profound: it involves removing the human "quants" from the equation, or more accurately, limiting their role.

Artificial intelligence or cognitive technologies are widely viewed as perhaps the most disruptive technological force that the world is facing today. It is less widely known that most cognitive tools are based on analytical or statistical models. There are a variety of different technologies under the cognitive umbrella, but *machine learning* is one of the most common ones, and it is largely statistical in nature. But in machine learning, the machine creates the models, determines whether they fit the data or not, and then creates some more models. For some forms of machine learning, one might say that the data itself creates the model, in that the model is trained by a set of data and can adapt to new forms of it.

To a large degree, the rise of machine learning is a response to the rapid growth of data, the availability of software, and the power of today's computing architectures. *Neural networks*, for example—a version of statistical machine learning—have been used since the 1950s, and were popular for business applications since the 1990s. But current versions—some of which are called *deep learning* because they have multiple layers of features or variables to predict or make a decision about something—require large amounts of data to learn on, and a high level of computing power to solve the complex problems they address. Fortunately, Moore's Law (which predicts that processing power will double every 18 months) has supplied the needed computing horsepower. Labeled data (used to train machine learning models) is somewhat harder to come by. But in many cases, there are data sources at the ready for training purposes. The ImageNet database, for example—a free database used for training cognitive technologies to recognize images—has over 14 million images upon which a deep learning system can be trained.

In terms of software, both proprietary and open-source software is widely available to perform various types of machine cognition. Google, Microsoft, Facebook, and Yahoo! have all made available open source machine learning libraries. Startups like DataRobot and Loop AI Labs have proprietary offerings for machine learning. And some of the world's largest IT companies are adding machine learning capabilities to their offerings. Cognitive technologies are available both as standalone software and increasingly as embedded capabilities within other types of software. SAS makes available machine learning methods to augment its traditional hypothesis-based analytical software. IBM has placed a big bet on Watson as either a stand-alone software offering, or a series of smaller programs (APIs) to link to others. Salesforce.com recently announced Einstein, a set of cognitive capabilities that are embedded within its "clouds" for sales, marketing, and service. We think that virtually every major software vendor will eventually embed cognitive capabilities in their business transaction systems.

In hardware, the most important computers are off-premise. The availability of virtually unlimited computing capability at reasonable prices in the cloud means that researchers and application developers can readily obtain the horsepower they need to crunch data with cognitive tools—without even buying a computer. And relatively new types of processors like graphics processing units (GPUs) are particularly well suited to addressing some cognitive problems such as deep learning. There are also emerging computational infrastructures that combine multiple processors in a mesh to enable an entire "stack" of complex cognitive algorithms and tools.

Leading analytical organizations, then, are rapidly making a strategic shift toward cognitive technologies in general, and machine learning in particular. In order to handle the amount of data they have at their disposal and to create the personalized, rapidly-adapting models they need, machine learning is generally the only feasible option.

These won't replace human analysts anytime soon, but at a minimum machine learning is a powerful productivity aid for them. With these semi-autonomous technologies, thousands of models can be created in the time that a human analyst historically took to create one. Building many models quickly means that an organization can be much more granular in its approach to customers and markets, and can react to rapidly-changing data. Machine learning models may be more accurate than those created by *artisanal* methods (analytics that are hypothesized and painstakingly modeled by human analysts) because they often consider more variables in different combinations. Some machine learning approaches can also test an "ensemble" of different algorithm types to see which ones best explain the factor in question. The downside of these approaches is that models generated by machine learning are often not very transparent or interpretable by their human users.

If your company already has an analytics group and is doing some work with statistical models in marketing, supply chain, human resources, or some other area, how might they transition to machine learning? Your company's analytics experts will need some new skills. Instead of slowly and painstakingly identifying variables and hypothesizing models, machine learning analysts or data scientists need to assemble large volumes of data and monitor the outputs of machine learning for relevance and reasonability.

They may also have to work with some new tools. As we've already noted, established vendors of proprietary analytics software are rapidly adding machine learning capabilities, but many algorithms are available in open-source formats that do the job, but may provide less support to users. And they may need to work with new hardware as well. Since machine learning models typically operate on large amounts of data and are computationally intensive, they may require in-memory architectures or cloud-based hardware environments that can be expanded as needed.

If there is already a central analytics group or center of excellence in place, it probably already has the statistical expertise in place to interpret machine learning models to some degree. But as we've suggested, full and logical interpretation is very difficult. If there are thousands of models and tens of thousands of variables being used to support a business process, it's probably impossible to interpret each one. And some variations on machine learning—neural networks and their more complex cousin, deep learning—are virtually impossible to interpret. We can say which variables (or *features*, as they are sometimes called in machine learning) predict an outcome, but we may not know why or know what the variables mean in human terms.

This "black box" problem—the difficulty of interpreting machine learning models—is both a cultural and a leadership challenge with the technology—particularly when the models are used in a highly regulated industry. Internal managers and external regulators may have to learn to trust models that they depend on, but don't fully understand. The key is to be vigilant about whether the models are actually working. If, for example, they no longer do a good job of successfully predicting sales from a marketing program or conversion rates from sales force attention to customers, it's probably time to revisit them.

To illustrate the movement from artisanal analytics to autonomous analytics, we'll provide an (anonymous) detailed example. The company involved is a big technology and services vendor. The company has over 5 million businesses around the world as customers, fifty major product and service categories, and hundreds of applications. Each customer organization has an average of four key executives as buyers. That's a lot of data and complexity, so in order to succeed the company needed to target sales and marketing approaches to each company and potential buyer. If a propensity score could be modeled that reflected each customer executive's likelihood of buying the company's products, both sales and marketing could be much more effective.

This approach is called *propensity modeling*, and it can be done with either traditional or autonomous analytics approaches. Using traditional artisanal modeling, the company once employed thirty-five offshore statisticians to generate 150 propensity models a year. Then it hired a San Diego-based company called Modern Analytics, which specializes in analytics that are created autonomously by what it calls the "Model Factory." Using machine learning let the company quickly bump the number of models up from 150 to 350 in the first year, 1,500 in the second, and now to about 5,000 models. The models use a mere 5 trillion pieces of information to generate over 11 billion scores a month, each predicting a particular customer executive's propensity to buy particular products or respond to particular marketing approaches. Eighty thousand different tactics are recommended to help persuade customers to buy. Achieving this level of granularity with traditional approaches to propensity modeling would require thousands of human analysts if it were possible at all.

Of course, there is still some human labor involved—but not very much. Modern Analytics uses fewer than 2.5 full-time employees to create the models and scores. Ninety-five percent of the models are produced without any human intervention, but analysts need to make adjustments to the remainder. The technology company does have to employ several people to translate and evangelize for the models to sales and marketing people, but far fewer than the thirty-five statisticians it previously used.

Going back to the presumption that your company already has some analytical skills, if so it may be able to do this sort of thing by itself. Cisco Systems' internal analysts and data scientists, for example, moved from creating tens of artisanal propensity models per quarter to tens of thousands of autonomously generated ones.

The world is a big and complex place, and there is increasingly data available that reflects its size and complexity. We can't deal with it all using traditional, artisanal analytical methods, so it's time to move to Analytics 4.0. Organizations with some experience and capabilities with traditional methods, however, will have an easier time transitioning to approaches involving greater autonomy.

What This Revolution Means for Organizations

Of course, all of these rapid changes in how analytics are done have important consequences for organizations. They mean new skills, new behaviors from employees, new ways of managing, and new business models and strategies. The details are still emerging, but we'll try to give you a sense of what's already visible.

First of all, so much change in such a short time means that organizations wanting to compete on analytics have to be very nimble. They have to integrate new technologies and new methods into their repertoires. For example, Capital One, the consumer bank that we profiled extensively in the first version of this book, was certainly a leader in 1.0 analytics. But it has kept pace with the times, and now is making extensive use of cognitive technologies for cybersecurity, risk, and marketing. The company has hired lots of data scientists and specialists in machine learning and artificial intelligence. And it uses all the latest open-source tools, from Hadoop to Python and a machine learning technology called H2O. It has no intention of retreating from its long-term goal of competing on analytics, in whatever form that may take.

The skills for doing analytics across the eras, unfortunately, are cumulative. That is, the skills necessary for doing Analytics 1.0 don't go away as we move to the next era. That's in part because companies still have a need for reporting and the other activities performed in 1.0, and also because the skills required for that era still apply in later eras. To be more specific, 1.0 quantitative analysts need to know statistics, of course, but also need to be able to integrate and clean data. They also require an understanding of the business, an ability to communicate effectively about data and analytics, and a talent for inspiring trust among decision-makers. For better or worse, none of these requirements go away when organizations move into Analytics 2.0.

But there are new skills required in the 2.0 era. As we noted above, data scientists in this environment need experimentation capabilities, as well as the need to transform unstructured data into structures suitable for analysis. That typically means a familiarity with open-source development tools. If the data scientists are going to help develop data products, they need to know something about product development and engineering. And for reasons we don't entirely understand, the time that big data took off was also the time that visual analytics took off, so a familiarity with visual display of data and analytics is also important.

And all of those 1.0 and 2.0 skills are still required in the 3.0 era. What gets added to them? Well, in addition to the new technologies used in combining big and small data, there's a lot of organizational change to be undertaken. If operational analytics means that data and analytics will be embedded into key business processes, there's going to be a great need for change management skills. At UPS, for example, the most expensive and time-consuming factor by far in the ORION project was change management—teaching about and getting drivers to accept the new way of routing.

Analytics 4.0, of course, involves a heavy dose of new technical skills—machine and deep learning, natural language processing, and so forth. There is also a need for work design skills to determine what tasks can be done by smart machines, and which ones can be performed by (hopefully) smart humans.

Thus far, we've described the skills for quantitative analysts and data scientists across the ages, but there is just as much change required of managers and executives. The shift to a data- and analytics-driven organizational culture falls primarily on them. And for many, it has not been an easy transition.

As an illustration of the problem, the consulting firm NewVantage Partners has for several years surveyed companies about their progress with big data. The most recent survey in late 2016 of fifty large, sophisticated companies had a lot of good news. For example, 80.7 percent of the respondents—business and technology executives—felt that their big data initiatives have been successful.[2] Forty-eight percent said that their firms had already achieved "measurable results" from their big data investments. Only 1.6 percent said their big data efforts were a failure; for some, it was still too early to tell.

But the organizational and human transitions were less successful. Forty-three percent mentioned "lack of organizational alignment" as an impediment to their big data initiatives: forty-one percent pointed specifically to middle management as the culprit; the same percentage faulted "business resistance or lack of understanding." Eighty-six percent say their companies have tried to create a data-driven culture, but only 37 percent say they've been successful at it.

The problem, we believe, is that most organizations lack strong leadership on these topics. Middle managers can't be expected to jump on the analytics bandwagon if no one is setting the overall tone for how this will improve their jobs and results. Culture change of any type seldom happens without committed leadership, and not enough leaders are committed to making decisions and competing in the marketplace on the basis of data and analytics. This situation has certainly improved over the past ten years, but it hasn't improved enough.

New management skills will also be required to create new strategies and business models. Many firms today feel the threat from digital startups—the Ubers and Airbnbs of the world—and are attempting to create new digital business models. They're also trying to harness new technologies like the Internet of Things and social media. What they need to realize is that digital business models are also analytical business models. Digital, data-rich strategies and processes aren't of much value unless the organization learns from the data and adopts new analytically driven behaviors and tactics. These are already second nature to digital startups, but often difficult for established firms to master.

Perhaps these changes in skills and strategies will require a generational change in company leadership. The physicist Max Planck said that "Science progresses one funeral at a time." The same might be said of analytical orientations in companies.

What's in This Book

We didn't invent the idea of competing on analytics, but we believe that this book (and the articles we wrote that preceded it) was the first to describe the phenomenon.[3] In this book, you'll find more on the topic than has ever been compiled: more discussion of the concept, more examples of organizations that are pursuing analytical competition, more management issues to be addressed, and more specific applications of analytics.

Part I of the book lays out the definition and key attributes of analytical competition, and discusses (with some analytics!) how it can lead to better business performance. The end of this part describes a variety of applications of competitive analytics, first internally and then externally, with customers and suppliers.

In chapter 1, we've attempted to lay out the general outlines of analytical competition and to provide a few examples in the worlds of business and sports. Chapter 2 describes the specific attributes of firms that compete on analytics and lays out a five-stage model of just how analytically oriented an organization is. Chapter 3 describes how analytics contribute to better business performance, and includes some data and analysis on that topic. Chapters 4 and 5 describe a number of applications of analytics in business; they are grouped into internally oriented applications and those primarily involving external relationships with customers and suppliers.

Part II is more of a how-to guide. It begins with an overall road map for organizations wishing to compete on their analytical capabilities. Whole chapters are devoted to each of the two key resources—human and technological—needed to make this form of competition a reality. We conclude by discussing some of the key directions for business analytics in the future.

There are a lot of words here, and we knew they wouldn't be the last on the topic. Since the initial publication of this book, we've been gratified to see how businesses and the public sector have embraced the concept of competing on analytics. Many academics and consultants have embraced the topic, too. Many excellent books and a raft of articles have helped advance the field. There are many books on how to implement business intelligence, leveraging big data, how to create and modify analytical models in such areas as supply chain and marketing, data visualization, machine learning, and how to do basic quantitative and statistical analysis. If analytics are to continue to prosper and evolve, the world will have to spend a lot of time and energy focusing on them, and we'll need all the guidance we can get.

We do our best to help organizations embark upon this path to business and organizational success. However, it's important to remember that this is just an overview. Our goal is not to give businesspeople all the knowledge they'll ever need to do serious analytical work, but rather to get you excited about the possibilities for analytical competition and motivated enough to pursue further study.

What's Changed in This Book

Since a lot of things have changed in the world of analytics over the last decade, we've changed a lot in this book as well. Other than this totally new introduction, we've maintained the first edition's chapter structure. But every chapter has been revised, with new content topics, new examples, new research, and so forth. Chapters 4 and 5, which include many examples of how analytics are used internally and externally within organizations, have both had their examples substantially updated. Chapter 8, on technology architecture, has changed dramatically, as any reader would expect. The future isn't what it used to be, so chapter 9, on the future of analytics, also isn't what it used to be. Throughout the book, we've added content on such topics as:

- Data scientists and what they do

- Big data and the changes it has wrought in analytics

- Hadoop and other open-source software for managing and analyzing data

- Data products—new products and services based on data and analytics

- Machine learning and other artificial intelligence technologies

- The Internet of Things (IoT) and its implications for analytics

- New computing architectures, including cloud computing

- Embedding analytics within operational systems

- Visual analytics

We've also added some content that has been around for a while, but that we hadn't developed yet when we wrote the first edition. The DELTA model is an easily (we hope) remembered acronym for the factors an organization has to address to get better at analytics. It's already in our book (with Bob Morison) *Analytics at Work,* but we still think it's a nifty framework and we've added it to this one too—primarily in chapters 2 and 6.

Like it or not, some things in the world of analytics haven't changed much. Issues like developing an analytical culture, the important role of leadership, and the critical need to focus your analytics on a pressing business problem, are all pretty similar to what they were in 2007. We've left all those lessons pretty constant in this edition, other than trying to find new examples of how important they are. They were the hardest things to pull off successfully a decade ago, and they're still the hardest today.

THE
NATURE OF
ANALYTICAL
COMPETITION

CHAPTER ONE

THE NATURE OF ANALYTICAL COMPETITION

USING ANALYTICS TO BUILD A DISTINCTIVE CAPABILITY

I N 1997, A THIRTY-SOMETHING MAN WHOSE RÉSUMÉ INCLUDED software geek, education reformer, and movie buff rented *Apollo 13* from the biggest video-rental chain on the block—Blockbuster—and got hit with $40 in late fees. That dent in his wallet got him thinking: why didn't video stores work like health clubs, where you paid a flat monthly fee to use the gym as much as you wanted? Because of this experience—and armed with the $750 million he received for selling his software company—Reed Hastings jumped into the frothy sea of the "new economy" and started Netflix, Inc.

Pure folly, right? After all, Blockbuster was already drawing in revenues of more than $3 billion per year from its thousands of stores across America and in many other countries—and it wasn't the only competitor in this space. Would people really order their movies online, wait for the US Postal Service (increasingly being referred to as "snail mail" by the late 1990s) to deliver them, and then go back to the mailbox to return the films? Surely Netflix would go the route of the many internet startups that had a "business model" and a marketing pitch but no customers.

And yet we know that the story turned out differently, and a significant reason for Netflix's success today is that it is an analytical competitor. The online content creation and distribution company, which has grown from $5 million in revenues in 1999 to $8.3 billion in 2016, is a prominent example of a firm that competes on the basis of its mathematical, statistical, and data management prowess. Netflix streams a wide range of content—including movies, television shows, documentaries, and original programming—to over 93 million subscribers in 190 countries worldwide. Every minute, Netflix customers stream 69,444 hours of video. Customers watch their cinematic choices at their leisure; there are no late fees.

Netflix employs analytics in two important ways, both driven by customer behavior and buying patterns. The first is a movie-recommendation "engine" called Cinematch that's based on proprietary, algorithmically driven software. Netflix hired mathematicians with programming experience to write the algorithms and code to define clusters of movies, connect customer movie rankings to the clusters, evaluate thousands of ratings per second, and factor in current website behavior—all to ensure a personalized web page for each visiting customer.

Netflix also created a $1 million prize for quantitative analysts outside the company who could improve the Cinematch algorithm by at least 10 percent. It was an innovative approach to crowdsourcing analytics, even if the winning algorithm was too complex to fully adopt. But no doubt Netflix's data scientists learned from the work and improved the company's own algorithms. CEO Reed Hastings notes, "If the Starbucks secret is a smile when you get your latte, ours is that the website adapts to the individual's taste."[1] Netflix analyzes customers' choices and customer feedback on the movies they have viewed—over 1 billion reviews of movies they liked, loved, hated, and so forth—and recommends movies in a way that optimizes the customer's taste. Netflix will often recommend movies that fit the customer's preference profile but that aren't in high demand. In other words, its primary territory is in "the long tail—the outer limits of the normal curve where the most popular products and offerings don't reside."[2]

Now that Netflix is solidly in the business of creating new entertainment, the company has used analytics to predict whether a TV show will be a hit with audiences before it is produced. The most prominent example of Netflix's predictive efforts is *House of Cards*, the company's first original series. The political drama stars Kevin Spacey and is now entering its fifth season. Netflix has spent at least $200 million producing it thus far, so it's a big decision. The company doesn't release viewership figures, but the show is widely regarded as a home run. And it's not by accident. Netflix employed analytics to increase the likelihood of its success. It used *attribute analysis*, which it developed for its movie recommendation system, to predict whether customers would like the series, and has identified as many as seventy thousand attributes of movies and TV shows, some of which it drew on for the decision whether to create it:

- Netflix knew that many people had liked a similar program, the UK version of *House of Cards*

- It knew that Kevin Spacey was a popular leading man

- It knew that movies produced or directed by David Fincher (*House of Cards*' producer) were well liked by Netflix customers

There was certainly still some uncertainty about investing in the show, but these facts made for a much better bet. The company also used predictive analytics in marketing the series, creating ten different trailers for it and predicting for each customer which one would be most likely to appeal. And of course, these bets paid off. Netflix is estimated to have gained more than 3 million customers worldwide because of *House of Cards* alone.

And while we don't know the details of Netflix's analytics about its other shows, it seems to be using similar approaches on them. Virtually all of the original shows Netflix produced were renewed after their first seasons—the company's batting average is well over .900. In addition, Netflix has had many shows nominated for Emmys and has won its fair share as well.

Like most analytical competitors, Netflix has a strong culture of analytics and a "test and learn" approach to its business. The chief product officer, Neil Hunt, notes,

> From product management all the way down to the engineering team, we have hired for and have built a culture of quantitative

tests. We typically have several hundred variations of consumer experience experiments running at once. For example, right now we're trying out the "Netflix Screening Room," which lets customers see previews of movies they haven't seen. We have built four different versions of that for the test. We put twenty thousand subscribers into each of four test cells, and we have a control group that doesn't get the screening room at all. We measure how long they spend viewing previews, what the completion rate is, how many movies they add to their queue, how it affects ratings of movies they eventually order, and a variety of other factors. The initial data is quite promising.[3]

Reed Hastings has a master's in computer science from Stanford and is a former Peace Corps math teacher. The company has introduced science into a notably artistic industry. As a *BusinessWeek* article put it, "Netflix uses data to make decisions moguls make by gut. The average user rates more than 200 films, and Netflix crunches consumers' rental history and film ratings to predict what they'll like . . . 'It's Moneyball for movies, with geeks like Reed [Hastings] looking at movies as just another data problem,' says Netflix board member Richard N. Barton."[4]

In its testing, Netflix employs a wide variety of quantitative and qualitative approaches, including primary surveys, website user testing, concept development and testing, advertising testing, data mining, brand awareness studies, subscriber satisfaction, channel analysis, marketing mix optimization, segmentation research, and marketing material effectiveness. The testing pervades the culture and extends from marketing to operations to customer service.

Netflix may seem unique, but in many ways it is typical of the companies and organizations—a small but rapidly growing number of them—that have recognized the potential of business analytics and have aggressively moved to realize it. They can be found in a variety of industries (see figure 1-1). Some are not widely known as analytical competitors. Others, like Netflix, Caesars Entertainment in the gaming industry, or the Oakland A's in baseball, have already been celebrated in books and articles. Some, such as Amazon and Google, are digital powerhouses that have harnessed the power of the internet

FIGURE 1-1

Analytic competitors are found in every industry

Financial Services
- American Express
- Barclays Bank
- Capital One
- Renaissance Technologies
- Royal Bank of Canada
- Visa

Consumer Products
- Anheuser-Busch InBev
- E. & J. Gallo Winery
- Nike
- Procter & Gamble
- Tesla

Hospitality and Entertainment
- Caesars Entertainment
- Chicago Cubs
- Disney
- Marriott International
- Netflix

Industrial Products
- CEMEX
- GE

Pharmaceuticals
- AstraZeneca
- Merck
- Vertex

Retail
- Amazon
- Tesco
- Walmart

Insurance
- Aetna
- Anthem
- Progressive Insurance
- United Healthcare

Transport
- Schneider National
- Uber
- UPS

Digital Business
- Facebook
- Google
- LinkedIn
- Zillow

to their analytical engines. Others, such as AB InBev and Procter & Gamble, have made familiar consumer goods for a century or more. These companies have only two things in common: they compete on the basis of their analytical capabilities, and they are highly successful in their industries. These two attributes, we believe, are not unrelated.

What Are Analytics?

By *analytics*, we mean the extensive use of data, statistical and quantitative analysis, explanatory and predictive models, and fact-based management to drive decisions and actions (see the box "Analytics Definitions" for some key terms). The analytics may be input for human decisions or may drive fully automated decisions.

As figure 1-2 shows, analytics may be descriptive, predictive, prescriptive, or autonomous. Each of these approaches addresses a range of questions about an organization's business activities. The questions that analytics can answer represent the higher-value and more proactive end of this spectrum.

In principle, analytics could be performed using paper, pencil, and perhaps a slide rule, but any sane person using analytics today would

ANALYTICS DEFINITIONS

Analytical competitor: An organization that uses analytics extensively and systematically to outthink and outexecute the competition.

Analytics: The extensive use of data, statistical and quantitative analysis, explanatory and predictive models, and fact-based management to drive decisions and actions:

- **Descriptive analytics** (aka *business intelligence* [BI] or *performance reporting*) provides access to historical and current data. It provides the ability to alert, explore, and report using both internal and external data from a variety of sources.

- **Predictive analytics** uses quantitative techniques (e.g., propensity, segmentation, network analysis and econometric forecasting) and technologies (such as models and rule-based systems) that use past data to predict the future.

- **Prescriptive analytics** uses a variety of quantitative techniques (such as optimization) and technologies (e.g., models, machine learning and recommendation engines) to specify optimal behaviors and actions.

- **Autonomous analytics** employs artificial intelligence or cognitive technologies (such as machine learning) to create and improve models and learn from data—all without human hypotheses and with substantially less involvement by human analysts.

employ a computer and software. The range of analytical software encompasses relatively simple statistical and optimization tools in spreadsheets (Excel being the primary example, of course), traditional statistical software packages (e.g., Minitab or Stata), complex data visualization and descriptive analytics suites (Qlik, Tableau, MicroStrategy, Oracle Hyperion, IBM Cognos), comprehensive descriptive, predictive and prescriptive analytics software (SAS, IBM), predictive industry applications (FICO), and the reporting and analytical modules of major enterprise systems (SAP BusinessObjects and Oracle). Open-source statistical programming capabilities (e.g., R, Python) are rapidly evolv-

FIGURE 1-2

**Potential competitive advantage increases
with more sophisticated analytics**

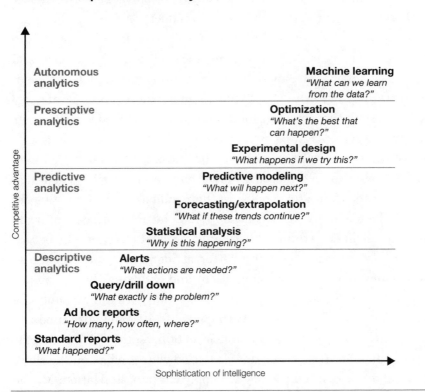

Autonomous
analytics

Machine learning
*"What can we learn
from the data?"*

Prescriptive
analytics

Optimization
*"What's the best that
can happen?"*

Experimental design
"What happens if we try this?"

Predictive
analytics

Predictive modeling
"What will happen next?"

Forecasting/extrapolation
"What if these trends continue?"

Statistical analysis
"Why is this happening?"

Descriptive
analytics

Alerts
"What actions are needed?"

Query/drill down
"What exactly is the problem?"

Ad hoc reports
"How many, how often, where?"

Standard reports
"What happened?"

Competitive advantage (vertical axis)

Sophistication of intelligence

ing to address both traditional statistical analysis and massive un-structured data. And as we'll describe later in the book, good analytical capabilities also require good information management capabilities to acquire, transform, manage, analyze, and act on both external and internal data. Some people, then, would simply equate analytics with an-alytical information technology. But this would be a huge mistake—as we'll argue throughout this book, it's the human and organizational aspects of analytical competition that are truly differentiating.

Why Compete on Analytics?

At a time when companies in many industries offer similar products and use comparable technology, high-performance business processes are among the last remaining points of differentiation. Many of the previous bases for competition are no longer available. Unique geographical advantage doesn't matter in global competition, and protective regulation is largely gone. Proprietary technologies are rapidly copied, and breakthrough innovation in products or services seems increasingly difficult to achieve. What's left as a basis for competition is to execute your business with maximum efficiency and effectiveness, and to make the smartest business decisions possible. And analytical competitors wring every last drop of value from business processes and key decisions. Analytics are even increasingly being embedded into their products and services.

Analytics can support almost any business process. Yet organizations that want to be competitive must have some attribute at which they are better than anyone else in their industry—a distinctive capability.[5] This usually involves some sort of business process or some type of decision, or perhaps a distinctive product offering. Maybe you strive to make money by being better at identifying profitable and loyal customers than your competition, and charging them the optimal price for your product or service. If so, analytics are probably the answer to being the best at it. Perhaps you sell commodity products and need to have the lowest possible level of inventory while preventing your customer from being unable to find your product on the shelf; if so, analytics are often the key to supply chain optimization. Maybe you have differentiated your products and services by incorporating some unique data and proprietary algorithms. Perhaps you compete in a people-intensive business and are seeking to hire, retain, and promote the best people in the industry. There too, analytics can be the key.

On the other hand, perhaps your operational business processes aren't much different from anybody else's, but you feel you compete on making the best decisions. Maybe you can choose the best locations for your stores—if so, you're probably doing it analytically. You may build scale through mergers and acquisitions, and select only the best candidates for such combinations. Most don't work out well, according to widely publicized research, but yours do. If so, you're probably not making those decisions primarily on intuition. Good decisions usually have systematically assembled data and analysis behind them.

Analytical competitors, then, are organizations that have selected one or a few distinctive capabilities on which to base their strategies, and then have applied extensive data, statistical and quantitative analysis, and fact-based decision making to support the selected capabilities. Analytics themselves don't constitute a strategy, but using them to optimize a distinctive business capability certainly constitutes a strategy. Whatever the capabilities emphasized in a strategy, analytics can propel them to a higher level. Capital One, for example, calls its approach to analytical competition "information-based strategy." Caesars' distinctive capabilities are customer loyalty and service, and it has certainly optimized them with its analytically driven strategy. GE is differentiating its industrial services processes by using sensor data to identify problems and maintenance needs before they cause unscheduled downtime.

Can any organization in any industry successfully compete on analytics? This is an interesting question that we've debated between ourselves. On the one hand, virtually any business would seem to have the potential for analytical competition. The cement business, for example, would seem to be as prosaic and non-analytical an industry as one could find. But the global cement giant CEMEX has successfully applied analytics to its distinctive capability of optimized supply chains and delivery times. We once believed that the fashion business might never be analytical, but then we found numerous examples of analytics-based predictions about what clothing styles and colors might sell out this season.

On the other hand, some industries are clearly more amenable to analytics than others. If your business generates lots of transaction data—such as in financial services, travel and transportation, or gaming—competing on analytics is a natural strategy (though many firms still don't do it). Similarly, if you can draw on the wealth of data available on the internet or on social media to get a unique insight into your customers and markets, competing on analytics is a great way to differentiate yourself. If your business model is based on hard-to-measure factors like style (as in the fashion business) or human relationships (as in the executive search industry), it would take much more groundbreaking work to compete on analytics—although, as we suggested, it's being done to some degree. Virtually every day we find examples of businesses that were previously intuitive but are now becoming analytical. The wine business, for example, was once (and in some quarters still is) highly intuitive and built on unpredictable consumer preferences. Today, however, it's possible to quantitatively analyze and predict the appeal of any wine, and large winemakers such as E. & J. Gallo are competing on analytics in such domains as sales, agriculture, and understanding of consumer preferences.[6]

How Did We Get Here? The Origins of Analytical Competition

The planets are clearly aligned for the move to analytical competition by organizations. At the same time that executives have been looking for new sources of advantage and differentiation, they have more data about their businesses than ever before. Enterprise resource planning (ERP) systems, point-of-sale (POS) systems, and mobile devices, websites and e-commerce, among other sources, have created more and better data than in the history of humankind. A new generation of technically literate executives—the first to grow up with computers—is coming into organizations and looking for new ways to manage them with the help of technology. Finally, the ability to make sense of data through computers and software has finally come of age. Analytical software makers have dramatically expanded the functionality of their products over the past several years, and hardware providers have optimized their technologies for fast analysis and the management of massive databases.

The use of analytics began as a small, out-of-the-way activity performed in a few data-intensive business functions. As early as the late 1960s, practitioners and researchers began to experiment with the use of computer systems to analyze data and support decision making. Called *decision support systems* (DSS), these applications were used for analytical, repetitive, and somewhat narrow activities such as production planning, investment portfolio management, and transportation routing. Two DSS pioneers, Peter Keen and Charles Stabell, argue that the concept of decision support arose from studies of organizational decision making done at Carnegie Tech (now Carnegie Mellon) by researchers such as Herbert Simon during the late 1950s and early '60s, and technical work on interactive computer systems, mainly carried out at MIT in the 1960s.[7] Others would argue that their origins were closely connected to military applications in and following World War II, although computers as we know them were not yet available for those applications.

Statistical analysis on computers became a much more mainstream activity in the 1970s, as companies such as SAS Institute and SPSS (now part of IBM) introduced packaged computer applications that made statistics accessible to many researchers and businesspeople. Yet despite the greater availability of statistics, DSS did not prosper in the period and evolved into *executive support systems*.[8] These applications involved direct use of computers and data by senior executives for monitoring and reporting of performance (with a lesser emphasis on decision making). This activity also never took off broadly, in part because of the reluctance of executives to engage in hands-on use.

Analytical technology became most frequently used for storing relatively small amounts of data and conducting ad hoc queries in support of decisions and performance monitoring. The focus on managing data became important because vast amounts of it were becoming available from transaction systems such as ERP and POS systems, and later from internet data. Versions of this data-oriented focus were referred to as OLAP (online analytical processing) and later *business intelligence*. The data management activities were known as *data warehousing*. Smaller data warehouses were called *data marts*.

Meanwhile, big data has its roots in a field originally known as "knowledge discovery and data mining" in 1989.[9] Before this time, the practice of data exploration without a guiding hypothesis was deemed too unfocused to be valuable to businesses. Technically speaking, the term *big data* refers to data that is too big, volatile, and unstructured to be manipulated and analyzed using traditional technologies. As we describe in the introduction, about a decade ago, Silicon Valley firms such as Google and LinkedIn developed new ways to process and make sense of all the data they capture. Once they made those tools publically available, big data and machine learning began to infiltrate analytical enterprises in other industries, too.

Today, the entire field is referred to by a variety of names such as *big data analytics* or *business intelligence and advanced analytics*, which generally encompass the collection, management, and reporting of decision-oriented data as well as the analytical techniques and computing approaches that are performed on the data. Business intelligence and analytics platforms are a broad and popular field within the IT industry—in fact, Gartner's 2016 survey of nearly three thousand chief information officers from eighty-four countries found that business intelligence and data analytics are the number-one technology priority for IT organizations for the fifth consecutive year.[10] Two studies of large organizations using ERP systems that we did in 2002 and 2006 revealed that better decision making was the primary benefit sought, and (in 2006) analytics was the technology most sought to take advantage of the ERP data.

Despite the variation in terminology, these movements—each of which lasted about a decade—had several attributes in common. They were largely technically focused, addressing how computers could be used to store, analyze, and display data and results of analysis. They were focused on fairly narrow problems—with the exception of the executive and performance monitoring systems, which displayed only the condition of the business. They were also relegated to the back office of organizations—used by technicians and specialists, with little visibility to senior executives. With only a few exceptions, they could rarely be said to influence the nature of competition.

Today, most large organizations have some sort of analytical applications in place and some analytics tools installed. But they are too often marginal to the success of the business and are managed at the departmental level. An insurance company, for example, may have some analytical tools and approaches in the actuarial department, where pricing for policies is determined. A manufacturing company may use such tools for quality management. Marketing may have some capabilities for lifetime value analysis for customers. However valuable these activities are, they are invisible to senior executives, customers, and shareholders—and they can't be said to drive the company's competitive strategy. They are important to individual functions but insignificant to competition overall.

Our focus in this book, however, is on companies that have elevated data management, statistical and quantitative analysis, predictive modeling, and fact-based decision making to a high art. These organizations have analytical activities that are hardly invisible; they are touted to every stakeholder and interested party by CEOs. Rather than being in the back room, analytics in these companies are found in the boardroom, the annual report, and in the press clippings. These organizations have taken a resource that is ostensibly available to all, and refined it to such a degree that their strategies (and increasingly, their products) are built around it.

When Are Analytical Decisions Appropriate?

There is considerable evidence that decisions based on analytics are more likely to be correct than those based on intuition.[11] It's better to *know*—at least within the limits of data and analysis—than to *believe* or *think* or *feel*, and most companies can benefit from more analytical decision making. Of course, there are some circumstances in which decisions can't or shouldn't be based on analytics. Some of these circumstances are described in Malcolm Gladwell's popular book *Blink*, which is a paean to intuitive decision making.[12] It's ironic that a book praising intuition became popular just when many organizations are relying heavily on analytics, but then perhaps that was part of its romantic appeal. The book is fun and has great stories, but it doesn't make clear that intuition is only appropriate under certain circumstances.

It's also clear that decision makers have to use intuition when they have no data and must make a very rapid decision—as in Gladwell's example of police officers deciding whether to shoot a suspect. Gary Klein, a consultant on decision making, makes similar arguments about firefighters making decisions about burning buildings.[13] Even firms that are generally quite analytical must sometimes resort to intuition when they have no data. For example, Jeff Bezos, CEO of Amazon, greatly prefers to perform limited tests of new features on Amazon, rigorously quantifying user reaction before rolling them out. But the company's "search inside the book" offering was impossible to test without applying it to a critical mass of books (Amazon started with 120,000). It was also expensive to develop, increasing the risk. In that case, Bezos trusted his instincts and took a flier. And the feature did prove popular when introduced.[14]

Of course, any quantitative analysis relies on a series of assumptions. When the conditions behind the assumptions no longer apply, the analyses should no longer be employed. For example, Capital One and other credit card companies make analytical predictions about customers' willingness to repay their balances under conditions of general economic prosperity. If the economy took a sharp downturn, the predictions would no longer apply, and it would be dangerous to continue using them. This is not just a hypothetical example; many banks that issued mortgage loans found that their assumptions about repayment were no longer valid in the 2008–2009 financial crisis, and those that didn't change their models quickly no longer exist.

The key message is that the frontier of decisions that can be treated analytically is always moving forward. Areas of decision making that were once well suited for intuition accumulate data and analytical rigor over time, and intuition becomes suboptimal. Today, for example, some executives still consider it feasible to make major decisions about mergers and acquisitions from their gut. However, the best firms are already using detailed analytics to explore such decisions. Procter & Gamble, for example, used a variety of analytical techniques before its acquisition of Gillette, including those for logistics and supply chains, drivers of stock market value, and human resources. In a few years, firms that do not employ extensive analytics in making a major acquisition will be considered irresponsible. Already, IBM is using algorithms to evaluate merger and acquisition candidates. Its M&A Pro tool both speeds deals and eliminates what the company views as the greatest source of problems in M&A work— human error.[15]

Indeed, trends point to a more analytical future for virtually every firm. The amount of data available will only continue to increase. Radio frequency identification (RFID) sensors will be put on virtually every pallet or carton that moves through the supply chain, generating vast amounts of new data for companies to collect and analyze. Every industrial machine and every vehicle will produce a vast amount of sensor data. Every mobile phone has a wealth of data about its user and her behavior. In retail, every shopping cart will be intelligent enough to gather data on "pickstreams," or a record of which products are taken off the shelves in what order (Amazon has already opened a grocery store where sensors permit it to know what is in your cart and automatically debit your account when you leave the store).[16] In oil exploration and mining, the amount of data—already massive—will expand geometrically. In advertising, more businesses are rapidly shifting to media such as the internet and cable television that can monitor which ads are seen by whom—again creating a huge new stream of data. And the decisions about what ad to run on what website are made by automated algorithms.

Analytical software will become more broadly available and will be in reach of every organization. Statistically oriented software firms such as SAS and IBM have made increasingly sophisticated analyses available to average companies and users for over forty years, and they will continue to do so. Enterprise systems vendors such as SAP, Oracle, and Salesforce.com are incorporating descriptive, predictive, and prescriptive analytics into their products, enabling managers to analyze their systems' data in real time and monitor the performance of the business. New industry applications targeting different business capabilities will become available from vendors such as FICO Corporation and MMIS, Inc. Open-source analytical tools (like R and RapidMiner) and computing frameworks (like Apache Hadoop and Spark), which originated in Silicon Valley, are rapidly evolving and proliferating across the corporate world. And Microsoft is incorporating increasing amounts of analytical capability into basic office productivity software. In the future, software availability will not be an issue in analytical competition, although the ability to use analytical software well won't ever be a commodity.

It's also safe to assume that hardware won't be a problem. Today, laptops and tablets that can do extensive quantitative analysis on large data sets are already readily available. Specialized computers and cloud platforms from providers such as Amazon, Microsoft, Teradata, Oracle, and IBM can easily manage petabytes or even exabytes of data. The cloud offers an infinitely expandable processing capability for data storage and analysis. No doubt even the smartphone of the near future will be able to perform serious analyses. The bigger issue will be how organizations control their data and analysis, and ensure that individual users make decisions on correct analyses and assumptions.

To remain an analytical competitor, however, means staying on the leading edge. Analytical competition will be something of an arms race, requiring continual development of new measures, new algorithms, new data sources, new data manipulation techniques, and new decision-making approaches. Firms embracing it will systematically eliminate guesswork from their processes and business models. Analytical competitors will have to conduct experiments in many aspects of their businesses and learn from each one of them. In order for quantitative decisions to be implemented effectively, analysis will have to be a broad capability of employees, rather than the province of a few "rocket scientists" with quantitative expertise.

We've developed a road map describing the primary steps needed to build an effective analytical competitor. It involves key prerequisites, such as having at least a moderate amount and quality of data about the domain of business that analytics will support, and having the right types of hardware and software on hand. The key variables are human, however. One prerequisite is that some manager must have enough commitment to analytics to develop the idea further. But the pivotal factor in how fast and how well an organization proceeds along the analytical path is sponsorship. Firms such as Netflix, Caesars, Capital One, and UPS have CEO-level sponsorship and even passion for analytical competition that lets them proceed on a "full steam ahead" path.

Other organizations that lack passionate executive sponsorship must first go through a "prove-it" path to demonstrate the value of analytical competition. This path is slower, and even those who take the prove-it path have to eventually arrive at strong executive sponsorship if they are to become true analytical competitors. We will discuss this road map—and the steps on each of the two paths—in detail in the second part of this book (chapter 6 in particular). For now, we simply want to emphasize that although analytics seem to be dispassionate and computer based, the most important factors leading to success involve passionate people.

Analytics in Professional Sports—and Their Implications for Business

We can perhaps best understand the progression of analytical competition across an industry by focusing on professional sports. While sports differ, of course, they have in common large amounts of data and talented but expensive human resources (the athletes). Sports also differ from businesses, but both domains of activity have in common the need to optimize critical resources and of course the need to win.

Perhaps the most analytical professional sport is baseball, which has long been the province of quantitative and statistical analysis. The use of statistics and new measures in baseball received considerable visibility with the publication of *Moneyball*, by Michael Lewis.[17] The book (and 2011 movie starring Brad Pitt) describes the analytical orientation of the Oakland A's, a professional team that had a record of consistently making the playoffs despite a low overall payroll (including the 2014 playoffs—although even the best analytical competitor doesn't win all the time, as in 2016). Lewis described the conversion of Oakland's general manager (GM), Billy Beane, to analytics for player selection when he realized that he himself had possessed all the traditional characteristics of a great player, according to major league scouts. Yet Beane had not been a great player, so he began to focus more on actual player performance as revealed in statistics than on the conventional wisdom of the potential to be great. Beane and the A's also began to make use of relatively new measures of player performance, eschewing the traditional "runs batted in," or RBIs, and focusing on "on-base percentage" and "on-base plus slugging percentage." Like analytical competitors in business, they invented new metrics that assessed and stretched their performance.

Yet Beane was not actually the first Oakland general manager to take a statistical orientation.[18] In the early 1980s, Sandy Alderson, then the GM (now CEO of the San Diego Padres, another 2006 playoff contender), adopted a more statistical approach for two reasons. First, Oakland had performed badly for a number of years before the decision and was on the brink of going out of business. Second, Alderson was offered an early version of a PC-based (actually, Apple II–based) statistical database and analysis package. Baseball statistics are widely available from firms such as STATS, LLC, and the Elias Sports Bureau, although the statistics were available to teams well before they started taking advantage of them. These reasons are typical of why businesses often adopt analytical competition: a combination of pressing business need, the availability of data, and IT that can crunch all the numbers.

The analytical approach to baseball has broadened dramatically over the last few years. Another team that has adopted the moneyball approach is the Boston Red Sox—a team with both analytical capabilities and the money to invest in expensive players. The Red Sox also had a business need, having failed to win the World Series for eighty-six years by the 2004 season. The Sox also exemplify another reason why organizations adopt analytical competition: new leadership. The team's two new principal owners in 2002 were John Henry, a quantitative hedge fund manager, and Tom Werner, a television producer who had previously owned the San Diego Padres. The appeal of analytics to Henry was obvious, but Werner had also realized with the Padres that the traditional baseball establishment didn't know as much about what led to championships as it purported to. The high level of executive sponsorship at the Sox let the team take the full-steam-ahead (discussed in chapter 6) approach to analytical competition.

The owners knew they needed a management team that shared their vision of using data analytics to outperform the competition. Werner brought Yale-educated Theo Epstein from the Padres and made him the youngest GM in baseball history. Epstein was joined by assistant GM Jed Hoyer. Epstein and Hoyer share a deep passion for baseball and a thirst for winning. But what made these two hires so crucial is that they also shared a deep commitment to ignoring conventional baseball beliefs in favor of detailed data analysis for decision making. Next, like other organizations committed to analytical strategies, the Red Sox quickly hired as a consultant the best analytical talent: Bill James, who was widely regarded as the world's foremost practitioner of *sabermetrics*, or baseball statistics (James even invented the term himself). The fact that no other team had seen fit to hire such an underemployed analytical genius suggests that analytical competition in baseball was not yet widespread. The analytical approach—along with some new and expensive talent—paid off for the Sox quickly, and they made the American League Championship Series (ALCS) against their perennial rivals, the New York Yankees, in 2003.

Yet one game in that series illustrates a key difficulty of analytical competition: it has to spread everywhere within an organization if analytical decisions are to be implemented. In the seventh and deciding game of the series, Red Sox ace Pedro Martínez was pitching. Sox analysts had demonstrated conclusively that Martínez became much easier for opposing batters to hit after about seven innings or 105 pitches (that year, the opposing team's batting average against Martínez for pitches 91–105 was .231; for pitches 106–120 it was .370). They had warned manager Grady Little that by no means should Martínez be left in the game after that point. Yet when Martínez predictably began to falter late in the seventh, Little let him keep pitching into the eighth (even against the advice of his pitching coach), and the Yankees shelled Martínez. The Yanks won the ALCS, and Little lost his job. It's a powerful story of what can happen if frontline managers and employees don't go along with the analytical program. Fortunately for long-suffering Red Sox fans (including one of the authors of this volume), the combination of numbers and money proved insurmountable in the 2004 season, and the Sox broke the eighty-six-year World Series championship drought. The Red Sox won it all again in 2007, and once more in 2013. One author of this book hopes they win again soon.

Still, some baseball pundits argued that the Red Sox's use of data analytics to build a better team and win games was not a reliable strategy. But the data does not support this belief. Nate Silver's data journalism website fivethirtyeight.com found that there was a considerable first mover advantage for teams that embraced analytics. It reported that "Teams with at least one analyst in 2009 outperformed their expected winning percentage by 44 percentage points over the 2012–14 period."[19] So it's no surprise that analytical talent has a much higher profile in MLB than it did ten years ago.

There is convincing evidence that all organizations, even those that are late adopters, can compete and win with analytics. The Chicago Cubs had been one of the teams that was slow to embrace data analytics. The team had not won the World Series in over a century—the longest drought in baseball history. But in 2009. the team was bought by the Ricketts family, who were determined to bring a championship to their hometown. Tom Ricketts, chairman of the Chicago Cubs, is a highly quantitative executive who has experienced firsthand the power of analytics to get superior results. Ricketts knew that he needed to bring in analytically minded leadership to transform the Cubs. So in 2011, he hired Red Sox alums Theo Epstein as president of Baseball Operations and Jed Hoyer as GM in 2011. He offered them the greatest challenge in professional baseball: to break the Cubs' "Curse of the Billy Goat."[20]

Ricketts gave Epstein a mandate to do whatever was needed to finally break the Curse. Epstein and Hoyer knew that data-driven insights would not be enough, since most major league teams had adopted them to some degree by 2011. But Ricketts promised time and resources to completely rebuild the entire team.

The management team began by creating "The Cubs Way"—a document that details the organization's philosophy and a detailed summation of everything the team had learned about winning. For example, it describes how teaching techniques and procedures must be consistent across the farm teams and the big leagues. The document gets quite detailed about the optimal way to perform specific movements. For example, it describes ". . . which foot hits the bag when players make a turn on the bases."[21]

Constructing a team from the ground up was a monumental task. Fortunately, while the salary cap restricted owners' ability to pay for on-field talent, there's no salary cap in the front office. The Cubs R&D group (led by Chris Moore, a PhD in psychology and neuroscience), was established to analyze every aspect of the game and the organization.

The team lost over a hundred games in the first year. But by 2016, they had the best record in professional baseball. And after 108 years, to the great joy of Cubs fans everywhere (including the other author of this volume), the Chicago Cubs won the 2016 World Series.

Using advanced data analytics has spread to every professional sport, including golf, hockey, and tennis. At the most analytical teams, baseball analysts are now being scouted and recruited just like players. Analyst hires and assessments of a team's capabilities are covered in ESPN magazine's annual "Analytics" issue, Nate Silver's fivethirtyeight.com website, and the mainstream media. And the MIT Sloan Sports Analytics Conference routinely draws from professional teams in every sport imaginable, and is attended by thousands.

One early adopter was in football. The New England Patriots, for example, have been particularly successful, winning five Super Bowls in the last fifteen years, most recently in 2017. The team uses data and analytical models extensively, both on and off the field. In-depth analytics help the team select its players and stay below the salary cap. The team selects players without using the scouting services that other teams employ, and it rates potential draft choices on such nontraditional factors as intelligence and willingness to subsume personal ego for the benefit of the team.

The Patriots also make extensive use of analytics for on-the-field decisions. They employ statistics, for example, to decide whether to punt or "go for it" on fourth down, whether to try for one point or two after a touchdown, and whether to challenge a referee's ruling. Both its coaches and players are renowned for their extensive study of game films and statistics, and head coach Bill Belichick has been known to peruse articles by academic economists on statistical probabilities of football outcomes. Off the field, the team uses detailed analytics to assess and improve the "total fan experience." At every home game, for example, twenty to twenty-five people have specific assignments to make quantitative measurements of the stadium food, parking, personnel, bathroom cleanliness, and other factors. External vendors of services are monitored for contract renewal and have incentives to improve their performance.[22]

Other NFL teams that make extensive usage of statistical analysis include the Atlanta Falcons, Baltimore Ravens, Dallas Cowboys, and Kansas City Chiefs. Other teams use analytics too, but more sparingly. For example, the Green Bay Packers analyzed game films of one running back with a fumbling problem, and determined that the fumbles only happened when the player's elbow wasn't horizontal to the ground when he was hit.[23] Despite the success of the Patriots and these other teams, some teams in the NFL have yet to grasp the nature and value of analytical competition.

In contrast, professional basketball was historically less quantitatively oriented than baseball, but the numeric approach is now revolutionizing the sport. Several teams, including the high-performing

San Antonio Spurs and the Golden State Warriors, have hired statistical consultants or statistically oriented executives. In 2007, the
Houston Rockets chose a young, quantitatively oriented executive who
previously managed information systems and analytics for the Boston
Celtics to be their GM. Daryl Morey, an MIT MBA and cofounder of
the MIT Sloan Sports Analytics Conference, considers baseball sa-
bermetrician Bill James to be his role model, and argues that analytics in basketball are similar to those for moneyball in baseball. "It's
the same principle. Generate wins for fewer dollars."[24] As in baseball and football, teams and their analysts are pursuing new measures, such as a player's value to the team when on the court versus
when off of it (called the Roland Rating after amateur statistician
Roland Beech).

Analytical competition is advancing rapidly in international sports.
Soccer (or football, as it is known outside the United States) teams
employ similar techniques. AC Milan, one of the most storied teams
in Europe, uses predictive models to prevent player injuries by analyzing physiological, orthopedic, and psychological data from a variety of
sources. Its Milan Lab identifies the risk factors that are most likely
to be associated with an injury for each player. The lab also assesses
potential players to add to the team. Several members of the 2006
FIFA World Cup–winning Italy national team trained at Milan Lab.

The level of analytical competition in professional soccer has accelerated dramatically over the past few years. Sports writer Graham
Ruthven describes the dramatic change that took place over the past
few years this way: "Every Premier League club now employs a team
of video and data analysts . . . graphs and pie-charts are now as much
a part of the sport as the dressing room blackboard."[25]

Oliver Bierhoff, manager of the 2014 FIFA World Cup Champion
German national football team, explains the big data challenge of
a fluid game like soccer: "In just 10 minutes, 10 players with three
balls can produce over seven million data points."[26] The team relies
on an array of sensors and on-field cameras along with a system called
Match Insights to make sense of the data, allowing it to tailor its
training and preparation for each match. Match Insights is used by
both coaches and players, almost like a video game, to assess individual opponent's capabilities and devise game strategies.

Why all this activity in professional sports, and what difference does it make for other types of organizations? There are many themes that could cut across sports and business. Perhaps the most important lesson from professional sports analytics is its focus on the human resource—on choosing, appropriately compensating, and keeping the best players. This is not a widespread practice in the business "talent management" domain, but it is growing rapidly. As executive and individual contributor salaries continue to rise, it may be time to begin to analyze and gather data on which people perform well under what circumstances, and to ensure that the right players are on the team. A few firms like Google have already adopted a more analytical approach to human resource management, but sports teams are still far ahead of most other organizations.

Analytical competition in sports also illustrates the point that analytics arises first when sufficient data is present to analyze. If there is a business area in which large amounts of data are available for the first time, it will probably soon become a playing field for analytical competition. Analytical innovators in professional sports also often create new measures, and businesspeople should do the same.

Finally, technology enables more opportunities for sports (and other businesses) to create entirely new types of data. This new data creates additional opportunities for competitive advantage. As Mark Cuban, owner of the Dallas Mavericks told ESPN.com, ". . . all teams now use all the data available to them to make personnel decisions, so the market has become more efficient. We have strived to introduce new and exclusive sources of data so that we can improve performance of our players."[27] Daryl Morey at the Houston Rockets was the earliest adopter of video data in the NBA for the same reason. Analytical teams have harnessed technologies that allow them to make more informed, data-driven, real time decisions during actual games. In the same way, analytical businesses are using cutting edge technological innovations to become more agile in changing market conditions.

While analytics is a somewhat abstract and complex subject, its adoption in professional sports illustrates the human nature of the process. When a team embraces analytical competition, it's because a leader makes a decision to do so. That decision can often be traced to the leader's own background and experiences. Analytical competition—whether in sports or business—is almost always a story involving people and leadership.

It's also no accident that the sports teams that have embraced analytical competition have generally done well. They won't win championships every year, of course, but analytical competitors have been successful in every sport in which they have arisen. However, as analytical competition spreads—and it spreads quickly—teams will have to continue innovating and building their analytical capabilities if they wish to stay in front. Whatever the approach to competition, no team (or firm) can afford to rest on its laurels.

CHAPTER TWO

WHAT MAKES AN ANALYTICAL COMPETITOR?

DEFINING THE COMMON KEY ATTRIBUTES OF SUCH COMPANIES

WHAT DOES IT MEAN TO COMPETE ON ANALYTICS? WE define an *analytical competitor* as an organization that uses analytics extensively and systematically to outthink and outexecute the competition. In this chapter, we'll describe the key attributes of companies that compete on analytics, and describe the levels and stages of these attributes that we found in researching actual organizations.

Among the firms we studied, we found that the most analytically sophisticated and successful had four common key characteristics: (1) analytics supported a strategic, distinctive capability; (2) the approach to and management of analytics was enterprise-wide; (3) senior management was committed to the use of analytics; and (4) the company made a significant strategic bet on analytics-based competition. We found each of these attributes present in the companies that were most aggressively pursuing analytical approaches to business. (see the box "The DELTA Model for Building Analytics Capability" for another version of attributes of analytical competitors).

THE DELTA MODEL FOR BUILDING ANALYTICS CAPABILITY

After publishing the first version of this book in 2007, we received many requests for an analytical capabilities framework that would be easy to communicate and apply. Tom then developed the DELTA model, which includes the following five attributes of analytical organizations, which was described in detail in our book *Analytics at Work*:[a]

- **Data:** Analytical companies require integrated, high-quality, and easily accessible data about their businesses and markets. The most analytical firms have distinctive sources and types of data.

- **Enterprise:** Instead of managing their analytics resources in disconnected silos, highly analytical firms manage these resources—including data, technology, and analysts—in a coordinated fashion across the enterprise.

- **Leadership:** One of the key factors driving success in analytics is strong, committed leaders who understand the importance of analytics and constantly advocate for their development and use in decisions and actions.

We don't know, of course, exactly how many analytical competitors there are, but early in our research, we found data allowing a good estimate. In a global survey of 371 medium to large firms, we asked respondents (IT executives or business executives familiar with their companies' enterprise IT applications) how much analytical capability their organizations had. The highest category was described by the statement "Analytical capability is a key element of strategy" for the business. Ten percent of the respondents selected that category. According to our detailed analysis of the data, perhaps half of these firms are full-bore analytical competitors.

The International Institute for Analytics (a research and advisory company on analytics cofounded by Tom) performs a systematic

- **Targets:** Organizations can't be equally analytical about all aspects of their businesses, so they need to target specific business capabilities and functions for the extensive use of analytics.

- **Analysts:** Analytical organizations succeed in part because they hire and train high-quality quantitative analysts and data scientists.

A subsequent version of the model—called DELTTA—added the *technology* factor, particularly for big data analytics environments requiring new and complex technology architectures. This model was described in the book *Big Data @ Work*.[b] More information on the DELTA model is provided in chapter 6.

a. Thomas H. Davenport, Jeanne G. Harris, and Robert F. Morison, *Analytics at Work: Smarter Decisions, Better Results* (Boston: Harvard Business Review Press, 2010).
b. Thomas H. Davenport, *Big Data @ Work* (Boston: Harvard Business Review Press, 2014).

Analytics Maturity Assessment on many companies using a five-point scale we describe later in this chapter, as well as the DELTA model factors. In a 2016 survey of fifty companies across several industries, the Institute found that most of the large, relatively sophisticated firms were not yet analytical competitors.[1] Only the "digital natives" (online and e-commerce businesses) in the survey approached analytical competitor levels on average; Amazon had the highest score of any company assessed. Financial services firms assessed were the second–most analytical industry, but were not at the analytical competitor level on average. Visa was the highest-ranking firm assessed in that industry. The lowest-ranking industries were health care providers and health insurance companies.

Primary Attributes of Analytical Competitors

Next, we'll describe how several of the companies we studied exemplify the four attributes of analytical competition. True analytical competitors exhibit all four; less advanced organizations may have only one or two at best.

Support of a Strategic, Distinctive Capability

It stands to reason that if analytics are to support competitive strategy, they must be in support of an important and distinctive capability. As we mentioned in the first chapter, the capability varies by organization and industry, and might involve supply chains, pricing and revenue management, customer service, customer loyalty, innovative products, or human resource management. At Netflix, of course, the primary focus for analytics is on predicting customer viewing preferences. At Caesars, it's on customer loyalty and service. Marriott International's primary analytical orientation is on revenue management. Walmart obviously emphasizes supply chain analytics. Professional sports teams generally focus on human resources, or choosing the right players.

Having a distinctive capability means that the organization views this aspect of its business as what sets it apart from competitors and as what makes it successful in the marketplace. In companies without this strategic focus, analytical capabilities are just a utility to be applied to a variety of business problems without regard for their significance.

Of course, not all businesses have a distinctive capability. They usually suffer when they don't. It's not obvious, for example, what Kmart's, Sears's, or JC Penney's distinctive capabilities are in the retail industry. To the outside observer, they don't do anything substantially better than their competitors—and their customers and potential shareholders have noticed. Without a distinctive capability, you can't be an analytical competitor, because there is no clear process or activity for analytics to support.

It's also possible that the distinctive capability an organization chooses would not be well supported by analytics—at least this has been true in the past. If the strategic decisions an organization makes are intuitive or experience based and cannot be made analytically, it wouldn't make sense to try to compete on statistics and fact-based decisions.

Management consulting has historically been characterized in this way, in that most consulting advice is based on experience rather than analytics. But in that industry, there is the potential for analytical competition; both Deloitte, which uses analytics internally and in its client services, and McKinsey Solutions, a business unit of that old-line firm, are breaking out in this regard. Operational consulting firms have already begun to include proprietary algorithms and benchmarking as a way to differentiate their services. Executive search firms, such as Korn Ferry, are beginning to build their businesses around a database of what kinds of executives perform well under certain circumstances. Auditors could apply analytics and artificial intelligence to their methodologies, as Deloitte and KPMG are doing aggressively.

In addition to developing distinctive capabilities, analytical competitors pay careful attention to measures of the chosen capabilities in their businesses. They engage in both *exploitation* and *exploration* of measures—they exploit existing measures to a considerable degree and are early to explore new measures. In chapter 1, we discussed professional baseball, where teams like the Oakland A's have moved to new measures of player performance. Consumer finance is another industry with a strong emphasis on developing new metrics.

Because there are many quantitative transactions in consumer financial services, it's relatively easy to employ measures in decision making. Perhaps the most commonly used measure in consumer finance is the credit or FICO score, which is an indicator of the customer's creditworthiness. There are many possible credit scores, but only one official FICO score. (FICO scores are based on an algorithm developed by Fair, Isaac and Company [now FICO] in 1989. Now, the three major credit bureaus have created a competitor called the VantageScore, that, unlike the FICO score, is consistent with all credit ratings; in Europe, some financial services firms employ credit scores from Scorex.)

Virtually every consumer finance firm in the United States uses the FICO score to make consumer credit decisions and to decide what interest rate to charge. Analytical banking competitors such as Capital One, however, adopted it earlier and more aggressively than other firms. Their distinctive capability was finding out which customers were most desirable in terms of paying considerable interest without defaulting on their loans. After FICO scores had become pervasive in banking, they began to spread to the insurance industry. Again, highly analytical firms such as Progressive determined that consumers with high FICO scores not only were more likely to pay back loans, but also were less likely to have automobile accidents. Therefore, they began to charge lower premiums for customers with higher FICO scores.

Today, however, there is little distinction in simply using a FICO score in banking or property and casualty insurance. The new frontiers are in applying credit scores in other industries and in mining data about them to refine decision making. Some analysts are predicting, for example, that credit scores will soon be applied in making life and health insurance decisions and pricing of premiums. At least one health insurance company is exploring whether the use of credit scores might make it possible to avoid requiring an expensive physical examination before issuing a health policy. One professor also notes that they might be used for employment screening:

> It is uncommon to counsel individuals with financial problems who don't have other kinds of problems. You're more likely to miss days at work, be less productive on the job, as well as have marriage and other relationship problems if you are struggling financially. It makes sense that if you have a low credit score that you are more likely to have problems in other areas of life. Employers looking to screen a large number of applicants could easily see a credit score as an effective way to narrow the field.[2]

Since credit scores are pervasive, some firms are beginning to try to disaggregate credit scores and determine which factors are most closely associated with the desired outcome. Progressive and Capital One, for example, are both reputed to have disaggregated and analyzed credit scores to determine which customers with relatively low scores might be better risks than their overall scores would predict.

One last point on the issue of distinctive capabilities. These mission-critical capabilities should be the organization's primary analytical target. Yet we've noticed that over time, analytical competitors tend to move into a variety of analytical domains. Marriott started its analytical work in the critical area of revenue management but later moved into loyalty program analysis and web metrics analysis. At Netflix, the most strategic application may be predicting customer movie preferences, but the company also employs testing and detailed analysis in its supply chain, new product development and its advertising. Caesars started in loyalty and service but also does detailed analyses of its slot machine pricing and placement, the design of its website, and many other issues in its business. Walmart, Progressive, and the hospital supply distributor Owens & Minor are all examples of firms that started with an internal analytical focus but have broadened it externally—to suppliers in the case of Walmart and to customers for the other two firms. Analytical competitors need a primary focus for their analytical activity, but once an analytical, test-and-learn culture has been created, it's impossible to stop it from spreading.

An Enterprise-Level Approach to and Management of Analytics

Companies and organizations that compete analytically don't entrust analytical activities just to one group within the company or to a collection of disparate employees across the organization. They manage analytics as an organization or enterprise and ensure that no process or business unit is optimized at the expense of another unless it is strategically important to do so. At Caesars, for example, when then-CEO Gary Loveman began the company's move into analytical competition, he had all the company's casino property heads report to him, and ensured that they implemented the company's marketing and customer service programs in the same way. Before this, each property had been a "fiefdom," managed by "feudal lords with occasional interruptions from the king or queen who passed through town."[3] This made it virtually impossible for Caesars to implement marketing and loyalty initiatives encouraging cross-market play.

Enterprise-level management also means ensuring that the data and analyses are made available broadly throughout the organization and that the proper care is taken to manage data and analyses efficiently and effectively. If decisions that drive the company's success are made on overly narrow data, incorrect data, or faulty analysis, the consequences could be severe. Therefore, analytical competitors make the management of analytics and the data on which they are based an organization-wide activity.

For example, one of the reasons that RBC Financial Group (the best-known unit of which is Royal Bank of Canada) has been a successful analytical competitor is that it decided early on (in the 1970s) that all customer data would be owned by the enterprise and held in a central customer information file. Bank of America attributes its analytical capabilities around asset and interest-rate risk exposure to the fact that risk was managed in a consistent way across the enterprise. Many other banks have been limited in their ability to assess the overall profitability or loyalty of customers because different divisions or product groups have different and incompatible ways to define and record customer data.

An enterprise approach is a departure from the past for many organizations. Analytics have largely been either an individual or a departmental activity in the past and largely remain so today in companies that don't compete on analytics. For example, in a survey of 220 organizations' approaches to the management of business intelligence and analytics (which, remember, also includes some nonanalytical activities, such as reporting), only 45 percent said that their use of business intelligence was either "organizational" or "global," with 53 percent responding "in my department," "departmental," "regional," or "individual." In the same survey, only 22 percent of firms reported a formal needs assessment process across the enterprise; 29 percent did no needs assessment at all; and 43 percent assessed business intelligence needs at the divisional or departmental level.[4] The reasons for this decentralization are easy to understand. A particular quantitatively focused department, such as quality, marketing, or pricing, may have used analytics in going about its work, without affecting the overall strategy or management approach of the enterprise. Perhaps its activities should have been elevated into a strategic resource, with broader access and greater management attention. Most frequently, however, these departmental analytical applications remained in the background.

Another possibility is that analytics might have been left entirely up to individuals within those departments. In such cases, analytics took place primarily on individual spreadsheets. While it's great for individual employees to use data and analysis to support their decisions, individually created and managed spreadsheets are not the best way to manage analytics for an enterprise. For one thing, they can contain errors. Research by one academic suggests that between 20 percent and 40 percent of user-created spreadsheets contain errors; the more spreadsheets, the more errors.[5] While there are no estimates of the frequency of errors for enterprise-level analytics, they could at least involve processes to control and eliminate errors that would be difficult to impose at the individual level.

A second problem with individual analytics is that they create "multiple versions of the truth," while most organizations seek only one. If, for example, there are multiple databases and calculations of the lifetime value of a company's customers across different individuals and departments, it will be difficult to focus the entire organization's attention on its best customers. If there are different versions of financial analytics across an organization, the consequences could be dire indeed—for example, extending to jail for senior executives under Sarbanes-Oxley legislation. Hence there are considerable advantages to managing key data and analytics at the enterprise level, so that there is only one version of critical business information and analytical results for decision making. Then, of course, the information and results can be distributed widely for use across the organization. Caesars, for example, calls its management approach for customer analytics "centrally driven, broadly distributed."

Enterprise management may take a variety of forms. For some organizations, it may mean only that central IT groups manage the data and procure and install the needed software. For others, it may mean that a central analytical services group assists executives with analysis and decision making. As we'll discuss in chapter 7, a number of firms have established such groups.

An increasingly common approach to enterprise-level analytics is to establish a *chief data and analytics officer* (alternatively called a *chief data officer* or *chief analytics officer*). The CDAO is a senior executive (often reporting directly to the COO, CMO, or CIO) While this is a relatively new role, Gartner estimates that there are over a thousand CDAOs today; it expects 90 percent of the world's largest organizations will have one by 2019.[6]

Job descriptions vary, but the CDAO is usually responsible for ensuring that the organization has the data, capabilities (human, financial, technical, and operational) and mindset needed to successfully leverage big data and analytics for competitive advantage. The role typically includes establishing strategic policies regarding data governance (including data policies and cybersecurity), determining investment priorities to enhance analytical capabilities, developing analytical talent, and building enterprise-wide analytic capabilities.

Charles Thomas, the chief data officer at Wells Fargo, says his team's "main purpose is to champion the enterprise's use of insight and action to drive business strategy, reduce risk, optimize performance, and increase value for Wells Fargo's customers, the company, its shareholders, and its team members."[7]

The CDAO may also head an "analytics hub," an enterprise-wide, deeply skilled, multidisciplinary team (analysts, data scientists, IT specialists, and data visualization experts) who tackle the most difficult and strategic challenges and opportunities on behalf of the organization.

For example, at Schneider National, a large trucking and logistics company, the central analytical group (called Engineering and Research) is a part of the chief information officer organization, and addresses advanced analytics and optimization, performance reporting, and data management functions as well as working with internal and external customers on analytical applications and problems.

Senior Management Commitment

The adoption of a broad analytical approach to business requires changes in culture, process, behavior, and skills for multiple employees. Such changes don't happen by accident; they must be led by senior executives with a passion for analytics and fact-based decision making. Ideally, the primary advocate should be the CEO (although COOs, CFOs, CIOs, and presidents have all successfully played this role). Indeed, we found several chief executives who were driving the shift to analytics at their firms. These included Gary Loveman, formerly CEO of Caesars; Jeff Bezos, the founder and CEO of Amazon; Rich Fairbank, the founder and CEO of Capital One; Reed Hastings of Netflix; and Barry Beracha, formerly CEO of Sara Lee Bakery Group. Each of these executives has stated both internally and publicly that their companies are engaged in some form of analytical competition. For example, Fairbank commented, "It's all about collecting information on 200 million people you'd never meet, and on the basis of that information, making a series of very critical long-term decisions about lending them money and hoping they would pay you back."[8]

Fairbank summarizes this approach as "information-based strategy." Beracha, before he retired as CEO of Sara Lee Bakery, simply kept a sign on his desk reading, "In God we trust; all others bring data" (a quote originally attributed to W. Edwards Deming). Loveman frequently asked employees, "Do we think, or do we know?" Anyone presenting ideas for initiatives or strategies is pressed for supporting evidence. Loveman also hired into Caesars a number of very analytical senior and middle managers. He also listed three reasons why employees could be fired from Caesars: ". . . you don't harass women, you don't steal, and you've got to have a control group."[9]

Loveman provides an excellent example of how a CEO (and ideally an entire executive team) who constantly pushes employees to use testing and analysis to make fact-based decisions can change an organization's culture. He's not just supportive of analytics—he's passionate on the subject. He's since moved to head a new division of Aetna focused on using data and analytics to transform consumer healthcare.

Without the push from the top, it's rare to find a firm making the cultural changes necessary to become an analytical competitor. We know it's a bit of a cliché to say that an idea needs the passionate support of the CEO or other senior general managers, but in our research on analytical competitors, we simply didn't find any without such committed and broad support from the executive suite. We found some firms, for example, in which single functional or business unit leaders (such as heads of marketing or research) were trying to engineer an analytically oriented shift in their firms but weren't able to sufficiently change the culture by themselves. This doesn't mean, of course, that such an executive couldn't lead a change like this under other circumstances, and we did find organizations in which lower-level advocates were making progress on changing the culture. Any cross-functional or cross-department change, and certainly any enterprise-wide effort, clearly requires the support and attention of executives senior enough to direct and coordinate efforts in those separate units.

How does an executive develop a passion for analytics? It helps, of course, if they learn it in school. We've mentioned the math teacher background of Reed Hastings at Netflix. Loveman of Caesars and Aetna has a PhD in economics from MIT and taught at Harvard Business School. Bezos from Amazon was a quantitatively oriented A+ engineering and computer science student at Princeton. Fairbanks and New England Patriots COO Jonathan Kraft were MBAs and analytically oriented management consultants before taking their jobs at their respective analytical competitors. Chris Lofgren, the president and CEO of Schneider National, has a PhD in operations research. It's obviously a desirable situation when a CEO can go toe to toe with the "propeller-heads" in the analytical department.

However, not every analytical executive has or needs such an extensive background. Statistics and data analysis are taught at virtually every college in the land. And a CEO doesn't have to be smarter or more quantitatively oriented than all of his or her employees. What is necessary is a willingness to delve into analytical approaches, the ability to engage in discussions with quantitative experts, and the fortitude to push others to think and act analytically.

There are several corollaries of the senior management commitment factor. CEO orientation drives not only the culture and mind share directed to analytics but also the level and persistence of the investment in people, IT, data, and so forth. It is no simple matter, as we will describe in subsequent chapters, to assemble these resources, and it can require substantial time.

Barclays's consumer finance organization, for example, had a "five-year plan" to build the unit's capabilities for analytical competition.[10] Executives in the consumer business had seen the powerful analytical transformations wrought by such US banks as Capital One, and felt that Barclays was underleveraging its very large customer base in the

United Kingdom. In adopting an analytical strategy, the company had to adjust virtually all aspects of its consumer business, including the interest rates it charges, the way it underwrites risk and sets credit limits, how it services accounts, its approach to controlling fraud, and how it cross-sells other products. It had to make its data on 13 million BarclayCard customers integrated and of sufficient quality to support detailed analyses. It had to undertake a large number of small tests to begin learning how to attract and retain the best customers at the lowest price. New people with quantitative analysis skills had to be hired, and new systems had to be built. Given all these activities, it's no surprise that it took five years to put the information-based customer strategy in place.

We've already mentioned the UPS ORION project, but this is probably a good time to describe its leader. Jack Levis is officially the senior director of Process Management at UPS, but in his forty years at the company, he's worn lots of hats. One of them was leading the ORION project, which started as a three- or four-person team and ended up as a seven-hundred-person behemoth. He also led the earlier Package Flow Technologies project, which provided the data environment for ORION. He's very analytical—he leads UPS's operations management group, for example—but he's no geeky propeller-head. He has a BA in psychology—a discipline that he's used to good advantage.

Levis modestly attributes the success of ORION to the great team that worked on it—in total thousands of UPSers. But we think he did a lot of things right. First, he started small in designing a new way of routing drivers at UPS. For five years, a small team designed the project and developed prototypes. He didn't give anyone much reason to cancel the project.

Later on, as ORION grew, Levis did an excellent job of accumulating senior management buy-in. He gives a lot of credit to his vice presidents, including Chuck Holland, the VP of Engineering. But Levis says that eventually every member of the UPS management committee was shown a prototype or given an "ORION ride."

Levis was also persistent. There were times when ORION was on the verge of being canceled because it didn't have the right algorithm, but Levis, his team and his "air cover" kept the vision alive and kept re-examining the algorithm rules and constraints until they made it work.

Finally, we'd argue that Levis succeeded because he was flexible. He realized midway into the project, for example, that deployment would be a major change management issue, so he set about winning the hearts and minds of the field and the drivers. "Once we came up with metrics and showed huge evidence of gains, people really started to get behind it," Levis notes. "By the time we got to deployment—where the really big ORION money was spent—we had enough results so that the senior management team kept asking us to speed things up. We went from 25 people on the deployment to 100 to 300 to 700."[11]

If you ask the leader of an analytics project how to orchestrate hundreds of millions of dollars and hundreds of people in order to save hundreds of millions a year, it might seem a bit overwhelming. Levis showed how to make such a massive project a reasonable ask of a dedicated and competent organization.

Large-Scale Ambition

A final way to define analytical competitors is by the results they aspire to achieve. The analytical competitors we studied had bet their future success on analytics-based strategies. In retrospect, the strategies appear very logical and rational. At the time, however, they were radical departures from standard industry practice. The founders of Capital One, for example, shopped their idea for "information-based strategy" to all the leaders of the credit card industry and found no takers. When Signet Bank accepted their terms and rebuilt its strategy and processes for credit cards around the new ideas, it was a huge gamble. The company was betting its future, at least in that business unit, on the analytical approach.

Not all attempts to create analytical competition will be successful, of course. But the scale and scope of results from such efforts should at least be large enough to affect organizational fortunes. Incremental, tactical uses of analytics will yield minor results; strategic, competitive uses should yield major ones.

There are many ways to measure the results of analytical activity, but the most obvious is with money. A single analytical initiative should result in savings or revenue increases in the hundreds of millions or billions for a large organization. There are many possible examples. One of the earliest was the idea of "yield management" at American Airlines, which greatly improved the company's fortunes in the 1980s. This technique, which involves optimizing the price at which each airline seat is sold to a passenger, is credited with bringing in $1.2 billion for American over three years and with putting some feisty competitors (such as People Express) out of business.[12] At Deere & Company, a new way of optimizing inventory (called "direct derivative estimation of nonstationary inventory") saved the company $1.2 billion in inventory costs between 2000 and 2005.[13] Procter & Gamble used operations research methods to reorganize sourcing and distribution approaches in the mid-1990s and saved the company $200 million in costs.[14] More recently, the ORION routing project at UPS is expected to save the company about half a billion dollars annually.

The results of analytical competition can also be measured in overall revenues and profits, market share, and customer loyalty. If a company can't see any impact on such critical measures of its non-financial and financial performance, it's not really competing on analytics. At Caesars (then Harrah's), for example, the company increased its market share from 36 percent to 43 percent between 1998 (when it started its customer loyalty analytics initiative) and 2004.[15] Over that same time period, the company experienced "same store" sales gains in twenty-three of twenty-four quarters, and play by customers across multiple markets increased every year. Before the adoption of these approaches, the company had failed to meet revenue and profit expectations for seven straight years. Capital One, which became a public company in 1994, increased earnings per share and return on equity by at least 20 percent each year over its first decade. Barclays's information-based customer management strategy in its UK consumer finance business led to lower recruitment costs for customers, higher customer balances with lower risk exposure, and a 25 percent increase in revenue per customer account—all over the first three years of the program. Kroger's analytics-based loyalty program helped the grocery retailer grow same-store sales for fifty-two straight quarters (and counting!). As we'll discuss in chapter 3, the analytical competitors we've studied tend to be relatively high performers.

These four factors, we feel, are roughly equivalent in defining analytical competition. Obviously, they are not entirely independent of each other. If senior executive leadership is committed and has built the strategy around an analytics-led distinctive capability, it's likely that the organization will adopt an enterprise-wide approach and that the results sought from analytics will reflect the strategic orientation. Therefore, we view them as four pillars supporting an analytical platform (see figure 2-1). If any one fell, the others would have difficulty compensating.

Of all four, however, senior executive commitment is perhaps the most important because it can make the others possible. It's no accident that many of the organizations we describe became analytical competitors when a new CEO arrived (e.g., Loveman at Caesars) or when they were founded by CEOs with a strong analytical orientation from the beginning (Hastings at Netflix or Bezos at Amazon). Sometimes the change comes from a new generation of managers in a family business. At winemaker E. & J. Gallo, when Joe Gallo, the son

FIGURE 2-1

Four pillars of analytical competition

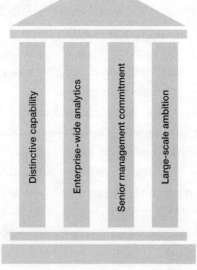

of one of the firm's founding brothers, became CEO, he focused much more than the previous generation of leaders on data and analysis—first in sales and later in other functions, including the assessment of customer taste. At the New England Patriots National Football League team, the involvement in the team by Jonathan Kraft, the son of owner Bob Kraft and a former management consultant, helped move the team in a more analytical direction in terms of both on-field issues like play selection and team composition and off-field issues affecting the fan experience.

Assessing the Degree of Analytical Competition

If these four factors are the hallmarks or defining factors of analytical competition, we can begin to assess organizations by how much or how little they have of them. To do so, we have identified five stages of analytical competition, as seen in figure 2-2. The key attributes for each stage are listed in table 2-1. Like the well-known "capability maturity model" for software development, these stages can describe the path

FIGURE 2-2

The five stages of analytical competition

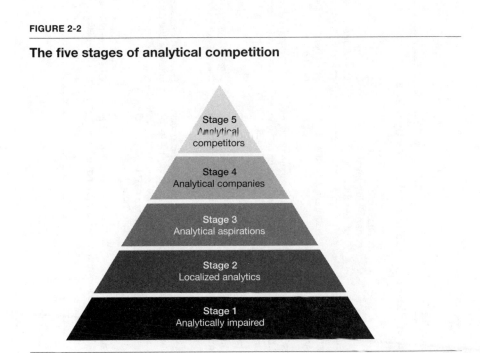

Stage 5
Analytical
competitors

Stage 4
Analytical companies

Stage 3
Analytical aspirations

Stage 2
Localized analytics

Stage 1
Analytically impaired

TABLE 2-1

Analytical competition: attributes by stage

	Distinctive capability/level of insights	Questions asked	Objective	Perceived value
Stage 1 **Analytically impaired**	Negligible; "flying blind"	What happened in our business?	Get accurate data to improve operations	None
Stage 2 **Localized analytics**	Local and opportunistic; may not be supporting company's distinctive capabilities	What can we do to improve this activity? How can we understand our business better?	Use analytics to improve one or more functional activities	ROI of individual applications
Stage 3 **Analytical aspirations**	Begin efforts for more integrated data and analytics	What's happening now? Can we extrapolate existing trends?	Use analytics to improve a distinctive capability	Future performance and market value
Stage 4 **Analytical companies**	Enterprise-wide perspective; able to use analytics for point advantage; know what to do to get to next level, but not quite there	How can we use analytics to innovate and differentiate?	Build broad analytic capability—analytics for differentiation	Analytics are an important driver of performance and value
Stage 5 **Analytical competitors**	Enterprise-wide, big results, sustainable advantage	What's next? What's possible? How do we stay ahead?	Analytical master—fully competing on analytics	Analytics are a primary driver of performance and value

that an organization can follow from having virtually no analytical capabilities to being a serious analytical competitor. In chapter 6, we describe the overall road map for moving through these stages.

Stage 5 organizations are full-blown *analytical competitors*, with high degrees of each of the four factors described earlier. Their analytical activities are clearly in support of a distinctive capability, they are taking an enterprise-wide approach, their executives are passionate and driving, and their analytical initiatives are aimed at substantial results. Some of the firms that fall into this category include Google, Caesars, Amazon, Capital One, Progressive, Netflix, Walmart, and UPS, as well as several sports teams we've discussed. These organizations could always apply their analytical capabilities even more broadly—and they are constantly doing so—but they already have them focused on the most significant capability their strategy requires. In our initial sample of thirty-two firms that are at least somewhat oriented to analytics, eleven were stage 5 analytical competitors. However, we sought out firms that fit in this category, so by no means should this be taken as an indicator of their overall prevalence. From our other research, we'd estimate that no more than 5 percent of large firms would be in this category overall (i.e., half of the percentage in our survey saying that "analytical capability is a key element of strategy"; the other half would be stage 4). This rough estimate is borne out by recent analytics maturity assessments by the International Institute for Analytics (IIA). Most of the stage 5 organizations we discovered, as might be predicted, were information-intensive services firms, with four firms in financial services. Several were also online firms. However, it's difficult to generalize about industries for analytical competition, since we found stage 5 organizations in several industry categories.

Stage 4 organizations, our *analytical companies*, are on the verge of analytical competition but still face a few minor hurdles to get there in full measure. For example, they have the skill but lack the out-and-out will to compete on this basis. Perhaps the CEO and executive team are supportive of an analytical focus but are not passionate about competing on this basis. Or perhaps there is substantial analytical activity, but it is not targeted at a distinctive capability. With only a small increase in emphasis, the companies could move into analytical competitor status. We found seven organizations in this category.

For example, one stage 4 consumer products firm we studied had strong analytical activities in several areas of the business. However, it wasn't clear that analytics were closely bound to the organization's strategy, and neither analytics nor the likely synonyms for them were mentioned in the company's recent annual reports. Analytics or information was not mentioned as one of the firm's strategic competencies. Granted, there are people within this company—and all of the stage 4 companies we studied—who are working diligently to make the company an analytical competitor, but they aren't yet influential enough to make it happen.

The organizations at stage 3 do grasp the value and the promise of analytical competition, but they're in the early stages of it. They typically face major capability hurdles and are a long way from overcoming them. Because of the importance of executive awareness and commitment, we believe that just having that is enough to put the organization at a higher stage and on the full-steam-ahead path that we describe in more detail in chapter 6. We found seven of thirty-two organizations in this position in our initial research, but they are more common now. Some have only recently articulated the vision and have not really begun implementing it. Others have very high levels of functional or business unit autonomy and are having difficulty mounting a cohesive approach to analytics across the enterprise.

One multiline insurance company, for example, had a CEO with the vision of using data, analytics, and a strong customer orientation in the fashion of the stage 5 firm Progressive, an auto insurance company with a history of technological and analytical innovation. But the multiline company had only recently begun to expand its analytical orientation beyond the traditionally quantitative actuarial function, and thus far there was little cooperation across the life and property and casualty business units.

We also interviewed executives from three different pharmaceutical firms, and we categorized two of the three into stage 3 at present. It was clear to all the managers that analytics were the key to the future of the industry. The combination of clinical, genomic, and proteomic data will lead to an analytical transformation and an environment of personalized medicine. Yet both the science and the application of informatics in these domains are as yet incomplete.[16] Each of our interviewees admitted that their company, and the rest of the industry, has a long way to go before mastering their analytical future. One of the companies, Vertex Pharmaceuticals, has made significant progress toward analytical competition—not by striving toward full-fledged analytical competition as we described it earlier, but by making more analytical decisions in virtually every phase of drug development and marketing.

Despite the implementation issues faced by stage 3 firms, because executive demand is one of the most important aspects of a company's analytical orientation—and because sufficient interest from executives can drive a great deal of change relatively quickly—we'd put these firms ahead of those that may even have more analytical activity but less interest from executives. We refer to them as having *competitive aspirations* with regard to analytics.

Stage 2 organizations exhibit the typical *localized analytics* approach to "business intelligence" in the past—that is, an emphasis on reporting with pockets of analytical activity—but they don't measure up to the standard of competing on analytics. They do analytical work, but they have no intention of competing on it. We found six of these firms in our initial study, although they would be much more common in a random sample. The IIA benchmarking suggests that this is the largest group.

By no means have analytics transformed the way these organizations do business. Marketing, for example, may be identifying optimal customers or modeling demand, but the company still markets to all customers and creates supply independent of the demand models. Their analytical activities produce economic benefits but not enough to affect the company's competitive strategy. What they primarily lack is any vision of analytical competition from senior executives. Several of the firms have some of the same technology as firms at higher stages of analytical activity, but they have not put it to strategic use.

Stage 1 organizations have some desire to become more analytical, but thus far they lack both the will and the skill to do so. We call them *analytically impaired* organizations. They face some substantial barriers—both human and technical—to analytical competition and are still focused on putting basic, integrated transaction functionality and high-quality data in place. They may also lack the hardware, software, and skills to do substantial analysis. They certainly lack any interest in analytical competition on the part of senior executives. To the degree that they have any analytical activity at all, it is both small and local. At a state government organization we researched, for example, the following barriers were cited in our interview notes from our initial study:

> [Manager interviewed] noted that there is not as great a sense in government that "time is money" and therefore that something needs to happen. Moreover, decision making is driven more by the budget and less by strategy. What this means is that decisions are as a rule very short-term focused on the current fiscal year and not characterized by a longer-term perspective. Finally, [interviewee] noted that one of the other impediments to developing a fact-based culture is that the technical tools today are not really adequate. Despite these difficulties, there is a great deal of interest on the part of the governor and the head of administration and finance to bring a new reform perspective to decision making and more of an analytical perspective. They are also starting to recruit staff with more of these analytical skills.

As a result of these deficiencies, stage 1 organizations are not yet even on the path to becoming analytical competitors, even though they have a desire to be. Because we only selected organizations to interview that wanted to compete on analytics in our initial study, we included only two stage 1 organizations—a state government and an engineering firm (and even that firm is becoming somewhat more analytical about its human resources). Today, many fewer organizations—at least among large corporations—would admit to being at stage 1. However, organizations at stage 2 probably still constitute the majority of all organizations in the world at large. Many firms today don't have a single definition of the customer, for example, and hence they can't use customer data across the organization to segment and select the best customers. They can't connect demand and supply information, so they can't optimize their supply chains. They can't understand the relationship between their nonfinancial performance indicators and their financial results. They may not even have a single definitive list of their employees—much less the ability to analyze employee traits. Such basic data issues are all too common among most firms today.

We have referred to these different categories as *stages* rather than *levels* because most organizations need to go through each one. However, with sufficiently motivated senior executives, it may be possible to skip a stage or at least move rapidly though them. We have had opportunities to observe the progress of analytical orientation at several firms over time. We've learned that an organization that was in a hurry to get to stage 5 could hire the people, buy the technology, and pound data into shape within a couple of years. The greatest constraint on rapid movement through the stages is changing the basic business processes and behaviors of the organization and its people. That's always the most difficult and time-consuming part of any major organizational change.

In chapter 3, we describe the relationship between analytical activity and business performance. We discuss analytical applications for key processes in the two subsequent chapters: chapter 4 describes the role that analytics play in internally oriented processes, such as finance and human resource management; chapter 5 focuses on using analytics to enhance organizations' externally oriented activities, including customer and supplier specific interactions. Before we get there, we will explore the link between organizations that have high analytical orientations and high-performance businesses.

CHAPTER THREE

ANALYTICS AND BUSINESS PERFORMANCE

TRANSFORMING THE ABILITY TO COMPETE ON ANALYTICS INTO A LASTING COMPETITIVE ADVANTAGE

IN THE 1980S, TWO FINANCIAL SERVICES CONSULTANTS, Richard Fairbank and Nigel Morris, identified a major problem in the credit card industry, as well as a potential solution. The problem was that the industry lacked a focus on the individual customer, and the solution came in the form of technology-driven analytics. Fairbank and Morris believed that insights from data analysis would enable a company to discover, target, and serve the most profitable credit customers while leaving other firms with less profitable customers. They pitched this idea, their "information-based market strategy," to more than fifteen national retail banks before Virginia-based Signet Bank hired them to work in its bank card division. Signet was hardly a leading competitor in credit cards at the time.

Over the next two years, the duo ran thousands of analytical tests on Signet's customer database—much to the chagrin of the company's previous, and largely intuitive, experts. They discovered that the most profitable customers were people who borrowed large amounts quickly and then paid off the balances slowly. At the time, the credit card industry treated such customers just as they treated people who made small purchases and paid their balances off in full every month. Recognizing an opportunity, the team created the industry's first balance-transfer card. As the first card that targeted debtors as valued, not just valuable, customers, it quickly took off within the industry. Ultimately, Fairbank and Morris's success with analytics led Signet to spin off its bank card division as a company called Capital One.

Today, Capital One runs about eighty thousand marketing experiments per year to improve its ability to target individual customers.[1] These tests provide a relatively low-cost way for the company to judge how successful products and programs would be before it engages in full-scale marketing. In its savings business, for example, Capital One found that its experiments in terms of CD interest rates, rollover incentives, minimum balances, and so forth had very predictable effects on retention rates and new money coming into the bank. Through such analyses, the savings business increased retention by 87 percent and lowered the cost of acquiring a new account by 83 percent.[2]

Through this analytical approach to marketing, Capital One is able to identify and serve new market segments before its peers can. The key to this ability is the company's closed loop of testing, learning, and acting on new opportunities. The firm's knowledge of what works and what doesn't forms the basis of a strategic asset that enables it to avoid approaches and customers that won't pay off. Few companies are truly set up to apply the principles of this test-and-learn approach, but Capital One's entire distinctive capability is built on it.

Capital One's analytical prowess has transformed the organization into a *Fortune* 200 company with an enviable record of growth and profitability. Analytics are at the heart of the company's ability to consistently outperform its peers and sustain its competitive advantage. Most recently, it has begun a focused initiative on artificial intelligence—the latest version of analytical technology. Rob Alexander, CIO of Capital One Financial, said in an interview with *InformationWeek*: "Machine learning will be a huge area of innovation within the banking industry . . . Banking is a rich environment in terms of the amount of data, the amount of interactions with customers, and the complexity of products and services you have. It's ripe for doing it better, and machine learning delivers tools to provide more tailored, customized products for your customers."[3]

Now consider a long-established company that has also become an analytical competitor: Marriott International, the global hotel and resort firm. Marriott's focus on fact-based decision making and analytics is deeply embedded in the corporate culture and lore. As one senior executive put it, "Everything is based on metrics here." This orientation was instilled as early as the 1950s, when founder J. Willard Marriott used to observe the occupancy of cars pulling into his motel's parking lot in order to charge the rate for a double room, if appropriate.

Over the last thirty years, Marriott has built on J. W. Marriott's early labor-intensive foray into *revenue management*—the process by which hotels establish the optimal price for their rooms (the industry's "inventory"). The economics are simple: if a hotel can predict the highest prices that will still lead to full occupancy, it will make more money than it would if too-high prices led to unoccupied rooms or too-low prices filled the building but essentially gave money back to customers unnecessarily. Marriott introduced revenue management to the lodging industry, and over the past three decades has continued to refine its capability with the help of analytics—even as most competitors are constantly a step behind in their ability to optimize revenues.

Recent enhancements make the system work faster so that pricing could be easily and frequently adjusted for hotel rooms, and they have allowed Marriott to extend revenue management into its restaurants, catering services, and meeting spaces—an approach Marriott calls "total hotel optimization." In late 2003, the company began using a new revenue management system and began to use a new metric—*revenue opportunity*—that relates actual revenues to optimal revenues. Only a couple of years later, Marriott had a revenue opportunity figure of 91 percent—up from 83 percent when it created the metric. While the company prefers its franchisees to use the system, it has given its regional "revenue leaders" the power to override the system's recommendations to deal with unanticipated local events, such as the arrival in Houston of a large number of Hurricane Katrina evacuees.

A successful revenue management system has helped Marriott achieve consistently strong financial performance. Marriott employs an enterprise-wide revenue management system called Total Yield. The system automates the business processes associated with optimizing revenue for more than 97 percent of the company's nearly six thousand properties.

Marriott has consistently been among the most profitable hotel chains, and executives and investment analysts attribute much of their success to analytical revenue management. The company has extended revenue management ahead of most competitors to additional areas of the business, including food and beverage and group room pricing.

In addition to revenue management, Marriott has embedded analytics into several other customer-facing processes. The company has identified its most profitable customers through its Marriott Rewards loyalty program and targets marketing offers and campaigns to them. It is an extensive user of web analytics, and pioneered the use of social media analytics in the lodging industry. Partly as a result of Marriott's analytical prowess, the company has been named the most admired firm in its industry for sixteen straight years in *Fortune* magazine's ranking.

Another analytical competitor whose innovations have kept it ahead of its rivals is Progressive. Progressive's top managers relentlessly hunt for undiscovered insurance markets and business models that have been ignored by companies that perform only conventional data analysis.

Progressive was the first insurance company to offer auto insurance online in real time and the first to allow online rate comparisons—the company is so confident in its price setting that it assumes that companies offering lower rates are taking on unprofitable customers.[4] It has even pioneered a program that would offer discounts to safer drivers who voluntarily used the company's Snapshot technology to measure such factors as how often they make sudden stops and the percentage of time they drive more than 75 miles per hour.[5] By digging deeper into customer information and doing it faster and earlier than the competition, the company uncovers new opportunities and exploits them before the rest of the industry takes notice. These and other tactics have enabled Progressive to continue to thrive in a highly competitive market, with a market capitalization of over $19 billion.

Analytical competitors run *thousands* of analytical experiments annually. Ben Clarke in *Fast Company* estimated the number of annual experiments at several analytical firms:

> Intuit: 1,300, P&G: 7,000–10,000, Google: 7,000, Amazon: 1,976, and Netflix: 1,000. And it isn't just quantity that's rising but the quality and pace of experimentation, too. These days, the true test of how innovative a company can be is how well it experiments.
>
> [. . .] Amazon chief Jeff Bezos has said, "Our success at Amazon is a function of how many experiments we do per year, per month, per week, per day . . . We've tried to reduce the cost of doing experiments so that we can do more of them. If you can increase the number of experiments you try from a hundred to a thousand, you dramatically increase the number of innovations you produce."[6]

What do the stories of Amazon, Capital One, Marriott International, and Progressive have in common? They demonstrate not only the concept of competing on analytics but also the connection between the extensive use of analytics and business performance. In this chapter, we will explore those links in greater detail and describe how several highly successful companies have transformed their ability to compete on analytics into a key point of differentiation and lasting competitive advantage.

Assessing the Evidence

Many researchers have found that fact-based decision processes are critical to high performance. In *Good to Great*, for example, Jim Collins notes that "breakthrough results come about by a series of good decisions, diligently executed and accumulated on top of another . . . [Good-to-great companies] made many more good decisions than bad ones, and they made many more good decisions than comparison companies . . . They infused the entire process with the brutal facts of reality . . . You absolutely cannot make a series of good decisions without first confronting the brutal facts."[7]

Researchers have also begun to document the returns that companies can earn from investments in specific analytical technologies or initiatives. For example, technology research firm International Data Corporation (IDC) found in one study that analytical projects aimed at improving production had a median ROI of 277 percent; those involving financial management had a median ROI of 139 percent; and those focused on customer relationship management, a median ROI of 55 percent.[8] The study also showed that the median ROI for analytics projects using predictive technologies was 145 percent, compared with a median ROI of 89 percent for projects without them.[9] Nucleus Research, a company that researches IT value, reported in 2014 on a multiyear study of the return on analytics investments. It found that a dollar spent on analytics returned $13 on average.[10]

Similarly, the consulting firm Bain & Company surveyed four hundred large companies around the world in 2013, and asked executive respondents about their firms' analytics capabilities. The consultants concluded that only 4 percent of the companies were "really good at analytics." But those analytical competitors were:

- Twice as likely to be in the top quartile of financial performance within their industries

- Three times more likely to execute decisions as intended

- Five times more likely to make decisions faster.[11]

To fill in the gaps of evidence about the effect of analytics on business performance, we conducted two surveys—the first an in-depth sample of thirty-two organizations that we rated in terms of their analytical orientations, and the second a much larger survey of firms that had made major investments in enterprise systems. In the first survey, we rated each firm's stage of analytical maturity (the same five-point scale described in chapter 2, with 1 equaling major challenges to analytical competition and 5 indicating analytical mastery). Then we gathered financial performance data on all the survey participants. After conducting a statistical analysis of the data, we found a significant correlation between higher levels of analytical maturity and robust five-year compound annual growth rates.[12]

In the second study, we surveyed more than 450 executives in 371 large and medium-sized companies. We limited this study to those companies that had already implemented at least two modules of an enterprise system and therefore had a sufficient quantity and quality of transaction data available for analysis.[13] Those companies represented eighteen industries in thirty-four countries.[14] This study was a follow-up to an earlier study on the value of enterprise systems and analytics.[15]

In the large survey, we found a direct relationship between enterprise systems and decision making. For example, while many organizations initially invest in enterprise systems to improve efficiency and streamline processes, we found that cost savings were not their primary objective. In both studies, a majority (53 percent) of respondents identified "improved decision making" as one of their top three business objectives. To help managers make more-informed and faster decisions, organizations initially invest in enterprise systems to deliver reliable transaction-level data and "a single version of the truth"—an important precursor to developing an analytical capability. Once a firm has established a solid foundation of high-quality transaction data, its managers are able to shift their focus to using the data and systems for better decision making.

We also found that companies are becoming more analytical over time and building their commitment to analytics. In the first study, nearly half (45 percent) of the companies we surveyed reported that they had minimal or no analytical capabilities. However, four years later, only 8 percent said they lacked basic analytical capabilities. Almost every large firm has those capabilities today.

Similarly, the number of organizations with significant or advanced analytical capabilities supported by extensive and integrated management information doubled from 28 percent to 57 percent.

Most important, we found (and subsequent studies by other researchers has confirmed) a striking relationship between the use of analytics and business performance. When we compared the responses of high performers (those who outperformed their industry in terms of profit, shareholder return, and revenue growth—about 13 percent of the sample) with those of low performers (16 percent of the sample), we found that the majority of high-performing businesses strategically apply analytics in their daily operations. And about 10 percent of executives cited analytics as a key element of their company's strategy. High performers were 50 percent more likely to use analytics strategically compared with the overall sample and five times as likely as low performers.

Further, we discovered a significant statistical association between an organization's commitment to analytics and high performance. Companies with strong analytical orientations (those who answered with a 4 or 5 on all our questions) represented 25 percent of the sample (ninety-three companies), and their orientations correlated highly with financial outperformance in terms of profit, revenue, and shareholder return.[16] In fact, one of the strongest and most consistent differences between low- and high-performance businesses is their attitude toward, and applications of, analytics (see figure 3-1).[17] For example, 65 percent of high performers indicated they have significant decision-support or real-time analytical capabilities versus 23 percent of low performers. Only 8 percent of low performers valued analytical insights to a very large extent compared with 36 percent of top performers. And while one-third of the low performers in our study believe that they have above-average analytical capability within their industries, 77 percent of top performers believe that. Finally, 40 percent of high performers employ analytics broadly across their entire organization, but only 23 percent of low performers do.

FIGURE 3-1

Importance of analytical orientation:
High performers versus low performers, 2006

	Low performers	High performers
Have significant decision-support/ analytical capabilities	23%	65%
Value analytical insights to a very large extent	8%	36%
Have above average analytical capability within industry	33%	77%
Use analytics across their entire organization	23%	40%

Subsequent studies reached similar conclusions. In 2010, *MIT Sloan Management Review* and IBM analyzed data from three thousand executives in over one hundred countries and thirty industries. They concluded that "top-performing organizations use analytics five times more than lower performers. Top performers approach business operations differently from their peers. Specifically, they put analytics to use in the widest possible range of decisions, large and small. They were twice as likely to use analytics to guide future strategies, and twice as likely to use insights to guide day-to-day operations. They make decisions based on rigorous analysis at more than double the rate of lower performers."[18]

After concluding a seven-year study of data from 864 respondents in nine countries and eight industries, Accenture and Professor David Simchi-Levi at the Massachusetts Institute of Technology (MIT), in 2015 concluded that "the stronger a company's commitment to analytics, the higher that company's performance" (see figure 3-2). Among their findings are that, compared to low performers:

- Twice as many high performers are using analytics in key areas to support decision making.

- Twice as many high performers are embedding analytics in decision making that leverages machine learning.

- High performers embed predictive analytics insights into key business processes at higher rates and keep monitoring decisions and course-correcting as needed.

- High performers are three times as likely to invest a substantial portion of their technology spend on analytics. In addition, more than twice as many high performers are spending more on investments in analytical human capital through training, investments in people and the use of consultants.[19]

The breadth and consistency of the associations described earlier suggest the wisdom of investing in analytics for any organization seeking to improve performance. Furthermore, our research confirms that while relatively few companies have adopted analytics as a competitive capability, many more aspire to do so. The leaders of these

FIGURE 3-2

Importance of analytical orientation:
High performers versus low performers, 2015

	Low performers	High performers
Achieve specific business outcomes from analytics	39%	79%
Embed predictive analytics insights into key business processes	34%	79%
Routinely monitor decisions and course-correct	32%	84%
Invest more than one-quarter of their total technology expenditure in analytics	17%	59%
Spend more on analytical talent (including hiring, training, consultants)	40%	82%

Source: Accenture/MIT study, Winning with Analytics, 2015.

companies have made the commitment to investing in analytics as a means of improving business performance.

Analytics as a Source of Competitive Advantage

Skeptics may scoff that analytics can't provide a sustainable competitive advantage, because any single insight or analysis eventually can be adopted by competitors. And it is true that an individual insight may provide only transient benefits. Yield management provided a big boost to American Airlines for a time, for example, but using that process is now just a cost of doing business in the airline industry.

Organizations can take several approaches to gain a competitive advantage with data. Some can collect unique data over time about their customers and prospects that competitors cannot match. Others can organize, standardize, and manipulate data that is available to others in a unique fashion. Still others might develop a proprietary algorithm that leads to better, more insightful analyses on which to make decisions. And some differentiate themselves by embedding analytics into a distinctive business process. Increasingly, both data and analytics are incorporated into innovative products and services.

Regardless of the approach, for companies to sustain a competitive advantage, analytics must be applied judiciously, executed well, and continually renewed. Companies that successfully compete on analytics have analytical capabilities that are:

- *Hard to duplicate.* It is one thing to copy another company's IT applications or its products and their related attributes (such as price, placement, or promotion), quite another to replicate processes and culture. For example, other banks have tried to copy Capital One's strategy of experimentation and testing, but they haven't been as successful. Banks that have been successful with a similar strategy, such as Barclays in the United Kingdom, have figured out their own route to analytical competition. While Capital One relentlessly seeks new customers, Barclays leverages analytics to increase "share of wallet" by cross-selling to its large customer base.

- *Unique.* There is no single correct path to follow to become an analytical competitor, and the way every company uses analytics is unique to its strategy and market position. For example, in the gaming industry, Caesars uses analytics to encourage customers to play in a variety of its locations. This makes sense for Caesars, because it has long had its casinos scattered around the United States. But that approach clearly would not be the right one for a single casino, such as Foxwoods Resort Casino in Connecticut. It's also less appealing for casino impresario Steve Wynn, who has translated his intuitive sense of style and luxury into the destination resorts Encore and the Wynn.

- *Capable of adapting to many situations.* An analytical organization can cross internal boundaries and apply analytical capabilities in innovative ways. Sprint, for example, easily adapted its analytical expertise in marketing to improve its human capital processes. The company applied its "customer experience life cycle" model to create an analogous "employee experience life cycle" model that helped it optimize employee acquisition and retention.

- *Better than the competition.* Even in industries where analytical expertise and consistent data are prevalent, some organizations are just better at exploiting information than others. While every financial services firm has access to the consumer risk information from FICO, for example, Capital One has analytical skills and knowledge that enables it to outperform the market by making smarter decisions about potentially risky credit customers. The company's managers refer to the concept of *deaveraging*—how can they break apart a category or a metric to get more analytical advantage?

- *Renewable.* Any competitive advantage needs to be a moving target, with continued improvement and reinvestment. Analytics are particularly well suited to continuous innovation and renewal. Progressive, for example, describes its competitive advantage in terms of the agility it gains through a disciplined analytical approach. By the time competitors notice that Progressive has targeted a new segment—such as older motorcycle drivers—it has captured the market and moved on to the next opportunity. By the time other insurers had adopted its approach to pricing based on credit scores, it was working on its Snapshot pay-as-you-drive system.

One caveat: companies in heavily regulated industries, or in those for which the availability of data is limited, will be constrained from exploiting analytics to the fullest. For example, outside the United States, pharmaceutical firms are prevented from obtaining data about prescriptions from individual physicians. As a result, pharmaceutical marketing activities in other parts of the world are generally much less analytical than those of companies selling in the US market. But in other cases, analytics can permanently and abruptly transform an industry or process. As *Moneyball* and *The Big Short* author Michael Lewis points out in talking about investment banking, "The introduction of derivatives and other new financial instruments brought unprecedented levels of complexity and variation to investment firms. The old-school, instinct guys who knew when to buy and when to sell were watching young MBAs—or worse, PhDs from MIT—bring an unprecedented level of analysis and brain power to trading. Within 10 years, the old guard was gone."[20]

Analytics in Government

We haven't written much thus far about analytics in government, because our focus in this book is on how organizations compete—and governmental organizations don't do that in the conventional sense of the term. The one area in which national governments do compete is war, and it's probably not surprising that the earliest uses of analytics in government involved national defense. The first computers were developed to calculate things like missile trajectories, and Robert McNamara introduced a broad range of analytical approaches to the military—not always with success—when he was secretary of defense in the 1960s. In the present military environment, analytics are used extensively for military intelligence, including automated analysis of text and voice communications (sometimes to considerable public controversy).

Today, however, analytics are widely used at many levels of government, from local to state to federal. They may not necessarily increase governments' abilities to compete, but they can certainly make governments substantially more efficient and effective. At the local level, for example, perhaps the most impressive accomplishment from analytics has been the use of crime statistics analysis to deter criminals. In New York City, the CompStat program associates crimes with particular geographical regions of the city and is used to guide decisions about where police officers should be stationed. It is also linked with an effort to push decisions down to the precinct level. CompStat has been widely praised for contributing to the reduction in crime in New York since its inception. However, several other factors changed during the same time, so it is difficult to isolate CompStat's effects alone.[21]

More recently, the Domain Awareness System (DAS), a joint initiative between the New York Police Department and Microsoft, is now being sold to other cities. The system harnesses the power of big data analytics to solve crimes faster and to prevent terrorist attacks. The amount of sensor and other data collected for DAS purposes is astounding, including:

- Images from nine thousand closed circuit video cameras

- Over 2 billion license plate reads from five hundred readers around the city

- Six hundred fixed and mobile (typically worn by officers) radiation and chemical sensors

- An extensive network of ShotSpotter audio gunshot detectors covering twenty-four square miles

- Speech-to-text data from 54 million 911 calls from citizens.

- The system also can draw from internal NYPD crime records, including 100 million summonses.[22]

Elsewhere in the United States, several city police departments are using predictive analytics to fight crime and deploy their personnel where they can have the greatest impact. In Atlanta, aggregate crime declined by 19 percent once a predictive policing solution was adopted.[23] Los Angeles experienced a 33 percent reduction in burglaries and a 21 percent reduction in violent crimes in city neighborhoods using the predictive model.[24]

Beyond crime prevention, there are many possible applications for analytics at the state level, some of which can amount to substantial savings when pursued effectively. Several states, including Massachusetts, have pursued revenue optimization approaches that have yielded hundreds of millions of dollars. These apply to tax and nontax payments. States have also pursued fraud detection to reduce improper payments for welfare, purchase cards, Medicare, and Medicaid. State departments of natural resources have used analytical approaches to model and optimize resources such as minerals, gas and oil, and parks.

Taxpayer compliance was among the US federal government's earliest nondefense applications of analytics. The Internal Revenue Service (IRS) initiated the Taxpayer Compliance Measurement Program in 1963 to analyze which taxpayers were likely to be cheating on their taxes and to close the "tax gap" between what is paid and what should be.[25] It was an effective program for the IRS, but data gathering was judged too expensive and invasive and was discontinued in 1988. The IRS rekindled its analytics efforts with the National Research Program in 2000, and continues to use it as a basis for analyzing compliance and for identifying returns to audit.

One of the most important applications of analytics in government involves health care. This is a major expense for the federal government—

its largest nondefense category of spending. Medicare and Medicaid are paid for by the US government but are administered by states. A large medical program that is run at the federal level is the Department of Veterans Affairs (VA) hospitals. The VA has employed electronic medical records and analytics based on them to become one of the most effective health care providers in the United States. As a *BusinessWeek* article about the VA hospitals titled "The Best Medical Care in the U.S." described, "In the mid-1990s, Dr. Kenneth W. Kizer, then the VA's Health Under Secretary, installed the most extensive electronic medical records system in the U.S. Kizer also decentralized decision-making, closed underused hospitals, reallocated resources, and most critically, instituted a culture of accountability and quality measurements."[26]

The VA hospitals employ such analytical approaches as predictive modeling of chronic disease, evidence-based medicine, automated decisions for treatment protocols and drug prescriptions, and many others. The VA's experience is one of the best indications that analytics can have as much of an effect on government as on the private sector.

While the VA hospitals have received criticism about the time veterans have had to wait for appointments, its standard of care has generally remained high. In 2014, Robert McDonald, the former CEO of Procter & Gamble and a strong analytics advocate, was named Secretary of Veterans Affairs. Among other data-driven initiatives, he established a central Data Analytics Division to make analytical expertise available throughout the VA.

Governments around the world are increasingly adopting predictive analytics. Singapore has an integrated city planning initiative called "Smart Nation" that is transforming how public policy decisions are made about issues ranging from strategic (e.g., economic planning) to operational (e.g., transportation planning) to tactical (e.g., determining which books to stock at local libraries).[27] Government agencies such as the Irish Tax and Customs Authority use predictive models to target fraudulent tax returns and thereby increase revenues.[28] Police forces in the United Kingdom, Singapore, the Netherlands, Uruguay, Brazil, Chile, and the United Arab Emirates are beginning to use predictive analytics to solve and deter criminal activity.[29] Emergency services personnel in the Philippines use predictive analytics to improve their preparedness for natural disasters.[30]

Serving the Market for Analytical Products and Services

While our focus in this book is on how companies can use analytics to optimize key business processes, there is another way to profit from analytics: by making available analytical products or services directly to customers—either as a stand-alone offering or to augment other products and services. For companies in a position to consider this an option, we take a brief detour here.

This focus on data products (which also invariably include analytics) came of age during the Analytics 2.0 era, as we mentioned in the introduction. Perhaps the best-known company of that era that augments its offerings with analytics is Google. In addition to providing analytics for search, which we discuss in chapter 4, and to advertisers, which we describe in chapter 5, Google acquired a web analytics business in 2005 and now makes its Google Analytics service available to anyone, providing data and analytical tools that can be used for search engine optimization (SEO), improving customer engagement, increasing click-throughs, and other marketing initiatives. The company offers Google Analytics with a unique business model: it gives many services away for free (although it has a "premium" version with more sophisticated analytics). Google's goal in offering the analytical service is to improve the understanding of the web and the internet by providing metrics on website results and user behavior. Rather than competing with other web analytics vendors, Google seeks to "lift all boats" and educate web publishers and advertisers on whether their efforts are working and how to profit from this relatively new channel. The more people who use web analytics well, the better the overall web experience will be, and Google will profit in the long run. Google even provides an online "Analytics Academy" to teach the basic principles of web analytics, in addition to publishing a blog and online articles, offering webinars, and providing public speakers on web analytics.

As we mentioned in the introduction, large firms have also begun to create data and analytics-based products and services. GE, for example, has made a multibillion-dollar bet on the "industrial internet," including such applications as predictive maintenance for turbines, jet engines, and locomotives; route optimization for locomotives; and clinical analytics in health care.[31] Verizon Wireless will analyze location data from its customers' mobile phones on behalf of sports, entertainment, and lodging companies to allow them to better target their ads and offers.[32] Philips offers a predictive analytics-based service called CareSage that lets health systems monitor and care for elderly patients by compiling data from wearable devices and home monitors (its own and those from competitors). It identifies patients most likely to have health issues so that clinicians can intervene before problems or hospitalizations occur. In short, if your organization generates data that is relevant to customers, you might want to figure out how best to analyze it and make it available to those customers in meaningful products and services.

Financial investing firms, of course, were among the earliest to employ analytics as a core element of their services. *Algorithmic trading* is used throughout the industry, and the general feeling is that the decisions in that sector involve too much data and need to happen too quickly to be done by humans. Hedge funds like Bridgewater Associates, Renaissance Technologies, Two Sigma, and others rely on analytics to make almost all trading decisions, and they have done well as a result. As one recent article put it: "Quant funds like those managed by Two Sigma and Renaissance Technologies have been consistently posting solid returns in recent years while most other hedge fund strategies centered around the trading decisions of human beings have struggled mightily."[33] The leaders of these hedge funds are among the highest-compensated businesspeople in the world, often making billions of dollars per year.

The move to analytics has also been reflected in the rise of analytical consulting. Accenture, Deloitte, IBM Global Services, and many other firms have identified analytical consulting as a growth area in response to client demands. These firms' consultants help clients address the broad strategic issues around building an analytical capability, or provide assistance building and supporting a particular business initiative (e.g., a customer loyalty program). They frequently tailor solutions for specific industries, such as automated underwriting in financial services. Quantitatively oriented consultants specialize in analytically intensive business solutions, such as supply chain optimization, while specialists in information management help clients develop a robust analytical technical environment. Consultants with particular industry and functional specialties (e.g., marketing or supply chain) work closely with clients while those with purely technical or statistical skills are increasingly based offshore, particularly in India.

Sometimes firms in analytical businesses take on related tasks, such as data management and consulting. In the retail sector, Dunnhumby (which describes itself as a "customer science" company using data and science to help retailers delight customers and build loyalty) worked closely with Tesco on the development of the giant grocery retailer's loyalty program Clubcard, an important tool in that firm's ability to use data to optimize its product mix (for more on Tesco, see chapter 5). The company has also worked closely with Kroger in the United States on similar loyalty programs.

Catalina also sells analytical services to the grocery industry that help it understand the effects of coupons and other promotions. The firm retrieves over 300 million transactions per week from more than fifty thousand retailers.[34] On behalf of those stores, Catalina manages one of the largest databases in the world, containing the purchase histories of over 260 million shoppers.[35] The company aggregates information about purchase behavior and customer demographics, attitudes, and preferences and sells that information to grocery store chains, in addition to offering personalized print and mobile coupons based on analytics. Catalina claims that its approach can increase a company's average coupon-redemption rates up to ten times higher than they would be with traditional promotion methods.

In many cases, selling data is not enough. Companies also need help interpreting and using the data, and hence buy consulting from external providers. Information Resources Inc. (IRI), for example, has long gathered data from retailers' point-of-sale terminals, from panels of almost 100,000 consumers, and from pantry audits to understand consumption patterns. More recently, however, IRI has grown its ability to help firms in the consumer packaged goods, retail, and pharmaceutical sectors analyze data to make smarter and more profitable marketing decisions. Sunil Garga, who was President of IRI's Global

Business & Consumer Insights, argues that because of the rise of analytics, "Marketing has changed more in the last twenty-four months than it has in the last twenty-four years, and that rate of change will continue. It's an analytic revolution."[36]

In the case of firms that sell data and analytics, the challenge is often to convince customers of the need for analytical capabilities. According to the managers we interviewed in these firms, a lack of understanding of the analytical methods and what they can accomplish, not cost, is the chief objection. This is one of the reasons why Google has taken such an evangelical and educational approach to web analytics with its Google Analytics offering.

In a variation of the "selling analytics" approach, many established companies are finding innovative ways to enhance physical products by incorporating analytics. For example, medical products companies are designing products with sensors so that an individual's health data can be analyzed remotely rather than at a clinic or hospital. Also on the horizon are copiers that can transmit data that allows the service provider to schedule preventive maintenance and avoid downtime. And washing machines in the near future will be able to "listen" to sensors embedded inside the clothes in order to determine the right temperature setting.

With the availability of wearable sensors, analytical products are even coming to golf, a sport that has not been a stranger to technological innovation in the past few decades. The Garmin TruSwing consists of a sensor that can be attached to any club and analytical software that runs on smartwatches, smartphones, and tablets. It measures and analyzes metrics based on the mechanics of a golfer's swing (such as ball flight, trajectory, and distance) to provide insights into each shot and improve performance. Golfers can get instant swing feedback from their wrist after each swing or use a mobile app that allows detailed 3D animations and more detailed analytics. Golfers not only have the ability to analyze individual swings: two swings can be overlaid on top of each other or, alternatively, run side-by-side for further comparison and analysis. Golfers also have the ability to share their performance data, either with friends or their golf pro, to get guidance on how to improve their swing.

When Analytics Aren't Enough

We wish we could argue that using analytics well is all an organization needs to improve business performance. But there are good examples that disprove that assertion. Large US airlines, such as American and United, are exhibit A. They are analytical competitors but struggled for many years nonetheless. Both airlines (American a bit more than United) were pioneers in adopting such analytical approaches as yield management for seat pricing, optimization of routes and resource scheduling, and the analysis of loyalty program data. While there's no doubt that these companies would be worse off without their use of analytics, both fared badly during much of the last two decades (although lower fuel prices and industry consolidation have helped them do much better recently, and they're both hard at work on new analytics approaches).

What happened? Two things kept these firms from succeeding with their analytical strategies over a couple of decades. One is that their analytics supported an obsolete business model. They pioneered analytics for yield management, but other airlines with lower costs could still offer lower prices (on average, if not for a particular seat). They pioneered analytics for complex optimization of routes with many different airplane types, but competitors such as Southwest saved both money and complexity by using only one type of plane. They pioneered loyalty programs and promotions based on data analysis, but their customer service was so indifferent and resources so constrained that loyalty to these airlines was difficult for frequent flyers.

The other problem with their analytical approaches was that other airlines adopted them. Even discount carriers such as Southwest and JetBlue make diligent use of yield management and crew-scheduling analytics. If the discounters lacked internal capabilities for analytics, they could buy them from providers such as Navitaire, PROS, or Sabre Airline Solutions (which used to be part of American but has now been spun out as a separate company). Industry data is widely available from associations and external providers to any airline that wants to analyze it.

In short, there are few barriers preventing any airline from employing standard analytical approaches, and airlines must work very hard to distinguish themselves in analytical competition at this point. Perhaps other frontiers of analytical orientation will emerge in that industry in the future.

Conclusion

The success of companies like Amazon, Capital One, Marriott, Progressive, and Google demonstrates that the use of analytics can lead to better business performance and, indeed, competitive advantage. Over a decade of research indicates that individual analytical projects pay major dividends, and survey data confirms that analytical approaches are correlated with high performance. We have also identified five factors that make an analytical approach a source of competitive advantage. In the next two chapters, we'll explore in more detail how certain companies are using analytics to outperform the competition. Chapter 4 addresses internal processes, and chapter 5 deals with external processes, such as those involving customers and suppliers.

CHAPTER FOUR

COMPETING ON ANALYTICS WITH INTERNAL PROCESSES

FINANCIAL, M&A, OPERATIONS, R&D, AND HUMAN RESOURCE APPLICATIONS

ANALYTICS CAN BE APPLIED TO MANY BUSINESS PRO-cesses to gain a competitive edge. We've divided the world of analytical support for business processes into two categories: internal and external. Chapter 5 will address external applications—customer and supplier-driven processes—and this one will focus on internal applications (refer to figure 4-1). It's not always a perfectly clean distinction; in this chapter, for example, the internal applications sometimes involve external data and entities, even though they are not primarily about supply and demand, customers, or supply chains. But the focus here is on such internally facing functions as general management, finance and accounting, operations, R&D, and human resource management. These are, in fact, the earliest applications of "decision support." The original intent was that this data and these systems would be used to manage the business internally. Only more recently have they been applied to working with customers and suppliers, as companies have accumulated better data about the outside world with which they interact.

The challenge, then, is not simply to identify internal applications of business analytics but to find some that are clearly strategic and involve

FIGURE 4-1

Application domains for analytics

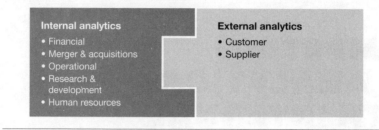

competitive advantage. Any company, for example, can have a financial or operational scorecard, but how does it contribute to a distinctive, strategic capability? Customer-related applications are more likely to be strategic almost by definition; internal applications have to work at it to make a strategic impact. They have to lead to measurable improvements to financial or operational performance. In the box "Typical Analytical Techniques for Internal Processes," we list some common approaches.

TYPICAL ANALYTICAL TECHNIQUES FOR INTERNAL PROCESSES

Activity-based costing (ABC). The first step in activity-based management is to allocate costs accurately to aspects of the business such as customers, processes, or distribution channels; models incorporating activities, materials, resources, and product-offering components then allow optimization based on cost and prediction of capacity needs.

Bayesian inference (e.g., to predict revenues). A numerical estimate of the degree of belief in a hypothesis before and after evidence has been observed.

Combinatorial optimization (e.g., for optimizing a product portfolio). The efficient allocation of limited resources to yield the best solution to particular objectives when the values of some or all of the variables (e.g., a given number of people) must be integers (because people can't be split into fractions) and there are many possible combinations. Also called *integer programming*.

Constraint analysis (e.g., for product configuration). The use of one or more constraint satisfaction algorithms to specify the set of feasible solutions. Constraints are programmed in rules or procedures that produce solutions to particular configuration and design problems using one or more constraint satisfaction algorithms.

Experimental design (e.g., for website analysis). In the simplest type of experiment, participants are randomly assigned to two groups that are equivalent to each other. One group (the program or treatment group) gets the program and the other group (the comparison or control group) does not. If the program results in statistically significant differences in the outcome variable, it is assumed to have the hypothesized effect.

Future-value analysis. The decomposition of market capitalization into current value (extrapolation of existing monetary returns) and future value, or expectations of future growth.

Genetic algorithms (e.g., for decryption/code breaking or product engineering/design). A class of stochastic optimization models and heuristic search techniques that use principles found in evolution and natural selection. Particularly useful when a large number of variables and complex constraints exist. External examples include: scheduling satellite communications, optimally loading cargo containers and optimizing delivery routes.

Monte Carlo simulation (e.g., for R&D project valuation). A computerized technique used to assess the probability of certain outcomes or risks by mathematically modeling a hypothetical event over multiple trials and comparing the outcome with predefined probability distributions.

Multiple regression analysis (e.g., to determine how nonfinancial factors affect financial performance). A statistical technique

(continued)

whereby the influence of a set of independent variables on a single dependent variable is determined.

Neural network analysis (e.g., to predict needed factory maintenance). Systems modeled on the structure and operation of the brain, in which the state of the system is modified by training until it can discriminate between the classes of inputs; used on large databases. Typically, a neural network is initially "trained," or fed large amounts of data and rules about data relationships—for example, "A grandfather is older than a person's father."

Simulation (e.g., in pharmaceutical "in silico" research). Manipulation of parameters using mathematics and/or rule bases to model how different values would generate a result. The simulated result can be used to obtain an optimal output or to predict a certain behavior. Pharmaceutical researchers might use biosimulation to study how cells or other living entities react to chemical or other interventions.

Textual analysis (e.g., to assess call center performance or mine Twitter data for customer sentiment). Analysis of the frequency, semantic relationships, and relative importance of particular terms, phrases, and documents in online text.

Yield analysis (e.g., in semiconductor manufacturing). Employing basic statistics (mean, median, standard deviation, etc.) to understand yield volume and quality, and to compare one batch of items with another—often displayed visually.

Financial Analytics

Despite being a quantitative field by nature, finance has trailed other functions like marketing, supply chain, operations, and even human resources in employing advanced analytics to make key decisions. Chief financial officers (CFOs) are generally thought of as the "numbers people" in their organizations. They are often articulate advocates for using predictive and prescriptive analytics for decision making—but usually when it is in some other department.

Finance groups, naturally, have long used reports, dashboards and scorecards, and online queries in the course of their work. The problem is that these descriptive analytics applications don't tell the user anything about underlying patterns in the numbers, and they only describe the past. Finance professionals may experiment with an occasional regression model in Excel, but for the finance function to make advanced analytics a core capability—on the same level as external reporting or the closing process—is quite rare.

We remain optimistic that this situation is beginning to change. As CFOs become more comfortable with the use of analytical models in the rest of the business, we expect more innovative analytical applications are being implemented in finance. At Intel, for example, a small number of finance professionals began to advocate for greater use of analytics three years ago. They presented to the senior finance team the idea of building a generalized competency in advanced analytics, and the reaction was positive. One early initiative was to compare Intel's finance analytics capabilities to those of leading firms in the area, and Intel found that some online or technology-focused firms in Silicon Valley (many of which have strong analytical orientations in general) had more advanced capabilities than it had. Intel started several specific initiatives in the forecasting area, including statistical forecasts of revenue and inventory levels, and prediction of impairments in Intel Capital's investments. The finance function at Intel has also embarked on a broad effort to educate finance professionals and managers about advanced analytics topics and is planning certification programs for them as well.

Given the amount of data available to finance functions and the level of insight that can be achieved, it seems inevitable that finance's use of advanced analytics will become more prevalent. In the following pages, we offer some examples of analytical financial applications, since they of course have the most direct tie to financial performance. There are several categories of financial analytics applications, including external reporting, enterprise performance management (management reporting and scorecards), cost management, and risk management.

External Reporting to Regulatory
Bodies and Shareholders

External reporting doesn't lead to competitive advantage under "business as usual" conditions. It's not normally an advantage to report more quickly and accurately beyond a certain level. Cisco Systems, for example, has touted over the years its ability to close the books instantaneously and to report its results almost immediately at the end of a financial period. But we often wondered why the company bothered; the SEC doesn't demand instantaneous closes, and it's not clear what else a company could do with financial results intended for external consumption. But it is a different story with the information used by managers to make better strategic, investment, and operational decisions.

Reporting and scorecards, both financial and operational, are some of the most common applications of business intelligence and decision support. They're obviously important to managing any business, and they're increasingly important (with the advent of Sarbanes-Oxley legislation, for example) to keeping senior executives out of jail. While organizations do not compete on the basis of their reporting and scorecards, having systems in place to monitor progress against key operating metrics and monitor progress against plan is critical to strategy execution.

New regulatory data requirements can become opportunity to create a rich data source to improve performance. For example, pharmaceutical companies routinely interact with healthcare professionals both as customers and as consultants, researchers, and marketing speakers. Due to the potential for a conflict of interest, more than forty countries have enacted "anti-kickback" regulations that require transparency into these relationships. As a result, companies must aggregate all physician spend data into a single location so that it can be reported appropriately to the correct jurisdiction. According to Everest Group, "The industry is viewing the increased regulatory supervision as a burden. However, the regulatory requirements are putting in place a foundation for data requirements that can be used to drive pharma and life sciences analytics. Organizations can extract additional value in a challenging market, and create competitive differentiation by utilizing this opportunity."[1] Medical device manufacturer Zimmer Biomet, for example, uses MediSpend's data and analytic dashboards to monitor compliance with global compliance laws. But it also leverages the data to create new business models that drive device and drug development.

As we argued in chapter 1, reporting activities have typically not made extensive use of analytics, but there are exceptions. One is the prediction of future performance.

Public companies have to make regular predictions of future performance for investors and analysts. The consequences of poor predictions can be dramatic; investors may severely punish companies that fail to "meet their numbers." Most companies make straightforward extrapolations of results from earlier periods to later ones. Yet in certain industries with a high degree of change and uncertainty, extrapolations can be problematic and yield poor predictions.

The information technology industry is one of those uncertain industries. Products and customer desires change rapidly, and disproportionate sales volumes take place at the ends of reporting periods. Hewlett-Packard found that it was very difficult to make accurate predictions of revenues in such an environment, and in one quarter of 2001 had a "nearly disastrous" revenue growth forecasting error of 12 percent.[2] Hewlett-Packard executives decided to put some of their quantitative researchers in HP Labs onto the problem of creating more accurate revenue forecasts.

The researchers used a Bayesian inference approach (see definition in the box earlier in this chapter) to predict monthly and quarterly revenues from data thus far in the period. After several adjustments, the algorithm yielded significantly better revenue predictions than the more straightforward approach used previously. Hewlett-Packard incorporated the new algorithm into its performance-reporting dashboard, and the company's (then) CFO, Bob Wayman, noted, "It is reassuring to have a solid projection algorithm. It's crisper and cleaner, it has rigor and methodology as opposed to my own algorithm."[3]

Better prediction of future performance from an operational standpoint also allows companies to take action sooner. Using "near-real-time" operational data, managers can quickly identify emerging trends, make predictions, and take prompt action. For example, during the last recession, Dell executives used predictive models to recognize months before their competitors how thoroughly sales were going to soften. They took preemptive action on prices and products, which resulted in better (or at least, less awful) financial performance during the downturn. More importantly, as the recession ended, they were able to adjust again to boost their market share.

Enterprise Performance Management and Scorecards

Another exception to financial reporting applications involving analytics is when companies try to explain financial performance from non-financial factors. A successful enterprise performance management initiative requires companies not just to predict performance accurately but also to come to grips with some broader questions: Which activities have the greatest impact on business performance? How do we know whether we are executing against our strategy? An organization needs quantifiable insight into the operational factors that contribute to business results and a way of measuring progress against them.

Over the past decade or so, the biggest advance in management reporting has been the shift from IT delivering structured reports or fairly static scorecards to giving managers unprecedented access to enterprise data. Information workers and managers are able to access and explore financial and operational information from across the organization using business intelligence applications that incorporate alerts, management dashboards, dynamic filters, and data visualization tools. As analytical tools incorporate artificial intelligence technologies like natural language generation, they are able to help managers understand and interpret the data, too. For example, Credit Suisse integrated Quill (an advanced natural language generation platform from Narrative Science) into HOLT, its investment data analytics platform. Credit Suisse analyzes both proprietary and market data to produce investment research reports that assess company expectations, upside and risk to help analysts, bankers, and investors make long-term investment decisions. Credit Suisse has achieved full analyst coverage on all five thousand companies profiled within its platform, increasing the number of companies that Credit Suisse analyzes by more than 300 percent. Because investment analysts no longer need to write summary reports themselves, they are able to focus more on their clients and on conducting more sophisticated analyses.

These performance management systems report not only on financial performance but also on such nonfinancial domains as customer relationships, employee learning and innovation, and operations. These have been a great step forward in understanding performance. But too many adopters of balanced scorecards still aren't very balanced, focusing primarily on financial reporting. It's great to add nonfinancial metrics to a scorecard, but if investors and regulators don't really care about them, it's natural to emphasize the financial numbers.

Another problem with most dashboards is that even when companies do include both financial and nonfinancial measures, they don't relate them to each other. Management professors David Larcker and Chris Ittner studied several companies that had adopted balanced scorecards.[4] None of the companies they examined had causal models that related nonfinancial to financial performance.

Nonfinancial or intangible resources (such as human knowledge capital, brand, and R&D capability) are growing in importance to both company business performance and external perceptions of company value.[5] Even the most favorable studies only show an explanatory power of approximately 50 percent for the effect of financial measures such as earnings per share, net income, economic profit, or return on invested capital on a company's market value.[6] In some industries, EPS accounts for less than 5 percent of value. We believe that a management team that manages all its sources of value—tangible and intangible, current and future—has a significant advantage over those who do not.

Some companies are working to develop a holistic understanding of both financial and nonfinancial value drivers. A few companies at the frontier are seeking to manage both their current and future shareholder value.[7] These organizations are exploring how to infuse their scorecards with data from Wall Street analysts and future-value analytics to gain better insight into the implications of decisions on shareholder value. Companies that develop such a capability might be well on the way to competitive advantage.

Reporting and scorecards are most likely to lead to competitive advantage when the business environment is changing dramatically. In those circumstances, it's particularly important to monitor new forms of performance. New measures need to be developed, new models of performance need to be created, and new management behaviors need to emerge. The speed and effectiveness of organizational trans-formation in such periods can certainly be or lead to a competitive advantage. For example, a property and casualty insurance company we worked with needed to transform itself. It was a poor financial performer, with losses over the last four years of well over a billion dollars. It paid out $1.40 in claims and expenses for every premium dollar it took in. The company had monitored its financial results, but it didn't have a handle on what was creating the poor performance.

As part of a major corporate transformation, the company focused on three key processes: producer (agent) relationships, profitable un-derwriting, and claims execution. In addition to redesigning those pro-cesses, the company created new measures of them and collected them in a balanced scorecard. The scorecard served as a means to rapidly communicate the performance of and changes in the processes, and the success of the change initiative overall, to the management team. The scorecard assessed the company's ability to deliver on such objectives as:

- Selecting profitable new markets to enter

- Attracting and selecting the right customers

- Driving pricing in accordance with risk

- Reducing the severity of claims

Reward systems for employees and managers at all levels of the company were changed to tie to performance on these objectives. Some automated analytics were embedded into underwriting systems to speed the process and improve the quality of pricing decisions.

The company used these process changes and reporting approaches to dramatically turn itself around. It began to make substantial amounts of profit and was eventually acquired by another insurance firm for $3.5 billion—up from perhaps zero value a few years earlier.

Cost Management

Although some might question whether cost management can lead to a competitive advantage, there are a still a few examples of organi-zations that have made effective analysis and management of costs a strategic capability.

In health care (at least in the United States), few hospitals even know their costs of treating patients, and are thus rarely able to control them. One exception is University of Utah Healthcare, which includes four academic medical centers and a variety of clinics and centers in the Salt Lake City area. UUHC embarked on a multiyear effort to accurately measure its costs. The project, called Value Driven Outcomes (VDO), used an activity-based costing approach. VDO fully integrates all available data regarding a patient encounter to provide a complete and comprehensive view of the care of patients. UUHC started by developing accurate cost accounting data using the actual acquisition costs of each item used in each patient encounter. Then comprehensive utilization methods were employed to assign all the costs to each patient encounter. Once cost information had been gathered, UUHC also developed key quality metrics and integrated the quality data with the cost and clinical data, so that a comprehensive analysis of cost-effectiveness could be used.

The hospital was then able to apply statistical methods to answer obvious—but previously impossible-to-answer—questions such as: What is the cost of poor quality? Where is there meaningful variation in cost or quality between physicians? Where is patient care over-utilizing labs or imaging where there is no additional quality or value as a result?

UUHC also engaged its physicians in the development and use of the VDO data and analytics tools. They developed self-service descriptive analytics tools with physician guidance, including continual feedback to ensure that what was being developed would meet their needs and answer their questions. The results are impressive: while costs at other academic medical centers in the area have risen by 2.9 on average annually over the past few years, UUHC's have declined by 0.5 percent a year.

Energy costs are another expensive resource for many organizations. Microsoft's five-hundred-acre corporate campus in Redmond, Washington, contains 14.9 million square feet of office space and labs. Seeking to save energy and reduce utility and maintenance costs, the company considered investing over $60 million to upgrade its incompatible networks of equipment and over thirty thousand sensors. Darrell Smith, director of Facilities and Energy, wanted to avoid a disruptive and expensive construction and replacement project. Additionally, the Microsoft team was concerned about displacing employees and the resulting loss in productivity. So instead, Smith and his team developed an "analytical blanket" to connect and weave together the diverse systems used to manage the campus buildings. The analytical layer enabled the team to string together data from thousands of sensors in the buildings, as well as in equipment such as HVAC, fans, and lighting systems. Soon they were accumulating billions of data points every week. Microsoft describes the benefits this way:

> That data has given the team deep insights, enabled better diagnostics, and has allowed for far more intelligent decision making. A test run of the program in 13 Microsoft buildings has provided staggering results—not only has Microsoft saved energy and millions in maintenance and utility costs, but the company now is hyper-aware of the way its buildings perform. . . . It's no small thing—whether a damper is stuck in Building 75 or a valve is leaky in Studio H—that engineers can now detect (and often fix with a few clicks) even the tiniest issues from their high-tech dashboard at their desks . . . rather than having to jump into a truck to go find and fix the problem in person.[8]

For example, in one garage, exhaust fans had been running continuously for a year (resulting in $66,000 of wasted energy). Within moments of coming online, the smart buildings solution detected the mistake and the problem was corrected. The software also informed engineers about a pressurization issue in a chilled water system in another building. It took less than five minutes to fix the problem, which saved about $12,000 each year.

The system also prioritizes problems to be fixed. Algorithms can balance out the cost of a fix in terms of the money and energy wasted with other factors such as the impact fixing the problem will have on employees who work in that building. So a lower-cost problem in a research lab with critical operations may be given higher priority than a higher-cost fix that directly affects few. According to Smith, almost half of the issues the system identifies can be corrected in under a minute.

Engineers appreciate being able to spend their time anticipating and preventing issues and solving problems instead of gathering data and reacting to emergencies. "I used to spend 70 percent of my time gathering and compiling data and only about 30 percent of my time doing engineering," notes facilities engineer Jonathan Grove. "Our smart buildings work serves up data for me in easily consumable formats, so now I get to spend 95 percent of my time doing engineering, which is great."

Microsoft is forecasting energy savings of 6–10 percent per year. And as each new algorithm comes online, the company finds new opportunities to save energy. For example, a "new algorithm for detecting when the air in a given building is being overcooled," can save fifteen minutes of air conditioning for each instance detected. The team seems confident that even greater energy and cost savings are on the horizon.

Risk Management

Identifying and minimizing risk is a priority for every organization. Risk managers have been using data and analytical tools to do their jobs for many years. Recent technical advances and new types of data are reinvigorating the use of predictive analytics to mitigate risk. While the specific risks vary by organization, two of the most active areas have been in fraud detection and cybersecurity.

A growing challenge for financial services firms is to protect their customers and themselves against fraudulent claims or purchases. The Coalition Against Insurance Fraud conservatively estimates that fraud costs insurers $80 billion a year.[9] Companies increasingly rely on sophisticated fraud detection algorithms to recognize fraudulent credit card purchases in real time. Credit card companies like Visa and American Express have been using advanced analytics methods for years to identify stolen credit cards and fraudulent purchases in real time. By combining point of sale, authorization, and geolocation information with past purchasing behavior, these companies are getting better at pinpointing suspicious behavior and alerting cardholders of potential problems.

Insurers are fighting back too, using predictive analytics to identify where they need to focus their attention. According to Bill Dibble, senior vice president of claims operations, Infinity Property & Casualty:

> We realized that automobile insurance claims could be scored in the same way as consumer credit applications, and that technology could significantly enhance that process by making specific inferences on behavior . . . We developed a process to assign different "scores" on fraud probabilities when claimants first report an accident. By using a rules engine that automatically scores claims based on its fraud probability, we could forward suspicious claims into the hands of investigators within a day or two for deeper analysis. As a result of using this technology, not only have we slashed the time it takes to identify potential fraudulent claims within 24 hours—it used to take between 30–60 days—and we have been more successful in catching fraud claims."[10]

In another example, Infinity analyzed its old adjusters' reports to develop a new algorithm that resulted in $12 million in subrogation recovery.[11]

IT groups historically have been better at creating predictive models for other parts of the business, but they have been slower to embrace analytics to manage their own function. That is changing as cybersecurity challenges proliferate and become more daunting. The number of threats to large organizations is growing rapidly, as is the number of hackers who create them and the number of systems at risk from cyberattacks. Data breaches are increasing, according to one report, by 85 percent a year, and in 2016, half a billion personal records were stolen or lost.[12]

And with the proliferation of connected devices, there is no doubt that the challenge of protecting an organization's data can only grow. Cybersecurity processes within companies are too often reactive to hacks and breaches; investigation and actions are taken only after (sometimes long after) a problem has occurred. The technology most commonly used to address cyberattacks employs "threat signatures" based on patterns of previous attacks. Of course, these approaches are of little value in preventing new types of attacks. Predictive analytical methods originally developed to detect and prevent credit card fraud—a form of anomaly detection—are now being applied to behaviors in cybersecurity attacks.[13] Some cognitive technologies, including deep learning, can also identify anomalies in transaction patterns. These approaches can identify emerging anomalies much faster than using threat signatures, and may be able to identify threats much earlier and prevent substantial hacks and data losses before they occur. Given the sensitivity of cybersecurity issues, humans will still be necessary to confirm and investigate threats, particularly when they are internal. But the amount of investigative labor can be substantially reduced through analytics. Organizations in both public and private sectors today are using analytics and—to a lesser degree—cognitive technologies and automation to improve their cybersecurity programs. It's unclear when these technical capabilities will be fully mature, but there should be no doubts about their necessity and the likelihood of their ultimate adoption.[14]

Merger and Acquisition Analytics

Mergers and acquisitions (M&A) have historically not been the focus of a lot of analytical activity, perhaps with the exception of detailed cash flow analyses. There is usually little attention paid to operational analytics involving supply chain efficiencies, predicted customer reactions, and impacts on costs within the combined organization. This may be a reason why a high proportion—estimates as high as 70 and 80 percent—of M&A deals are not terribly successful in terms of producing economic value.

We haven't found any firm that really differentiates itself on the quality of its M&A analytics. But that might be starting to change. A 2015 Deloitte survey of five hundred corporate executives found 68 percent were using data analytics for M&A (although only 40 percent saw it as a core capability for M&A), and more than 80 percent saw data analytics becoming increasingly important in the future of M&A.[15] The most common uses were to understand customers, markets, workforces, and compensation. But some more advanced organizations were using predictive analytics for identification and realizing potential synergies.

Certainly, some M&A deals must be done so quickly that extensive analytics would be difficult or impossible. When Bank of America was given the opportunity to acquire Fleet Bank, for example, it had about forty-eight hours to make a decision. But for most deals, there's plenty of time to undertake analyses. At Procter & Gamble, for example, the acquisition of Gillette was considered for more than a year before the deal was announced. P&G's analysis identified significant savings (in its supply chain, through workforce reductions, and potential gains from customer synergies), which were used to determine how much P&G offered for Gillette in the deal. Similarly, CEMEX, the global cement company, uses analytics to quantify expected benefits from increased market share and improved profitability by enforcing its processes and systems on the takeover target.

One company attempting to inject more analytical rigor into its M&A integration activity is IBM. IBM has been on an acquisition spree lately, and to improve the odds of achieving its goals, it has developed a machine learning algorithm called M&A Pro. The system produces visualizations quantifying key integration risks, offers qualitative advice and creates a financial dashboard comparing performance of past deals against their initial business plan. Paul Price, IBM's director of M&A Integration says, "Not everyone is an M&A process expert. But what we have done is create a common language, an Esperanto, for deal execution across the organization . . . Our business now is much more grounded in economic and operational reality."[16]

Operational Analytics

One analytical domain that has long existed in companies is operations, especially manufacturing, quality, safety, and logistics. This was the original home, for example, of Total Quality Management and Six Sigma, which, when done seriously, involve detailed statistical analysis of process variations, defect rates, and sources of problems. Manufacturing and quality analytics have had an enormous impact on the global manufacturing industries, but until recently their impact has been less revolutionary for service industries and nonmanufacturing functions within manufacturing companies. For many organizations, it still seems difficult to summon the required levels of discipline and rigor to apply statistical quality control or even a strong process orientation outside of manufacturing. This means, of course, that it becomes difficult for firms to compete broadly on the basis of analytics, since they are often limited to the manufacturing function and generally focused on achieving productivity improvements rather than innovations to gain a competitive advantage.

Manufacturing

Real analytical competitors in manufacturing, then, are those that go beyond just manufacturing. There are a few great examples of this approach. One is at a small steel manufacturer in the United States, and it illustrates that analytical competition applies both to smaller firms and to the manufacture of commodity goods. Rocky Mountain Steel Mills, a steel rail-, rod-, and bar-making division of Oregon Steel, faced a critical decision about manufacturing capacity in early 2005. It had shut down its seamless pipe mill in 2003 because of price pressures, but the primary customers for seamless pipe were oil drillers, and by 2005 oil prices had risen enough to make Rob Simon, the company's vice president and general manager, consider reopening the pipe mill. However, he found the rules of thumb and standard costing/volume analyses previously used for such decisions to be too simplistic for a fast-changing mix of demand, pricing, production constraints, and industry capacity.

Simon decided to turn to a more analytical approach, and Rocky Mountain installed an analytical software tool called Profit InSight. He began to work with monthly analyses to determine whether the plant should be reopened. Potential customers and other managers thought that the high prices for pipe clearly justified the capital outlay that would be needed to reopen, but Simon's analyses suggested that increased revenues for pipe would be offset by lower production of rod and bar, and would not be profitable. Only when pipe prices continued to rise throughout 2005 did Simon decide to reopen the plant in December of that year. Even when production started, his models suggested holding off on taking orders because prices were predicted to rise. Indeed, by January 2006 they had risen by 20 percent over the previous quarter.

Rocky Mountain estimates that in addition to the higher prices it received, it averted a $34 million loss it would have faced from production constraints had it reopened the plant earlier in 2005. The success with the new pipe mill was also a key factor in a substantial rise in Oregon Steel's stock price. Profit InSight is now used as a weekly strategic planning tool, and Rocky Mountain Steel Mills has completely abandoned its previous "rhetorical" sales planning and forecasting approach for the new analytical methods. They are measurably superior, but Simon still had to demand that everyone listen to what the analyses show and quit second-guessing using the old approaches.

Engineers involved in product design have been using computer-aided design (CAD) for decades. But recent advances using parametric modeling permit more flexible, individually customized designs that also cut manufacturing time. Firewire Surfboards, a manufacturer of high-performance, premium surfboards wanted to give customers more freedom to customize their board without sacrificing board performance or overwhelming their design and manufacturing processes. Firewire boards are constructed through proprietary methods and a combination of high-tech materials previously not offered by other commercial surfboard manufacturers. But Firewire's CEO Mark Price knew that this wasn't enough to be a market leader. Hardcore surfers want customized boards—made for them specifically to suit their personal style and local wave conditions. But the complexity of Firewire's production process made customization through its computer-aided design system extremely labor-intensive. Firewire worked with ShapeLogic and Siemens' NX 3D CAD software to develop advanced parametric models of its stock and added specific rules that control how the customer's changes affect the board's curves to ensure peak performance.

Online customers begin by selecting one of Firewire Surfboards' standard models and then altering the design to fit their needs. Once the customer orders a custom board, a precise solid model is sent directly to Firewire's factory, where it is used to run the machines that manufacture the board. The model makes it possible to quickly machine custom boards to about 97 percent of their net shape, which minimizes the required finishing processes, manufacturing time, and costs.[17] As more powerful and sophisticated (yet consumer-friendly) CAD solutions become more accessible, we expect customer customization of bicycles, sports equipment, automobiles and even medical devices will become commonplace.

For internet-based businesses, *operations* means churning out the basic service for which customers visit a website. Successful online businesses use analytics to test virtually all aspects of their sites before implementing them broadly. For example, because the primary reason customers visit Google is to use its search capabilities, the company has a very extensive program of testing and analytics with regard to its search engine. Google employs a wide range of operational and customer data and analytics to improve search attributes, including relevance, timeliness, and the user experience. The company developed many of its own proprietary measures of search relevance. Most of the metrics are gathered in an automated fashion, such as the percentage of foreign results, how deeply users go in the retrieved items list, the percentage of users who go to each page of the search result, and the measures of search latency or timeliness. But Google also collects human judgments on the search process, and even observes individual users (at Google headquarters and in users' homes) as they use the site for individual queries and entire sessions. One technique employed is *eye tracking*, from which "heat maps" are created showing which areas of a page receive the most attention.

Google is heavily committed to experimentation before making any change in its search site. As Google's Bill Brougher put it:

> Experiments are a requirement of launching a new feature. It's a very powerful tool for us. We have been experimenting for years and have accumulated a lot of institutional knowledge about what works. Before any new feature ships, it has to pass through a funnel involving several tests. For example, any change to our search algorithms has to be tested against our base-level search quality to make sure the change is a substantial improvement over the base. A little blip in quality isn't significant enough to adopt.[18]

Google's methods for analytical operations are as rigorous as any firm's, and the nature of the business makes a large amount of data available for analysis.

Another key aspect of manufacturing analytics is to ensure that the right products are being manufactured. We'll refer to it as the *configuration problem*—making sure that the products offered to the market are those that the market wants. The configuration problem, like the ones described earlier at Rocky Mountain Steel and Firewire Surfboards, is cross-functional; it takes place at the intersection of sales and manufacturing, and usually also involves the company's supply chain, financial, and even human resource processes. To compete on the basis of configuration is thus by definition an enterprise-wide activity. Configuration is highly analytical. It involves predictive modeling of what customers want to buy, as well as complex (usually rule-based) analysis of what components go with what other components into what finished products.

What companies compete on the basis of configuration? Some high-technology companies, such as Dell, are known for their configurable products. Wireless telecommunications companies may have many different service plans; some have developed automated analytical applications to find the best one for each customer. They also tailor their services to each corporate account. Automobile companies need to compete on configuration, though US and European manufacturers have traditionally done it poorly. Since manufacturing a car from scratch to a customer's specification is viewed as taking too long (at least outside of Japan, where it is commonly done), car companies have to forecast the types of vehicles and options customers will want, manufacture them, and send them to dealers. Far too often, the mixes of models and option packages have not been what customers want, so cars have to be substantially discounted to be sold during promotions or at the end of a model year. The mismatch between consumer desires and available product has been one of the biggest problems facing Ford and General Motors.

Both companies are trying to do something about configuration, but Ford is probably the more aggressive of the two. The company has shifted its focus from producing whatever the factory could produce and worrying later about selling it, to trying to closely match supply and demand. As part of this initiative, Ford is using configuration software to maintain rules about options and components, which will reduce the number of production mistakes and more closely match dealer orders to production schedules. Ford's Smart Inventory Management System (SIMS) optimizes inventory for nearly three thousand Ford and Lincoln dealerships in North America. SIMS uses advanced analytics to produce dealer-specific vehicle order recommendations to ensure that dealers have the right number and mix of inventory to accommodate customer preferences and demand. As a result, annual revenue has increased and Ford dealerships are confidently making smart and cost-effective inventory ordering decisions.[19] Ford has not yet entirely mastered the art of competing on configuration, but it is clearly making strides in that direction.

Quality

Analytics can also be applied to assess manufactured quality. Honda, for example, has long been known for the quality of its automobiles and other products. The company certainly has analytical individuals in its manufacturing quality department. However, it goes well beyond that function in identifying potential quality problems. Honda instituted an analytical "early warning" program to identify major potential quality issues from warranty service records. These records are sent to Honda by dealers, and they include both categorized quality problems and free text. Other text comes from transcripts of calls by mechanics to experts in various domains at headquarters and from customer calls to call centers. Honda's primary concern was that any serious problems identified by dealers or customers would be noticed at headquarters and addressed quickly. So Honda analysts set up a system to mine the textual data coming from these different sources. Words appearing for the first time (particularly those suggesting major problems, such as *fire*) and words appearing more than predicted were flagged for human analysts to look at. Honda won't go into details about any specific problems it's nipped in the bud, but says that the program has been very successful.

Toshiba Semiconductor Company is another business that has made extensive use of analytics—in particular, visual representation of statistical analysis—in manufacturing quality. The initial applications focused on advanced analysis for new product and technology development, but they expanded quickly into other areas such as sales, marketing, development, production, and quality assurance.

The semiconductor business unit's executives are strong advocates of analytics, and have led the company by the concept for over fifteen years. Toshiba's overall approach is encompassed by a broader initiative entitled Management Innovation Policy and Activity.

The visual analytics approach was first used by engineers in several semiconductor fabrication plants (fabs) for yield analysis—a key problem in the industry. According to Shigeru Komatsu, the company's chief knowledge officer (it is rare for analytics to be addressed in such a role, but they are at Toshiba Semiconductor), "We have worked on standardizing performance indicators, we have built shared databases, we have made efforts to share analysis cases and results, and we have implemented analytic software such as Minitab and [TIBCO] Spotfire DecisionSite in order to increase our efficiency in analytics."[20] Toshiba Semiconductor continues to invest in yield analytics, most recently by incorporating artificial intelligence into analytical models used to determine the root cause of defects and further boost production quality.[21]

Safety

Safety was not the earliest area to apply data and analytics, but it's growing rapidly today. It turns out that certain types of accidents are—at least to some degree—predictable. They are a function of the people, equipment, and company settings involved. If you have data on past safety incidents and the attributes associated with them, it's not a huge stretch to predict when they will happen in the future, and intervene to try to prevent them.

Safety analytics is one of the specialties of the boutique analytics consulting firm First Analytics, which Tom helped to found in 2009. A manager at a large railroad read the original "Competing on Analytics" article, and contacted First Analytics CEO Mike Thompson in 2010. They began discussing how the company could improve its safety using analytics.

The railroad manager explained that safety was a top priority for the company and that it had improved considerably on this front, but it got harder to keep improving. He said the company had already used some data to identify likely risks, but there was a lot more that could be explored.

The railroad and First Analytics began with a proof of concept project to take existing data on the company's train operators and score how likely they were to be at risk. The available data included location, job position, weather conditions, work schedule, absenteeism, scores on rules tests and training exercises, previous rules violations, and more. The data eventually came from about twenty different databases across the company. The railroad had previously used a risk scoring system based on reasonable logic, but the new one based on analytics improved upon it dramatically.

Since the proof of concept had worked well, the railroad worked with First Analytics to expand the analysis to other safety areas; for example, an analysis was created to identify and prioritize the most at-risk railroad grade crossings. The personnel safety analytics were extended beyond those operating the trains to the personnel maintaining the tens of thousands of miles of track. The overall result of these efforts was a dramatic improvement in safety. The company's vice president of safety recently discussed the improvements with customers:

> Big data. We're into it big time. We think it's driving these last eighteen months [of safety results]. There are twenty-five hundred operating managers . . . there's no way we can look, spend time with, teach all the employees, all the time, every day. This is about focusing management attention on those who exhibit more risk. We're on our fourth iteration of this model; we're constantly fine-tuning it . . . If you were to take a look at our control charts, it's been a nice downward trend for a decade. Since we turned a lot of this on, it's been a step function: a full standard deviation from our normal run rate.[22]

Some companies in other transportation industries have adopted similar approaches to safety analytics. This is facilitated by the increasing ease of capturing driving data. Schneider National, Inc., for example, a large trucking firm, captures driver behaviors such as speed, acceleration and deceleration, and driving times. A predictive safety algorithm alerts supervisors that drivers are at risk for accidents even before they have had one.

Other industries that have taken aggressive approaches to safety analytics include mining, energy, and manufacturing. As sensors become more pervasive, we're likely to see many more companies and industries adopt these approaches.

Logistics

When you invest in operational analytics at the level of hundreds of millions of dollars—and more importantly, deliver value at multiples of that sum—it's safe to assume that you are competing on analytics. UPS has a long history of measurement and improvement through industrial engineering. Today, UPS captures information on the 18.3 million packages and documents, on average, that it delivers daily, and it receives 69.4 million tracking requests a day. The company has a deep, long-standing commitment to using analytics for decision making.

Jack Levis, the company's senior director of process management, who also leads the Operations Research and Advanced Analytics groups, leads the ORION project. ORION, an acronym that stands for On-Road Integrated Optimization and Navigation, may be the largest commercial analytics project ever undertaken.[23] ORION is a prescriptive analytics logistical model for UPS's fifty-five thousand drivers in the United States (the international rollouts will come soon). Before drivers start their routes, ORION analyzes the packages to be delivered that day and determines an optimal routing for the "package cars." Handheld computers tell the drivers where to go next.

UPS is a big company, and the benefits of ORION are commensurately large. Jack Levis likes to say "Big savings come from attention to detail." Shortening each driver's route by one mile daily translates into $50 million to the UPS bottom line annually. Every minute saved per driver daily is worth $14.6 million, and preventing one minute of idle time daily saves $515,000. As a result, what seem like small incremental improvements can yield big savings. For example, savings in driver productivity and fuel economy by driving more efficient routes add up to about $400 million a year. By cutting routes just a fraction of a mile here and there, UPS is driving 100 million fewer miles, with a resulting reduction in carbon emissions of 100,000 metric tons a year. You don't see those levels of benefit from an analytics project very often, and these have been confirmed through intensive measurement and reported to Wall Street analysts.

ORION required a sustained commitment over more than a decade on the part of UPS management. The system took more than a decade from inception to fully roll out, and more than $250 million of investment. So the company clearly went all in on this project. What took so long? First, the sheer volume of data and the complexity of the math needed to optimize routes are truly staggering. Consider that for a single driver making 120 deliveries, the number of potential routes is 120 factorial, which is a sum greater than the age of the earth—in seconds.[24] Now imagine computing the optimal route for every driver, every day.

The optimization algorithm itself was difficult to develop, but that aspect of the work paled in comparison to the other challenges. UPS had to develop its own maps to ensure that the drivers would be directed to the right place every time, and to the correct location for package drop-off or pickup. No commercially available maps could do that for the 250 million different locations to which UPS delivers. Next, telematics sensors were installed in more than forty-six thousand company trucks, which track metrics including speed, direction, braking, and drivetrain performance.

But it was the change management challenges that were the most complex to address. Imagine communicating and inculcating a new way of performing a core daily task to fifty-five thousand skilled union workers. UPS devoted six days of training and support to each driver. Most of the drivers wanted to know how the system worked before they would give up their time-honored routes, and so considerable effort was devoted to turning the "black box" algorithm into a "glass box." To their credit, most of the drivers were enthusiastic about the new approach once they had experienced it.

ORION's benefits to date are only the beginning for UPS. There is, of course, the global rollout of these tools. And to maintain a level of simplicity for drivers, ORION only optimizes routes at the beginning of the workday. More sophisticated programs down the road will re-optimize during the day, taking factors such as traffic patterns and weather into account. UPS plans to continue to extend ORION's capabilities. Levis explains that future enhancements will also make other decisions to improve customer service without sacrificing efficiency. "If a customer calls with a request while drivers are on road, ORION will look at all drivers and determine the best choice. ORION will then put it in their handheld computer and adjust their route accordingly."

There aren't many companies that have made bets on analytics to this degree. But with the ORION initiative, UPS has truly transformed itself from a trucking company that uses technology to a "technology company with trucks."

Managing the logistics of a global supply chain is another fertile area for investing in analytics. Caterpillar's Global Supply Network Division (GSND) is responsible for overseeing an interdependent supply network with over eleven thousand suppliers and 150 facilities. But for thirty years, Caterpillar's supplier performance appeared stagnant, with no sustainable improvements. GSND personnel were hampered by outdated manual processes, data unavailability, and network complexity. Users became accustomed to making decisions on assumptions and incomplete data. "We were trying to manage a supply network in the dark on spreadsheets."[25]

To solve this problem, in 2012 Caterpillar began to develop the Assurance of Supply Center (ASC). The ASC is a data analytics and visualization platform that captures and transforms supply network data from dozens of systems into a suite of powerful business tools that is used to drive both every day decisions and strategic network design decisions. Three years later, the transformation has been remarkable. CEO Doug Oberhelman told shareholders, "[ASC] simplifies the supply network—a network that involves thousands of suppliers shipping more than a million parts and components every year. Now Caterpillar can see orders from production to delivery—by facility, business unit and cost."[26]

Using mobile devices, users are able to see data on inventory, transportation, suppliers, performance, network footprint, defects, and tariffs. A shipment occurs every ninety seconds, producing millions of new data points every day that are analyzed, visualized to support decisions to over 10,000 users. The system incorporates a library of over 100 million data points feeding 45,000 predictive and prescriptive models, including data on 640,000 part numbers from over 7,000 suppliers, shipping to 127 facilities across the globe. All this data enables them to answer important questions such as:

- Where is my inventory?

- Are we ready for an upturn?

- Why is supplier X performing poorly?

- What is the network impact of a major natural disaster?

- Factoring in projected demand, consumption, and performance, what should our parts inventory be for all part numbers next year?

- How could I change my network to make it more cost-effective and profitable?

Caterpillar shares its data and insights with suppliers and works with them to improve their performance. In just three years, the results have been dramatic: in 2012, 67 percent of schedules were shipped on time; now it is 93 percent. Quality defects have been reduced by 50 percent. The organization now has the ability to keep the network moving even when disaster strikes. Users are able to resolve network performance issues in minutes rather than months. And ASC has become a continuing source of competitive advantage for Caterpillar as it continues to introduce more innovative analytic solutions to its business.

Research and Development Analytics

Research and development (R&D) has been perhaps the most analytical function within companies. It was the primary bastion of the scientific method within companies, featuring hypothesis testing, control groups, and statistical analysis.

Of course, some of this highly analytical work still goes on within R&D functions, although much of the basic research in R&D has been supplanted by applied research (which can still use analytical methods) and the creation of extensions of existing products. In several industries, research has become more mathematical and statistical in nature, as computational methods replace or augment traditional experimental approaches. For example, automaker Tesla's connected cars share a steady stream of information with the company, which it uses to identify problems and create software fixes that are then automatically downloaded.

We'll describe the analytical environment for R&D in one industry that's changing dramatically with regard to analytics. In the pharmaceutical industry, analytics—particularly the analysis of clinical trials data to see whether drugs have a beneficial effect—always have been important. Over the last several years, however, there has been a marked growth in systems biology, in which firms attempt to integrate genomic, proteomic, metabolic, and clinical data from a variety of sources, create models and identify patterns in this data, correlate them to clinical outcomes, and eventually generate knowledge about diseases and their responses to drugs. This is a considerable challenge, however, and firms are just beginning to address it. We interviewed three pharmaceutical firms—one large "big pharma" company and two smaller, research-oriented firms—and found that all of them have efforts under way in this regard, but they are a long way from achieving the goal. This field is rapidly changing, however, and several firms are now attempting to use artificial intelligence—specifically IBM's Watson—to help develop new drug compounds.

Analytics is also being used effectively to address today's challenges in R&D, and this is one way that Vertex Pharmaceuticals, Inc. competes. Vertex, a global biotech firm headquartered in Boston, Massachusetts, has taken a particularly analytical approach to R&D, and its results are beginning to show the payoff. Vertex's co-founder and retired CEO, Joshua Boger, is a strong believer in the power of analytics to raise drug development productivity. As early as 1988 (when he left Merck & Co. to found Vertex) he argued that, "What you need in this business is more information than the other guy. Not more smarts. Not more intuition. Just more information."[27]

Vertex has undertaken a variety of analytical initiatives—in research, development, and marketing. In research, Vertex has focused on analyses that attempt to maximize the likelihood of a compound's success. This includes developing multiple patent lead series per project and ensuring that compounds have favorable drug-like attributes.

Vertex's approach to drug design is known as rational or structural. This approach seeks to "design in" drug-like properties from the beginning of a drug development project and it enables Vertex to determine as early as possible whether a compound will have drug-like attributes.

More of Vertex's efforts in using analytics have gone into the development stage of R&D, where its analyses indicate that most of the cost increases in the industry have taken place. One particularly high cost is the design of clinical trials. Poor clinical trial design leads to either ambiguous trial results or overly large clinical trials. This causes substantial delays and raises costs. Vertex has addressed this challenge by developing new trial simulation tools. These tools enable Vertex to design more informative and effective clinical trials in substantially less time. Vertex can now perform trial simulations hundreds of times faster than were previously possible. With these simulations, Vertex can also reduce the risk of failed or ambiguous trials caused by faulty trial design. This simulation advantage allows Vertex to optimize trial design in a fraction of the time it takes using industry standard design tools, thereby shortening the trial cycle time.

Clinical trial operation also represents some of the highest cost increases across the pharmaceutical industry. The operation of clinical trials, as with trial design, takes place within the development stage of R&D. Operational activities that are not automated lead to significant costs. Vertex uses analytics to automate and enhance clinical trial operations; examples include tools for patient accruals and electronic data capture (EDC).

Whether in R&D or elsewhere, the company begins with the right metric for the phenomenon it needs to optimize. Analysts determine how to obtain the appropriate data and what analyses to conduct. With these findings, Vertex constantly compares itself to competitors and to best practice benchmarks for the pharmaceutical industry. "We compete on analytics and culture," says Steve Schmidt, Vertex's former chief information officer. "We encourage fearless pursuit of innovations but we ruthlessly measure the effect these innovations have on our core business. We're always looking for new meaningful analytic metrics, but where we look is driven by our strategy, our core corporate values and strengths, and our understanding of the value proposition to our business."[28] Vertex is a great example of applying analytics to product R&D, and as a result the company has an impressive array of new drugs in all stages of development.

The pharmaceutical industry is also pursuing analytical approaches that don't even involve the laboratory. So-called in silico research uses computational models of both patients and drugs to simulate experiments more rapidly and cheaply than they could be performed in a lab. One systems biology firm, Entelos, Inc., has produced computer program platforms to simulate diseases and treatments in the areas of cardiovascular diseases, diabetes, inflammations, and asthma, among others. Entelos partners with pharmaceutical companies and other research organizations to identify and test new compounds. The goal is to use computational simulations to reduce the very high cost, long cycle times, and high failure rates of conventional laboratory research in the pharmaceutical industry. One collaboration on a diabetes drug between Entelos and Johnson & Johnson, for example, led to a 40 percent reduction in time and a 66 percent reduction in the number of patients necessary in an early-phase clinical trial.[29]

Of course, R&D today involves not only product innovation but also innovation in other domains: processes and operations; business models; customer innovations such as marketing, sales, and service; and new management approaches. In a very important sense, the idea behind this book is that each area in which an organization does business can be one in which R&D is conducted. In chapter 3, we noted how Capital One identifies new offerings through its test-and-learn market research approach. At internet-oriented firms such as Amazon, Facebook, and Google, every change to a web page is treated as a small R&D project. What's the baseline case for measures such as page views, time spent on the site, and click-throughs? How does the change work on a small scale? How does it work when it is scaled more broadly? This test-and-learn approach to operational R&D is just as important as R&D on products.

Operational, business-model R&D also doesn't have to involve the internet. In health care for example, despite the seemingly scientific nature of medicine, several studies suggest that only one-quarter to a third of medical decisions are based on science. A growing industry of health care providers, insurance companies, and third-party data and analytical service providers are working to make health care more efficient and effective through analytics. One of the most aggressive adopters of this approach is Intermountain Healthcare, a Utah-based association of twenty-two hospitals. Brent James, a physician with a master's degree in statistics, began proposing small "science projects" to see which clinical interventions led to the best outcomes at Intermountain. These projects eventually evolved into a broad set of ten clinical programs based on research and evidence. Each clinical program is supported by information systems that incorporate recommended care protocols and keep track of patient costs. Intermountain has become a model for the effective provision of health care at a reasonable cost, and has trained many other physicians and administrators around the world.

A key aspect of analytical health care is population health, or the analysis of health outcomes for groups of people. One increasingly common approach to population health, for example, is to try to predict the likelihood that members of a health plan will develop higher risk for more severe disease over time. Healthways is one company that works with insurers to make such predictions and to identify ways to improve health outcomes and thereby reduce the likely cost to the insurer. Healthways uses data on members' demographic, claims, prescription, and lab procedures to predict (using artificial intelligence neural network technology) which ones will be at highest risk for greater future total medical expenditures over the next year. Healthways employs more than fifteen hundred registered nurses who then provide telephonic and direct mail interventions from one of its ten call centers nationwide to help members develop healthy behaviors which reduce the severity of the disease, improve outcomes, and reduce the cost to the health plan. This approach to risk management can also reduce ongoing health maintenance costs and lower the risk of disease recurrence.[30] The health insurance giant United Healthcare goes one step further by not only determining whether a patient is at risk for acquiring a particular disease, but also by using analytics to determine how likely a patient will be to adopt and follow disease management interventions.

Human Resource Analytics

The final internal analytical application we'll discuss in this chapter is in human resources. Once a lagging area for analytics, leading-edge companies are now adopting sophisticated methods of analyzing employee data in order to get the most value from their people. Google, eBay, Walmart and others are using predictive analytics to increase productivity, to compensate and incent their employees appropriately, to help employees succeed in their jobs, and to reduce retention.

As with other parts of organizations, the tools for employing analytics in HR are becoming widely available. Most large organizations now have in place human resource information systems (HRIS), which record basic HR transactions such as hiring date, compensation, promotions, and performance ratings. Some go well beyond that level, and record skill levels on a variety of aptitudes and learning programs undertaken to improve those skills. Companies increasingly have the ability to relate their investments in human capital to their returns on financial capital. Whether they have the desire, however, is another question. People may be "our most important asset," and even our most expensive asset, but they are rarely our most measured asset. Many companies may be beginning to employ HR analytics, but they are hardly competing on them.

The most conspicuous exception, of course, is in professional sports. Baseball, football, basketball, and soccer teams (at least outside the United States) pay high salaries to their players and have little other than those players to help them compete. Many successful teams are taking innovative approaches to the measurement of player abilities and the selection of players for teams. We've already talked about the analytical approach to player evaluation in baseball that was well described in Michael Lewis's *Moneyball*. In American professional football, the team that most exemplifies analytical HR is the New England Patriots, the 2017 Super Bowl champions and winners of five Super Bowls over the last fifteen years.

The Patriots take a decidedly different approach to HR than other teams in the National Football League (NFL). They don't use the same scouting services that other teams employ. They evaluate college players at the smallest, most obscure schools. They evaluate potential draft selections on the basis of criteria that other teams don't use—intelligence, for example, and a low level of egotism. As head coach Bill Belichick puts it: "When you bring a player onto a team, you bring all that comes with him. You bring his attitude, his speed, strength, mental toughness, quickness. Our evaluation is comprehensive. Scott Pioli [then vice president of player personnel] and the scouting department do a great job of getting a lot of details by going into the history of a player, his mental and physical makeup as well as attitude and character. He eventually receives one grade and that establishes his overall value to the team."[31] Belichick often refers to the nonphysical attributes of players as "intangibles," and he is perfectly comfortable discussing them with players and media representatives. Anyone who witnessed the Patriots' unprecedented overtime win of the 2017 Super Bowl probably knows that one particular intangible—mental toughness—was a key element in their victory. The Patriots measure and actively develop this trait in their players with the help of behavioral and emotional intelligence testing using the Troutwine Athletic Profile (TAP). Belichick says, "I've been familiar with [the TAP] for over 15 years . . . I'm telling you from experience this gives you tremendous insight into players, yourself, and your program."[32]

The Patriots manage the potential player data in a Draft Decision Support System, which is updated daily with new reports from scouts. Cross-checkers at the team's offices check the scout ranking by comparing West Coast scout ratings with similar East Coast ratings (i.e., does the 6'7" UCLA receiver compare with the 6'7" Georgia Tech receiver?). No detail that can provide an edge is overlooked.

With the success of analytics in other domains, business leaders have high (but thus far mostly unmet) expectations for how analytics should revolutionize HR as well. Many HR departments have taken small steps to catch up to their peers in other parts of the organization. Companies are measuring more consistently across global HR processes and putting the information in systems. There are varying approaches to quantitative HR, including 360-degree evaluations, forced rankings, predictions about attrition, and so forth. None of these approach "rocket science," but they do connote a much more disciplined and methodical approach. At American Express, for example, which has employees in eighty-three countries, an HR executive in

Asia commented, "Everything that we touch has a metric attached. Whatever we do we use globally consistent processes, measurements and databases. We do things in a methodical, thought out, consistent manner, and we have consistent platforms."[33]

Other firms are taking more modest steps to managing their talent. One manufacturing company we interviewed, for example, has developed a "talent management index" from four proprietary measures, and it uses the index to evaluate how each organizational unit manages its investments in human capital. Goldman Sachs, which, like professional sports teams, pays its employees extremely well, is beginning to apply analytical approaches to its workforce. GE, Accenture, Capital One, and Procter & Gamble seek quantitative reasoning abilities in potential recruits. Caesars, another analytical competitor in general, also uses HR analytics extensively in the recruiting process.

Digital companies are adopting more analytical techniques to retain their highly skilled and mobile workforce. In 2014, when eBay was preparing to spin off PayPal, managers were concerned about the effect on their workforce. Management asked Katie Meger, senior manager of talent analytics at eBay (and a psychology PhD) to help identify at-risk employees and to help them determine the best ways to prevent unwanted attrition. As the *Wall Street Journal* reported, Meger developed a predictive model, using survival analysis, a statistical technique for predicting death:

> At the time, as eBay prepared to spin out PayPal, managers lobbied for more money to keep good employees from leaving, she recalled. But compensation wasn't in the top five variables that indicated someone was at risk for quitting, the model showed. It also revealed that attrition was contagious, especially on small teams, she said. One remedy eBay enacted: If an employee resigned, HR software would automatically send an email to his former manager explaining the contagion factor and offering suggestions for staying close to remaining employees.[34]

Another factor driving the shift to HR analytics is increasing rigor in staffing and recruiting processes. Companies are increasingly viewing these processes as activities that can be measured and improved; people are almost becoming just another supply chain resource. This is particularly noticeable in relationships with external staffing firms. Apex Systems, a division of On Assignment, is a major IT staffing firm. It has observed a long-term move among its clients to greater use of more rigorous processes and metrics, and it's trying to stay ahead of the trend by adopting more analytical measures and management approaches in its own business. Apex looks at a variety of staffing metrics, including:

- Time to respond with a first, second, and third qualified candidate

- How many candidates does a customer see?

- Frequencies of payroll errors or customer invoice defects

- Speed of customer issue resolution

- Overall customer satisfaction levels

Apex's customers are increasingly using analytics themselves to track the efficiency and effectiveness of staffing processes, so the company needs to establish and understand its own analytics to stay ahead of demand.

Three companies that rival the New England Patriots as analytics powerhouses for talent management are Google, Capital One, and Walmart. Google's highly analytical culture and practices are evident in its human resources function. Google's People Operations group operates very differently than the typical HR department. Its motto is: "All people decisions should be informed by data and analytics." To achieve its goal, Google created a people analytics function with its own director and staff of over sixty researchers, analysts, and consultants who study employee-related decisions and issues.

In naming Laszlo Bock, Google's former vice president of people operations, the HR Professional of the Decade in 2016, ERE Recruiting notes that Bock views data as a way to seek truth and unique insights. In contrast to the typical HR organization, Bock's former group behaves like an applied R&D function that experiments and finds solutions for people management challenges: Google's People Management frequently goes significantly beyond the usual HR metrics and scope, using predictive analytics to find ways to improve its managerial performance, recruiting, retention, employee well-being, and health. Google's People Operations researchers even found ways for employees to eat better and consume fewer calories. Data and experiments on improving employee health led to the company switching to smaller plates at their eating facilities.[35]

The People and Innovation Lab (PiLab) is the R&D group within People Operations that conducts focused investigations on behalf of internal clients. As Google analyzes different HR issues, it has often moved in new directions as a result. The PiLab has determined what backgrounds and capabilities are associated with high performance and what factors are likely to lead to attrition—such as an employee's feeling underutilized at the company. It has set the ideal number of recruiting interviews at four, down from the previous average of ten. One such project was Google's Project Oxygen—so named because good management keeps the company alive. The objective of this project was to determine the attributes of successful managers. The PiLab team analyzed annual employee surveys, performance management scores, and other data to divide managers into four groups according to their quality. It then interviewed the managers with the highest and lowest scores (interviews were double-blind—neither interviewer nor managers knew which category the managers were in) to determine their managerial practices. Google's HR analytics team ultimately identified eight behaviors that characterized good managers and five behaviors that every manager should avoid. A year after the team shared its findings, Google measured significant improvement in 75 percent of low-performing managers.

Google's talent value models address questions such as "Why do employees choose to stay with our company?" to calculate what employees value most, then apply those insights to boost retention rates, design personalized performance incentives, decide whether to match a competitor's job offer, or determine when to promote someone. Google also uses employee performance data to determine the most appropriate ways to help both high- and low-performing employees become more successful. Bock told us, "We don't use performance data to look at the averages but to monitor the highest and lowest performers on the distribution curve. The lowest 5 percent of performers we actively try to help. We know we've hired talented people, and we genuinely want them to succeed." The company's hypothesis was that many of these individuals might be misplaced or poorly managed, and a detailed analysis supported that idea. Understanding individual's needs and values allow the People Operations team to successfully address a number of difficult situations. The team has the data to prove it. Bock noted, "It's not the company-provided lunch that keeps people here. Googlers tell us that there are three reasons they stay: the mission, the quality of the people, and the chance to build the skill set of a better leader or entrepreneur. And all our analytics are built around these reasons."[36]

Capital One uses analytics extensively in the hiring process, requiring potential employees at all levels to take a variety of tests that measure their analytical abilities. The company uses mathematical case interviewing, a variety of behavioral and attitudinal tests, and multiple rounds of interviewing to ensure that it gets the people it wants. The process applies at all levels—even to the senior vice presidents who head business functions. For example:

> When Dennis Liberson flew into Washington to interview for the top human resources position at Capital One Financial Corp., he was told that his interviews with the 16 top executives would have to wait. First, he was whisked off to a hotel room to take an algebra exam and write a business plan. Liberson, who jokes nearly seven years later that he might have been "the only HR guy who could pass their math test," got the job and is now one of the company's executive vice presidents. He also got an early taste of Capital One's obsession with testing.[37]

Liberson is no longer the head of HR, but the focus on testing remains. A candidate for a managerial role at Capital One, for example, is still asked to review a set of financial statements and charts for a publishing company and then answer questions like these:

> What was the ratio of sales revenue to distribution costs for science books in 2016? (Round to nearest whole number):
>
> A. 27 to 1   B. 53 to 1   C. 39 to 1   D. 4 to 1   E. Cannot say

Without some quantitative skills, even the most senior executive need not apply.

Walmart employs a lot of people—over 2.2 million associates worldwide. Saba Beyene heads Walmart's global People Analytics team of seventy dedicated analysts. Gaining insight into the business implications of staff turnover was a big priority for the group: "Like all retail organizations, Walmart has a big turnover issue. We were trying to understand what we could do to make the organization understand that this is big. They were thinking if somebody moves I will get to hire somebody at a lower cost. What they did not understand is the cost of hiring, the cost of on-boarding, the cost of training. We were able to quantify all that and make it clear that when you lose an associate within 90 days or less they did not get their money back from hiring that associate."[38]

In light of these findings, it is not surprising that Walmart took a closer look at compensation for new hires. The company is investing billions to improve its training processes, increase starting salaries, and give raises to associates that have been with the company for 6 months.

Overall, however, other than these few companies and professional sports teams, few organizations are truly competing on HR analytics. Perhaps this emphasis will come with time, but what seems to be lacking most is the management desire to compete on HR in the first place. Perhaps as people costs continue to rise and constitute higher percentages of organizations' total costs, and as executives realize that their people are truly their most critical resource, analytics will catch on and proliferate in HR.

This chapter has considered a wide variety of internal applications of analytics. In each case, our objective was to illustrate not just that analytics are possible in a particular function but that they can be the basis for a different approach to competition and strategy. We hope these examples will drive senior executives to think about their own strategies and how they perform their internal activities. Chapter 5, which addresses the use of analytics in external (e.g., customer and supplier) relationships, offers even more possibilities for competition.

CHAPTER FIVE

COMPETING ON ANALYTICS WITH EXTERNAL PROCESSES

CUSTOMER AND SUPPLIER APPLICATIONS

ANALYTICS TOOK A GREAT LEAP FORWARD WHEN COM-panies began using them to improve their external processes—those related to managing and responding to customer demand and supplier relationships. Once kept strictly segregated, the boundaries between customer relationship management (CRM) processes such as sales and marketing, and supply chain management (SCM) processes such as procurement and logistics have been broken down by organizations seeking to align supply and demand more accurately. Unlike internal processes that lie completely within the organization's direct control, externally focused processes require cooperation from outsiders, as well as their resources. For those reasons, managing analytics related to external processes is sometimes a greater challenge.

Despite the challenge, many companies in a variety of industries are enhancing their customer and supplier relationships with predictive analytics, and they are enjoying market-leading growth and performance as a result.

FIGURE 5-1

Application domains for analytics

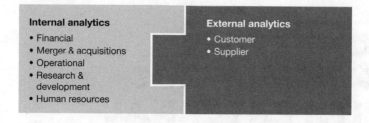

Many companies generate descriptive statistics about external aspects of their business—average revenue per customer, for example, or time spent on a website. But analytical competitors look beyond basic statistics and do the following:

- They use predictive modeling to identify the most profitable customers—as well as those with the greatest profit potential and the ones most likely to cancel their accounts.

- They integrate data generated in-house with data acquired from outside sources (third-party data providers, social media, and so forth) for a comprehensive understanding of their customers.

- They optimize their supply chains and can thus determine the impact of unexpected glitches, simulate alternatives, and route shipments around problems.

- They analyze historical sales and pricing trends to establish prices in real time and get the highest yield possible from each transaction.

- They use sophisticated experiments to measure the overall impact or "lift" (improvement in customer conversion rates) as well as attribution of particular interventions of advertising and other marketing strategies, and then apply their insights to future analyses.

Strange Bedfellows?

At first glance, supply chain management and customer relationships would seem to have little in common. Supply chain management, on the one hand, seems like a natural fit for an analytical focus. For years, operations management specialists have created algorithms to help companies keep minimal levels of inventory on hand while preventing stockouts—among other supply chain challenges. And manufacturing firms have long relied on sophisticated mathematical models to forecast demand, manage inventory, and optimize manufacturing processes. They also pursued quality-focused initiatives such as Six Sigma and *kaizen*, tools for which data analysis is an integral part of the methodology.

Customer relationships may once have seemed less amenable to analytical intervention, but they have been the focus of an explosion of marketing, sales, and service analytics. The traditional perspective in sales was on the personal skills of salespeople—their ability to form long-term relationships and to put skeptical potential customers at ease. Marketing was long viewed as a creative function whose challenge has been to understand customer behavior and convert that insight into inducements that will increase sales. Service was often viewed as an activity to be minimized as a cost of doing business, and was rarely the target for analytics.

In fact, analytics usage has its roots in the customer side of the business as much as on the supply side. Thirty years ago, consumer products firms like Procter & Gamble began using analytical software and databases to analyze sales and determine the parameters of product promotions. These companies invented the discipline of marketing-mix analytics to track the impact of individual investments such as trade promotions and coupon offers. They collected and analyzed data from vendors like ACNielsen and Information Resources, Inc. (IRI) to understand how their customers' (grocers) and consumers' behavior was influenced by different channels. These early innovators are being joined today by companies in virtually every industry, including retailers such as 7-Eleven Japan, manufacturers like Samsung, phone companies such as Verizon and AT&T, and pharmaceutical companies such as Merck and AstraZeneca. More recently, marketing organizations have radically increased their analytical orientations with the rise of campaign management software. Quantitatively oriented marketers can now use these tools to experiment with different campaigns for different groups of customers and learn which campaigns work best for which audiences.

Analytical competitors, however, take the use of analytics much further than most companies. In many cases, they are also sharing data and the results of analyses with their customers. Our survey data suggests that they are also integrating their systems more thoroughly and sharing data with their suppliers.[1] As companies integrate data on products, customers, and prices, they find new opportunities that arise by aligning and integrating the activities of supply and demand. Instead of conducting post hoc analyses that allow them to correct future actions, they generate and analyze process data in near–real time and adjust their processes dynamically.

At Caesars Entertainment casinos, for example, customers use loyalty cards that capture data on their behavior. Most other casinos also have loyalty cards, but Caesars is unusual in making extensive use of them for analytics. The data is used in near–real time by both marketing and operations to optimize yield, set prices for slots and hotel rooms, and design the optimal traffic flow through the casinos. Tim Stanley, Caesars' chief information officer during its initial shift to analytics, described the change in orientation: "We are in a transition from analytical customer-relationship management, where customer data is analyzed and acted upon at a later time, to real-time customer analytics at the point of sale in the casino, where . . . action is taken on data as it is being collected."[2]

How does this work in practice? One example can be seen when a customer loses too much money too fast. Caesars' systems can identify this problem and almost immediately send a message (electronically or through a service representative, sometimes called the "luck fairy") to the customer at a slot machine, such as, "Looks like you're having a tough day at the slots. It might be a good time to visit the buffet. Here's a $20 coupon you can use in the next hour." Caesars is also using real-time marketing interventions over smartphones (with customer permission) that help customers manage their entire vacation experience in Las Vegas, where the company owns several adjacent properties. "There are two seats left for the Celine Dion concert to-night," a text message might say, "and we're making them available at half price because of your loyal play at Caesars! Text 'yes, 2' if you'd like both tickets."

In the remainder of this chapter, we'll explain how other companies are taking advantage of their analytical abilities to optimize their customer and supplier processes.

Customer-Based Processes

Companies today face a critical need for robust customer-based processes. For one thing, acquiring and retaining customers is getting more expensive, especially in service-based industries such as tele-communications and financial services. And for another, consumers are harder to satisfy and more demanding.[3] To compete successfully in this environment, analytical competitors are pursuing a range of tactics that enable them to attract and retain customers more effectively, engage in "dynamic pricing," optimize their brand management, translate customer interactions into sales, manage customer life cycles, and differentiate their products by personalizing them across multiple channels (refer to the box "Typical Analytical Techniques in Marketing").

Attracting and Retaining Customers

There are, of course, a variety of ways to attract and retain customers, and analytics can support most of them. One traditional means of attracting customers has been advertising. This industry has already been, and will continue to be, transformed by analytics. Two factors are most closely associated with the transformation. One is the econometric analysis of time series data to determine whether advertising is statistically associated with increased sales of a product or service. The other is the "addressable" and relatively easily analyzed nature of digital advertising, as exemplified by Google and other firms. We'll describe each of these briefly.

Econometric analysis has begun to address the age-old problem with advertising in traditional media, as described around the turn of the twentieth century by department store pioneer John Wanamaker

TYPICAL ANALYTICAL TECHNIQUES IN MARKETING

CHAID. An abbreviation of *Chi-square automatic interaction detection*, a statistical technique used to segment customers on the basis of multiple alternative variables. The analysis creates a segmentation "tree" and continues to add different variables, or branches, to the tree as long as it is statistically significant.

Conjoint analysis. Typically used to evaluate the strength and direction of customer preferences for a combination of product or service attributes. For example, a conjoint analysis might be used to determine which factors—price, quality, dealer location, and so on—are most important to customers who are purchasing a new car.

Econometric modeling. Adapting theories, quantitative methods, and models developed for the study of economics in order to gain insight into complex market trends and the variables that affect market demand, supply, and costs.

Lifetime value analysis. This analysis employs analytical models to assess the profitability of an individual customer (or a class of customers) over a lifetime of transactions. Sophisticated models generate accurate estimates of the costs incurred by the customer in buying and making use of the product, including the cost of the buying channel, the likelihood of returns, the expense from calls for customer service, and so on.

Market experiments. Using direct mail, changes in a website (known as A/B tests), promotions, and other techniques, marketers test variables to determine what customers respond to most in a given offering. Normally involves different treatments based on assumed causal variables for different (ideally randomized) groups, with an outcome measure and a comparison from which the effect of the treatment can be observed.

Multiple regression analysis. The most common statistical technique for predicting the value of a dependent variable (such as sales) in relation to one or more independent variables (such as the number of salespeople, the temperature, or the day of the month). While basic regression assumes linear relationships, modifications of the model can deal with nonlinearity, logarithmic relationships, and so forth. Forms of this set of methods are used in econometrics and time series analysis.

Price optimization. Also known as *yield* or *revenue management*, this technique assumes that the primary causal variable in customer purchase behavior is price. The key issue is usually price elasticity, or the response (changes in demand) of the buyer to increases or decreases in product price. Price optimization initiatives typically construct price elasticity curves in order to understand the impact of price across a range of changes and conditions.

Search engine optimization (SEO). Statistical methods and activities designed to improve a website's ranking in search engines such as Google.

Support vector machine (SVM). This machine learning method uses training data to classify cases into one category or another. It is often used for customer segmentation and churn analysis.

Time series experiments. These experimental designs follow a particular population for successive points in time. They are used to determine whether a condition that applied at a certain point led to a change in the variables under study. This approach might be used, for example, to determine the impact of exposure to advertising on product purchases over time.

Uplift modeling. A predictive modeling technique that directly assesses the incremental impact of a treatment (such as a promotion or other type of marketing initiative) on a customer's behavior.

(or attributed in Europe to Lever Brothers founder Lord Leverhulme): "Half the money I spend on advertising is wasted; the trouble is, I don't know which half."

Sir Martin Sorrell, CEO of WPP plc, one of the world's largest advertising agencies, calls econometrics the holy grail of advertising. He noted in an interview, "There is no doubt in my mind that scientific analysis, including econometrics, is one of the most important areas in the marketing-services industry."[4]

Most large advertising agencies have created groups of econometrics experts to do such analyses for clients. These firms gather data for their clients, build data warehouses and Hadoop-based data lakes, and analyze the data to find answers to a variety of questions on advertising effectiveness. The questions include such issues as which medium is most effective, whether the additional cost of color is worthwhile in print advertising, and what days of the week are best to run ads. Typically, a great deal of data must be gathered to rule out alternative explanations of advertising lift.

The other dramatic change in advertising is the rise of digital ads. These are revolutionary, of course, because whether someone clicks on an ad can be tracked. There are a variety of web-based advertising approaches—banners, pop-ups, search-based, and more—and the effectiveness of each can be easily tracked. Analytical algorithms are also used to determine which digital ads are placed on which sites for each user. The ads are personalized (at least to some degree), and the decisions about placement are largely automated. The combination of digital and analytical advertising has led mainstream IT-oriented consulting firms like Accenture, Deloitte, and IBM to enter these businesses, largely through acquisitions.

Of course, one of the most powerful forms of online advertising is the search-based ad exemplified by Google. By having the industry-leading search engine, Google can serve ads that correspond to search terms (AdWords) used by a potential customer. Google also serves ads onto other companies' online properties through its AdSense network. One of the primary reasons Google has been successful with advertisers is its extensive use of analytics. Because Google advertising is done for a large client base for small payment increments (a few cents per click-through), much of the analytics must be automated and highly scalable. Google employs self-learning algorithms that are constantly analyzing the efficacy (typically in conversion rates) of different keywords (the primary advertising medium on Google's own properties), placement on the page, creative material, and so forth. The learning is input for an optimization engine that develops suggestions for advertisers without any human intervention. Advertisers can see the suggestions when they look at the reports for activity relative to their ads. The suggestions may differ for different types of sites, such as entertainment versus publishing. Large Google advertisers also have account managers who can work with the advertiser and provide analytics-based advice. Google's philosophy is that analytics and metrics will make advertisers more successful in working with the company, so they try to provide as much analytical sophistication as advertisers can use. The current challenges in online advertising involve how to deliver personalized ads in an omnichannel environment and how to determine attribution for a sale across online and offline channels.

Other approaches to customer analytics primarily focus on retention and cross-selling. For example, the Norwegian bank DnB NOR has built analytics on top of a Teradata warehouse to more effectively build customer relationships. The bank uses "event triggers," based on customer life events, in the data warehouse to prompt customer relationship analysts to offer one or more tailored services based on the event. For example, if a customer receives a substantial inheritance, a bank representative will call on the customer to offer investment products. DnB NOR has a set of automated tools that match customer profiles and events and then generate a set of suggested products. Based on customers' past experience, DnB then chooses the most effective channel through which to contact a customer about the most appropriate products. Using these tools, the company has achieved a conversion rate on cross-selling between 40 and 50 percent and has halved its marketing budget while increasing customer satisfaction.[5]

Of course, organizations need to be careful that their event triggers don't violate customer privacy. The best-known example of this issue is when Target analysts recognized that pregnant women were a "fertile" target for direct marketing, buying a wide variety of items in Target stores. They realized that they could identify a pregnant woman early on by her shopping habits. When one teenager received a targeted circular with pregnancy-oriented items, her father— enraged at the assumption that his unwed daughter was pregnant— complained to Target. Though the daughter turned out to actually be pregnant, Target rapidly discontinued this particular event trigger marketing approach.[6]

One of the most impressive users of analytics to retain customers is Tesco. Founded in 1924, Tesco is now the largest food retailer in the United Kingdom and one of the world's largest retailers. Located in eleven countries, it operates in every form of retail food channel— convenience, specialty, supermarket, and hypermarket. Tesco's spectacular transformation began in 1995, when it introduced its Clubcard loyalty program. The card functions as a mechanism for collecting information on customers, rewarding customers for shopping at Tesco, and targeting coupon variations for maximum return. Customers earn points that are redeemable at Tesco at a rate of 1 percent of purchase amounts. Tesco estimates it has awarded points worth several billon British pounds.

The results are impressive. While the direct marketing industry's average response is only 2 percent, Tesco and its in-house consultant Dunnhumby achieve average redemption rates between 8 percent and 20 percent. The Tesco CEO who founded the program, Sir Terry Leahy, believes the Clubcard program is also responsible for the company's success with its internet business. The world's largest internet grocer, Tesco has delivered food to more than a million homes and serves four hundred thousand repeat customers. All online Tesco customers must have a Clubcard, so Tesco can know what they purchase and target online promotions accordingly. By analyzing Clubcard data, combined with a rigorous program of experimentation, Tesco's internet business has seen sales surge for nonfood items including home furnishings, music downloads, and homeowner and automobile insurance. The company has also established a bank that makes use of Clubcard data.

Tesco uses the data it collects on purchases to group customers according to lifestyle. It has aggressively pursued a classification system to determine what products will appeal to customers with adventurous, healthy, or penny-pinching, etc., tastes. Some attributes, such as whether a product is frozen or what it costs per kilogram, can be pulled from its product databases. But others involving taste and lifestyle are more difficult to classify. When Tesco wants to identify products that appeal to adventurous palates, for example, it will start with a product that is widely agreed to be an adventurous choice in a given country—say, Thai green curry paste in the United Kingdom—and then analyze the other purchases made by people who bought the paste. If customers who buy curry paste also frequently buy squid or wild rocket (arugula) pesto, these products have a high coefficient of relatedness and so probably also appeal to adventurous customers.

Tesco says that it issues 12 million targeted variations of product coupons a year, driving the coupon redemption rate, customer loyalty, and ultimately financial performance to market-leading heights.[7] When Leahy retired, Tesco's performance deteriorated a bit, but there is no evidence that Clubcard and analytics were the problem. Kroger, which uses a similar approach (and the same consultant, Dunn-humby), has an industry-leading loyalty card usage rate and coupon redemption rate in the United States, and Kroger has had fifty-two straight quarters of positive sales growth.

Firms also use analytics to avoid bad customers while attracting the few customers who defy conventional measures of suitability or risk—an approach known as "skimming the cream off the garbage." As we mentioned in chapter 3, Progressive and Capital One both es-chew the traditional industry-standard risk measures. At Progres-sive, for example, instead of automatically rating a motorcycle rider as a high risk, analysts take into account such factors as the driver's employment history, participation in other high-risk activities (such as skydiving), and credit score. A driver with a long record with one employer who is also a low credit risk and avoids other risky activities will be rated as a low-risk customer.

Capital One has improved on conventional approaches to attracting so-called subprime customers—those individuals who by their credit rating are considered to be a high risk for bankruptcy or default. Cap-ital One employs its own proprietary consumer creditworthiness as-sessment tool to identify and attract those customers it sees as less risky than their credit scores would indicate.

Pricing Optimization

Pricing is another task that is particularly susceptible to analytical manipulation. Companies use analytics for a competitive advantage by pricing products appropriately, whether that is Walmart's everyday low pricing or a hotelier's adjusting prices in response to customer demand. Analytics also make it easier to engage in *dynamic pricing*—the practice of adjusting the price for a good or service in real time in response to market conditions such as demand, inventory level, competitor behavior, and customer history. This tactic was pioneered in the airline industry but now has spread to other sectors.

Retail prices, for example, have historically been set by intuition. Today, however, many retailers (and even business-to-business firms) are adopting analytical software as part of "scientific retailing." Such software works by analyzing historical point-of-sale data to determine price elasticity and cross-elasticity (a measure of whether one good is a substitute for another) for every item in every store. An equation is calculated that determines the optimal price to maximize sales and profitability.

Retailers usually begin by using pricing analytics to optimize markdowns—figuring out when and by how much to lower prices. Some then move on to pricing for all retail merchandise and to analysis of promotions, category mix, and breadth and depth of assortments. Most retailers experience a 5 to 10 percent increase in gross margin as a result of using price optimization systems. Some yield even greater benefits. According to a Yankee Group report, "Enterprises have realized up to 20 percent profit improvements by using price management and profit optimization (PMPO) solutions. No other packaged software can deliver the same type of top-line benefits and address bottom-line inefficiencies. PMPO is the best kept secret in enterprise software."[8]

Virtually all retailers today have adopted some version of analytical pricing software. Many adopted it initially for discount pricing, and later moved to all item pricing. Some companies, such as Macy's, have combined it with in-memory analytics software to rapidly reprice merchandise based on factors like weather and competitors' prices. The department store chain has been able to reduce the time to optimize pricing of its 73 million items for sale from over twenty-seven hours to just over one hour.

Analytically based pricing software is spreading to other industries as well. Many vendors offer price optimization software, and many industries are taking advantage of it. The San Francisco Giants, for example, pioneered the optimization of baseball game ticket prices. If the team is playing a popular rival or if the pitching matchup is considered a good one, prices can go up almost tenfold. In addition to professional baseball, pricing optimization is used by some professional football, basketball, hockey, and soccer teams.

It has also been successfully applied in casinos. Gary Loveman, the former CEO of Caesars Entertainment, wrote about it in the foreword to the first edition of this book:

> In short, opportunities abound to employ simple analytic methods to marginally or substantially increase profitability, especially in large businesses such as mine where a single insight can ring the cash register literally thousands or millions of times. Examples abound in casino resort entertainment, including yield management, game pricing, customer relationship management, loyalty programs, and procurement. To take perhaps the easiest and biggest opportunity in my tenure, we found that a ten-basis-point movement of slot pricing toward the estimated demand curve for a given game could enhance our profitability by an eight-figure amount and be unobservable to the guest.[9]

One cautionary note: pricing changes are not always unobservable. Most consumers are used to the idea of dynamic pricing in the context of changing market conditions—resorts that lower room prices during the off-season and raise them during peak demand, for example—and probably find it fair. However, companies can face a backlash when they use demand elasticity (the fact that loyal customers will pay a higher price for something than fickle customers) to make pricing decisions. For example, for a time, Amazon priced its DVDs higher to people who spent more. When that practice became known to the public, Amazon was forced to retreat by the resulting outcry.

Brand Management

Just as analytics bring a heightened level of discipline to pricing, they also bring needed discipline to marketing activities as a whole. Leading companies have developed analytical capabilities that enable them to efficiently design and execute highly effective multichannel marketing campaigns, measure the results, and continually improve future campaigns. Many are using econometric modeling and scenario planning to predict performance outcomes depending on overall budget levels or how much is spent in different channels.

The great challenge for brand managers in the current age, however, is developing a *closed loop* of analytics describing how customers interact with a brand across multiple channels. With this information, brands can learn not only what ads and promotions customers see, but how they react in terms of click-throughs, conversions, and service. Most companies find it difficult to marshal all this data and make sense of it with analytics.

One company that does do it well, however, is Disney's Parks and Resorts business unit. The business has long been highly analytical, optimizing hotel prices, ride times, and marketing offers. Now, however, due to a "vacation management" project called MyMagic+ that cost over $1 billion and began in 2008, it is able to close the loop on how all that marketing translates into a customer experience.[10] The ambitious goal of MyMagic+ is to provide a more magical, immersive, seamless and personal experience for every single guest. From the beginning of planning a Disney park or hotels reservation, the customer is encouraged to register and to supply an email address. The customer can plan a family trip (and, at the same time, register all family members or friends participating in the trip) with the MyDisneyExperience website or app. Disney is then able to learn what activities the customer is considering and what web pages engage different family members. Customers are also encouraged to sign up for the FastPass+ service, which offers them shorter wait times; in exchange, they share information about the park attractions, entertainment options, and even greetings from Disney characters they intend to experience.

What really closes the loop for Disney, however, is the MagicBand. Rolled out in 2013, these wristbands are typically mailed to a family before its visit starts. From the customer's standpoint, it allows access to the park and hotel rooms, FastPass+ entry to attractions at specific times, and in-park and hotel purchases. It also stores photos taken with Disney characters, and allows the characters to have personalized interactions with kids. From Disney's standpoint, it provides a goldmine of data, including customer locations, character interactions, purchase histories, ride patterns, and much more. If customers opt in, Disney will send personalized offers to them during their stay and after they return home.

The scale and expense of the MyMagic+ system is reflective of the fact that the ante has been raised for competing on analytics. It may take a while for Disney to recoup its billion-dollar investment in this closed-loop system, but the company has already seen operational benefits in being able to admit more customers to parks on busy days. There is also a belief that the system will deter customers from visiting competitor parks. Key to the ultimate value of the program, however, will be extensive analytics on how marketing and branding programs translate into actual customer activity.

Converting Customer Interactions into Sales

The strategies described so far relate to marketing and branding, but it is also possible to use analytics to improve the face-to-face encounters between customers and salespeople. This process—previously one involving plenty of intuition—is becoming increasingly analytical. Many sales processes, such as lead streams, pipelines, and conversion rates, are now addressed analytically. In the early days of sales analytics, almost all methods were descriptive. A bar chart would be considered state-of-the-art. Today, however, companies such as Salesforce.com have embedded predictive and prescriptive analytics into their mainstream transactional systems. Instead of deciding which lead to address, for example, a salesperson might resort to a *predictive lead scoring system.*

Consider how Capital One Health Care, which sells financing services through medical practices for uninsured medical procedures (like cosmetic surgery), outsmarts competitors. Most financing firms market their credit services to doctors the same way many pharmaceutical reps do—known in the business as "pens, pads, and pizza."

By stopping by at lunchtime, representatives hope they can entice the doctor out for a quick lunch break and an even shorter sales pitch. At Capital One, however, reps don't randomly chase down prospects and hope that a few freebies will clinch the deal. Instead, analysts supply the company's reps with information about which doctors to target and which sales messages and products are most likely to be effective.

Boston-based publisher HMH, perhaps better known as Houghton Mifflin Harcourt, has been publishing books since the 1830s.[11] Now, however, much of its content is electronic or software-based, and the company's leaders wanted to similarly transform sales processes. Like many companies, HMH used a transactional CRM system—one from Salesforce.com. But it had few analytics to inform and motivate salespeople and sales management.

HMH's salespeople primarily call on school districts, and they used to track their sales opportunities and forecasts in Excel. But this approach didn't facilitate communications about sales processes, and it was only descriptive analytics. But when sales became a key focus of the company's executives, HMH began a collaboration between the marketing organization—responsible for lead generation—and sales, which has responsibility for converting them. Part of the initiative involved acquiring new software for descriptive sales analytics and a different system for lead scoring.

HMH improved the entire process for lead management, including capturing leads from events and webinars as well as salespeople. It launched a predictive lead scoring and routing system that prioritized leads for sales, which eventually reduced days leads outstanding from thirty days to six. The company also built an attribution model for leads across the sales funnel to determine the optimal channel mix for lowest cost-per-lead and cost-per-conversion. A series of new reports addressed such metrics as days leads outstanding, lead survival curve, estimated lead value, and funnel conversion velocity.

Sometimes sales analytics have little to do with a sales force. Caesars, for example, is able to use the information it collects to improve the experience of the customer while simultaneously streamlining casino traffic. Customers hate to wait; they may be tempted to leave. Worse, from the casino's perspective, a waiting customer is not spending money. When bottlenecks occur at certain slot machines, the company can offer a customer a free game at a slot machine located in a slower part of the casino. It can also inform waiting customers of an opening at another machine. These prompts help redirect traffic and even out demand. According to Wharton School professor David Bell, Caesars is able to tell "who is coming into the casino, where they are going once they are inside, how long they sit at different gambling tables and so forth. This allows them to optimize the range, and configuration, of their gambling games."[12]

Managing Customer Life Cycles

In addition to facilitating the purchases of a customer on a given day, companies want to optimize their customers' lifetime value. Predictive analytics tools help organizations understand the life cycle of individual customer purchases and behavior. Best Buy's predictive models enable the company to increase subsequent sales after an initial purchase. Someone who buys a digital camera, for example, will receive a carefully timed e-coupon from Best Buy for a photo printer.

Sprint also takes a keen interest in customer life cycles. It uses analytics to address forty-two attributes that characterize the interactions, perceptions, and emotions of customers across a six-stage life cycle, from initial product awareness through service renewal or upgrade. The company integrates these life cycle analytics into its operations, using twenty-five models to determine the best ways to maximize customer loyalty and spending over time.

Sprint's goal is to have every customer "touch point" make the "next best offer" to the customer while eliminating interactions that might be perceived as nuisances. When Sprint discovered, for example, that a significant percentage of customers with unpaid bills were not deadbeats but individuals and companies with unresolved questions about their accounts, it shifted these collections from bill collectors to *retention agents*, whose role is to resolve conflicts and retain satisfied customers.

According to Sprint, the group responsible for these analytics has delivered more than $1 billion of enterprise value and $500 million in revenue by reducing customer churn, getting customers to buy more, and improving satisfaction rates.

Personalizing Content

A final strategy for using analytics to win over customers is to tailor offerings to individual preferences. In the mobile network business, for example, companies are vying to boost average revenue per user by selling subscribers information (such as news alerts and stock updates) and entertainment services (such as music downloads, ringtones, and video clips). But given the small screen on mobile devices, navigating content is a real challenge.

O2, a mobile network operator in the United Kingdom, uses analytics to help mobile users resolve that challenge. The company pioneered the use of artificial intelligence software to provide subscribers with the content they want before they know they want it. Analytical technology monitors subscriber behavior, such as the frequency with which users click on specific content, to determine personal preferences. The software then places desirable content where users can get to it easily.

The vast majority (97 percent) of O2's subscribers have opted to use personalized menus and enjoy the convenience of having a service that can predict and present content to match their tastes. Today, O2 has more than 50 percent of the mobile internet traffic in the United Kingdom, and the company continues to explore new ways to use analytics; for instance, it is investigating new collaborative filtering technology that would analyze the preferences of similar customers to make content suggestions. Hugh Griffiths, formerly O2's vice president of digital products, services and content, believes that "personalization is [O2's] key service differentiator."[13]

Personalization is also being applied to contexts like gaming and education. At the Strata + Hadoop World conference, online game developer Jagex Games Studio described its model that analyzes a decade of game content and 220 million player accounts to provide recommendations to its players in real time. One of its most popular games, RuneScape, is a free, massively multiplayer online role-playing game (MMORPG). By incorporating recommendations that point players to the most interesting and relevant content during the game, Jagex increased revenues (from advertising, paid subscriptions, and in-game purchases) while also improving player engagement and quest completion rates.[14]

The eLearning company Skillsoft is using big data to improve the effectiveness of its technology-delivered education solutions to its 6000 customers and 19 million learners worldwide. Customer learning recommendations and content are personalized by analyzing detailed data about how and when individuals use over sixty thousand learning assets, as well as other factors such as survey data and direct email response behavior. Though sophisticated personalization of both content and recommendations, Skillsoft has realized a 128 percent improvement in user engagement. According to John Ambrose, Senior Vice President, Strategy, Corporate Development and Emerging Business, "We're building a powerful new big data engine that will enable us to optimize learning experiences and uncover new learning patterns that can be applied immediately so that the system is continually improving. This is the perfect application of big data—harness it and apply it to improve individual and organizational performance."[15]

Supplier-Facing Processes

Contemporary supply chain processes blur the line between customer- and supplier-oriented processes. In some cases, customers penetrate deep into and across an organization, reaching all the way to suppliers. In other cases, companies are managing logistics for their customers (refer to the box "Typical Analytical Techniques in Supply Chains").

Connecting Customers and Suppliers

The mother of all supply chain analytics competitors is Walmart. The company collects massive amounts of sales and inventory data (over 30 terabytes as of 2015) into a single integrated technology platform. Its managers routinely analyze manifold aspects of its supply chain, and store managers use analytical tools to optimize product assortment; they examine not only detailed sales data but also qualitative factors such as the opportunity to tailor assortments to local community needs.[16]

The most distinctive element of Walmart's supply chain data is not the sophistication of the analytics, but rather the availability of data and descriptive analytics to suppliers. Walmart buys products from

TYPICAL ANALYTICAL TECHNIQUES IN SUPPLY CHAINS

Capacity planning. Finding and optimizing the capacity of a supply chain or its elements; identifying and eliminating bottlenecks; typically employs iterative analysis of alternative plans.

Combinatorics. A sophisticated mathematical technique that models components in a supply chain, typically with a goal of optimizing them or their attributes.

Demand–supply matching. Determining the intersections of demand and supply curves to optimize inventory and minimize overstocks and stockouts. Typically involves such issues as arrival processes, waiting times, and throughput losses.

Location analysis. Optimization of locations for stores, distribution centers, manufacturing plants, and so on. Increasingly uses geographic analysis and digital maps to, for example, relate company locations to customer locations.

Modeling. Creating models to simulate, explore contingencies, and optimize supply chains. Many of these approaches employ

more than sixty thousand suppliers in eighty countries, and each one uses the company's Retail Link system to track the movement of its products—in fact, the system's use is mandatory. In aggregate, suppliers run tens of millions of queries on the data warehouse every year, covering such data as daily sales, shipments, purchase orders, invoices, claims, returns, forecasts, radio frequency ID deployments, and more.[17] Suppliers also have access to the Modular Category Assortment Planning System, which they can use to create store-specific modular layouts of products. The layouts are based on sales data, store traits, and data on ten consumer segments. Some suppliers have created more than one thousand modular layouts.

As Walmart's data warehouse introduced additional information about customer behavior, applications using Walmart's massive data-

some form of linear programming software and solvers, which allow programs to seek particular goals, given a set of variables and constraints. More recent approaches involve machine learning applications.

Routing. Finding the best path for a delivery vehicle around a set of locations. Many of these approaches are versions of the "traveling salesman problem."

Scheduling. Creating detailed schedules for the flow of resources and work through a process. Some scheduling models are *finite* in that they take factory capacity limits into account when scheduling orders. So-called advanced planning and scheduling (APS) approaches also recognize material constraints in terms of current inventory and planned deliveries or allocations.

Simulation. Supply chain simulations model variation in supply flows, resources, warehouses, and various types of constraints. They allow for both optimization and visualization of complex supply chains.

base began to extend well beyond its supply chain. Walmart now collects more data about more consumers than anyone in the private sector. Its marketers mine this data to ensure that customers have the products they want, when they want them, and at the right price. For example, they've learned that before a hurricane, consumers stock up on food items that don't require cooking or refrigeration. The top seller: Strawberry Pop Tarts. We expect that Walmart asks Kellogg's to rush shipments of them to stores just before a hurricane hits. In short, there are many analytical applications behind Walmart's success as the world's largest retailer.

Walmart may be the world's largest retailer, but at least it knows where all its stores are located. Amazon's business model, in contrast, requires the company to manage a constant flow of new products, suppliers, customers, and promotions, as well as deliver orders directly to its customers by promised dates.

Amazon is pretty quiet about all its analytics projects, but over the years, we've been able to glean a few details. The company is best known for its "collaborative filtering" analytics that recommend products to customers, but it has also worked diligently on supply chain analytics. It has integrated all the elements of its supply chain in order to coordinate supplier sourcing decisions. To determine the optimal sourcing strategy (determining the right mix of joint replenishment, coordinated replenishment, and single sourcing) as well as manage all the logistics to get a product from manufacturer to customer, Amazon applies advanced optimization and supply chain management methodologies and techniques across its fulfillment, capacity expansion, inventory management, procurement, and logistics functions.

For example, after experimenting with a variety of packaged software solutions and techniques, Amazon concluded that no existing approach to modeling and managing supply chains would fit their needs. They ultimately invented a proprietary inventory model employing nonstationary stochastic optimization techniques, which allows them to model and optimize the many variables associated with their highly dynamic, fast-growing business. An Amazon job description supplies some detail on the methods the company uses:

> When customers place orders, our systems use real time, large scale optimization techniques to optimally choose where to ship from and how to consolidate multiple orders so that customers get their shipments on time or faster with the lowest possible transportation costs. This team is focused on saving hundreds of millions of dollars using cutting edge science, machine learning, and scalable distributed software on the Cloud that automates and optimizes inventory and shipments to customers under the uncertainty of demand, pricing and supply.[18]

Amazon sells over thirty categories of goods, from books to groceries to industrial and scientific tools to home services, and its own electronic products Kindle, Fire, and Echo. The company has a variety of fulfillment centers for different goods. When Amazon launches a new goods category, it uses analytics to plan the supply chain for the goods and leverage the company's existing systems and processes. To do so, it forecasts demand and capacity at the national level and fulfillment center level for each SKU. Its supply chain analysts try to optimize order quantities to satisfy constraints and minimize holding, shipping, and stockout costs. In order to optimize its consumer goods supply chain, for example, it used an "integral min-cost flow problem with side constraints"; to round off fractional shipments, it used a "multiple knapsack problem using the greedy algorithm" (if you know what that means, perhaps you should be working for Amazon). The company even obsesses over the optimized way to load a truck.

One of the Amazon's more recent supply chain innovations was a patent it filed in 2012 for a "method and system for anticipatory package shipping." That means that Amazon sometimes predicts what customers will order, and ships packages to a geographical area without knowing exactly where they will end up. It's a unique combination of predictive sales and supply chain management.

Amazon is also planning to take over many aspects of its supply chain, bypassing cargo brokers and even shippers. Amazon would then be "amassing inventory from thousands of merchants around the world and then buying space on trucks, planes and ships at reduced rates," according to Bloomberg Technology.[19] The company has already received approval from China and the United States to act as a wholesaler for ocean container shipping. While the analytics implications of this are as yet unclear, it's likely that Amazon will bring a new level of data-based insights to that traditional business.

Logistics Management

Sometimes a service company uses analytics with such skill and execution that entire lines of business can be created. UPS took this route in 1986, when it formed UPS Logistics, a wholly owned subsidiary of UPS Supply Chain Solutions. UPS Logistics provides routing, scheduling, and dispatching systems for businesses with private fleets and wholesale distribution.[20] The company claims to have over one thousand clients that use its services daily. This approach, captured in the "Don't You Worry 'Bout a Thing" campaign, is enabling UPS to expand its reputation from reliable shipping to reliable handling of clients' logistics value chains. UPS has also entered into the data product business, charging customers extra for the My Choice option to reroute, reschedule, or authorize delivery of packages en route.

Of course, UPS has been an analytical competitor in supply chains for many years. In 1954 its CEO noted, "Without operations research we'd be analyzing our problems intuitively only."[21] The company has long been known in its industry for truck route optimization and, more recently, airplane route optimization. Mike Eskew, UPS's CEO from 2002 to 2007, founded UPS's current operations research group in 1987. By 2003 he announced that he expected savings from optimization of $600 million annually. He described the importance of route optimization: "It's vital that we manage our networks around the world the best way that we can. When things don't go exactly the way we expected because volume changes or weather gets in the way, we have to think of the best ways to recover and still keep our service levels."[22] UPS has built on these capabilities over time to develop the ORION real-time routing application that we've described in detail in chapter 4.

FedEx has also embraced both analytics and the move to providing full logistics outsourcing services to companies. While UPS and FedEx both provide customers with a full range of IT-based analytical tools, FedEx provides these applications to firms that do not engage its full logistics services, leading one analyst to observe, "FedEx is as much a technology company as a shipping company."[23] UPS and FedEx have become so efficient and effective in all aspects of the logistics of shipping that other companies have found it to their economic advantage to outsource their entire logistics operations.

Another company helping its customers manage logistics is CEMEX, the leading global supplier of cement. Cement is highly perishable; it begins to set as soon as a truck is loaded, and the producer has limited time to get it to its destination. In Mexico, traffic, weather, and an unpredictable labor market make it incredibly hard to plan deliveries accurately. So a contractor might have concrete ready for delivery when the site isn't ready, or work crews might be at a standstill because the concrete hasn't arrived.

CEMEX realized that it could increase market share and charge a premium to time-conscious contractors by reducing delivery time on orders. To figure out how to accomplish that goal, CEMEX staffers studied FedEx, pizza delivery companies, and ambulance squads. Following this research, CEMEX equipped most of its concrete-mixing trucks in Mexico with global positioning satellite locators and used predictive analytics to improve its delivery processes. This approach allows dispatchers to cut the average response time for changed orders from three hours to twenty minutes in most locations.[24] Not only did this system increase truck productivity by 35 percent, it also wedded customers firmly to the brand.[25] CEMEX has also used analytics to optimize other aspects of its business, including factory production, the size of its truck fleet, electricity consumption, and inventory management. Its disciplined and analytical approach to operations has made it one of the fastest-growing and most profitable cement companies in the world. And if you can be analytical about cement—one of the world's oldest commodities—you can apply it to any business.

Conclusion

Analytical competitors have recognized that the lines between supply and demand have blurred. As a result, they are using sophisticated analytics in their supply chain and customer-facing processes to create distinctive capabilities that help them serve their customers better and work with their suppliers more effectively.

The discipline of supply chain management has deep roots in analytical mastery; companies that have excelled in this area have a decades-long history of using quantitative analysis and "operations management" to optimize logistics. Companies getting a later start, however, have clear opportunities to embrace an analytical approach to marketing, customer relationship management, and other demand processes.

In part I of this book, we have described the nature of analytical competition. In part II, we lay out the steps companies need to take and the key technical and human resources needed for analytical competition.

PART 2

BUILDING AN ANALYTICAL CAPABILITY

CHAPTER SIX

A ROAD MAP TO ENHANCED ANALYTICAL CAPABILITIES

PROGRESSING THROUGH THE FIVE STAGES OF ANALYTICAL MATURITY

BY THIS POINT, DEVELOPING AN ANALYTICAL CAPABILITY may seem straightforward. Indeed, some organizations such as Marriott, GE, and Procter & Gamble have been using intensive data analysis for decades. Others, such as Google, Amazon, Netflix, Zillow and Capital One, were founded with the idea of using analytics as the basis of competition. These firms, with their history of close attention to data, sponsorship from senior management, and enter prise use of analytics, have attained the highest stage of analytical capability.

The overwhelming majority of organizations, however, have neither a finely honed analytical capability nor a detailed plan to develop one. For companies that want to become analytical competitors, a quick and painless journey cannot be promised. There are many moving pieces to put in place, including software applications, technology, data, processes, metrics, incentives, skills, culture, and sponsorship. One executive we interviewed compared the complexity of managing the development of analytical capabilities to playing a fifteen-level chess game.

Once the pieces fall into place, it still takes time for an organization to get the large-scale results it needs to become an analytical competitor. Changing business processes and employee behaviors is always the most difficult and time-consuming part of any major organizational change. And by its nature, developing an analytical capability is an iterative process, as managers gain better insights into the dynamics of their business over time by working with data and refining analytical models. Our research and experience suggests that it takes eighteen to thirty-six months of regularly working with data to start developing a steady stream of rich insights that can be translated into practice. Many organizations, lacking the will or faced with other pressing priorities, will take much longer than that.

Even highly analytical companies have lots of work left to do to improve their analytical capabilities. For example, Sprint, which used analytics to realize more than $1 billion of value and $500 million in incremental revenue over five years, believes that it has just scratched the surface of what it can accomplish with its analytical capability. And managers at a bank that has been an analytical competitor for years reported that different units are slipping back into silos of disaggregated customer data. Analytical competitors cannot rest on their laurels.

Nevertheless, the benefits of becoming an analytical competitor far outweigh the costs. In this chapter, we will introduce a road map that describes how organizations become analytical competitors and the benefits associated with each stage of the development process.

Overview of the Road Map

The road map describes typical behaviors, capabilities, and challenges at each stage of development. It provides guidance on investments and actions that are necessary to build an organization's analytical capabilities and move to higher stages of analytical competition.

Figure 6-1 provides an overview of the road map to analytical competition and the exit criteria for each stage.

FIGURE 6-1

Road map to becoming an analytical competitor

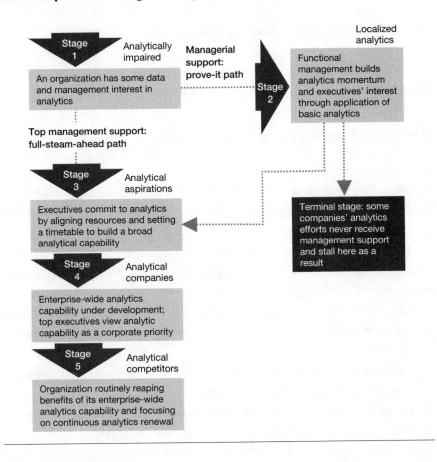

Stage 1: Prerequisites to Analytical Competition

At stage 1, organizations lack the prerequisites for analytics. These companies need first to improve their transaction data environment in order to have consistent, quality data for decision making. If a company has poor-quality data, it should postpone plans for analytical competition and fix its data first. Dow Chemical's path is instructive. It began installing one of the first SAP systems in the United States in the late 1980s but did not begin serious initiatives to use data analytically until enough transaction data had been accumulated.

Even if an organization has some quality data available, it must also have executives who are predisposed to fact-based decision making. A "data-allergic" management team that prides itself on making gut-based decisions is unlikely to be supportive. Any analytical initiatives in such an organization will be tactical and limited in impact.

Once a company has surmounted these obstacles, it is ready to advance to a critical juncture in the road map.

Assessing Analytical Capabilities

Once an organization has some useful data and management support in place, the next task is to take stock and candidly assess whether it has the strategic insight, sponsorship, culture, skills, data, and IT needed for analytical competition.

One financial services executive offers sage advice to anyone getting started: "Begin with an assessment—how differentiated is your offering versus what you and your customers want it to be? Big data and analytics can be a real game changer. But you must have a clear vision of what value looks like if you are going to figure out how to unleash that vision."

While each stage of the road map reflects the ability of an enterprise to compete on analytics, different parts of the organization may be in very different stages of development. For example, actuarial work requires an appreciation of statistical methods that may not exist to the same extent in other parts of an insurance company. Or a pharmaceutical firm's marketing analytics in the United States may be far more sophisticated than they are in other countries or regions simply because the US operation has greater access to data and an analytically minded manager in charge.

Just as some business units or processes may be more or less advanced than others in the enterprise, some aspects of the business are likely to be more analytically astute than others. For example, an organization may have a tightly integrated, highly standardized, and flexible IT environment but little demand for analytics, or, conversely, the demand for analytics far outstrips the capabilities of the IT organization. A utility might use machine learning capabilities to manage its electrical grid but not elsewhere in the enterprise. There may be many user departments and even individuals with their own analytical applications and data sources but little central coordination or synergy.

Organizations need to assess their level of analytical capability in three main areas. (Table 6-1 provides an overview of these key attributes, each of which is equally vital to successful analytical competition.) One cautionary note: executives are often tempted to just obtain the data and analytical software they need, thinking that analytics are synonymous with technology. But unless executives consciously address the other elements, they will find it difficult to progress to later stages.

We'll address the organizational issues in this chapter and go into greater detail on the human factors in chapter 7 and the technical ones in chapter 8.

A company needs a clear strategy in order to know which data to focus on, how to allocate analytical resources, and what it is trying to accomplish (what we refer to as "targets" in the DELTA model that we describe in chapter 2 and later in this chapter). For example, the business strategy at Caesars Entertainment dictated the company's analytical strategy as well. When the explosion of newly legalized gaming jurisdictions in the mid-1990s ground to a halt, Caesars (then Harrah's) managers realized that growth could no longer come from the construction of new casinos. They knew that growth would need to come from existing casinos and from an increase of customer visits

TABLE 6-1

The key elements in an analytical capability

Capabilities	Key elements
Organization	• Insight into performance drivers • Choosing a distinctive capability • Performance management and strategy execution • Process redesign and integration
Human	• Leadership and senior executive commitment • Establishing a fact-based culture • Securing and building skills • Managing analytical people
Technology	• Quality data • Analytic technologies

CHOOSING A STRATEGIC FOCUS OR TARGET

Organizations initially focus on one or two areas for analytical competition:

- **Caesars:** Loyalty plus service
- **New England Patriots:** Player selection plus fan experience
- **Intuit:** Customer driven innovation plus operational discipline
- **Dreyfus Corporation:** Equity analysis plus asset attrition
- **UPS:** Operations plus customer data
- **Walmart:** Supply chain plus marketing
- **Owens & Minor:** Internal logistics plus customer cost reduction
- **Progressive:** Pricing plus new analytical service offerings

across Caesars' multiple properties. To achieve this goal, the company set a new strategic focus to drive growth through customer loyalty and data-driven marketing operations. This strategic focus enables Caesars to concentrate its investments on the activities and processes that have the greatest impact on financial performance—its distinctive capability. Implementing this strategy required the company to expand and exploit the data it had amassed on the gaming behaviors and resort preferences of existing customers. (See the box "Choosing a Strategic Focus or Target" for examples of where companies chose to focus their initial analytical investments.)

To have a significant impact on business performance, analytical competitors must continually strive to quantify and improve their insights into their performance drivers—the causal factors that drive costs, profitability, growth, and shareholder value in their industry (only the most advanced organizations have attempted to develop an enterprise-wide model of value creation). In practice, most organizations build their understanding gradually over time in a few key areas, learning from each new analysis and experiment.

To decide where to focus their resources for the greatest strategic impact, managers should answer the following questions:

- How can we distinguish ourselves in the marketplace?

- What is our distinctive capability?

- What key decisions in those processes, and elsewhere, need support from analytical insights?

- What information really matters to the business?

- What are the information and knowledge leverage points of the firm's performance?

As organizations develop greater insights, they can incorporate them into analytical models and adapt business processes to leverage them and increase competitive differentiation. These strategically focused insights, processes, and capabilities form the basis of the organization's distinctive capability.

Analytical competitors design effective decision making into their processes to ensure that analytical insights get translated into action and ultimately enhance business performance. They incorporate a way of thinking, putting plans into place, monitoring and correcting those plans, and learning from the results to help shape future actions.[1] For example, UK police analysts learned that they could predict from early behaviors which juveniles were likely to become adult criminals. The analysis concluded that if the UK police could proactively intervene when kids began to pursue the criminal path and prevent them from going in that direction, they could dramatically reduce the number of crimes ultimately committed.[2] However, in order for this insight to have any impact on crime rates requires more than awareness; it requires a close collaboration between police, educators, and human services workers to establish programs and practices aimed at eliminating the root causes of crime.

Finally, to ensure that strategy is converted into operational results, organizations must define and monitor metrics that are tied to strategic enterprise objectives, and align individual incentives and metrics with business objectives.

Choosing a Path

After an organization has realistically appraised its analytical capabilities, it must next choose which path to pursue. Organizations blessed with top management commitment and passion for analytics can move quickly through the "full steam ahead" path, while the rest are forced to take the slower "prove-it" detour.

Full Steam Ahead

A committed, passionate CEO can put the organization on the fast track to analytical competition. To date, firms pursuing this path have usually been digital businesses (e.g.: Google, Amazon, LinkedIn, Zillow) whose strategy from the beginning has been to compete on analytics, although occasionally a new CEO at an established firm (such as Gary Loveman of Caesars or the new general managers at the Chicago Cubs and Boston Red Sox in baseball) has led a major organizational transformation with analytics.

For a startup, the primary challenge on this path is acquiring and deploying the human and financial resources needed to build its analytical capabilities. Established companies face a more complex set of challenges because they already have people, data, processes, technology, and a culture. The existence of these resources is a double-edged sword—they can either provide a head start on building an analytical capability or be a source of resistance to using new methods. If organizational resistance is too great, it may be necessary to take a slower path to build support by demonstrating the benefits of analytics.

The organization going full steam ahead is easily recognized, because the CEO (or other top executive) regularly articulates the burning platform for competing on analytics. He or she consistently invests and takes actions designed to build the organization's strategic analytical capability. At such firms, the top priority is integrating analytics into the organization's distinctive capability, with an eye to building competitive differentiation. Success is characterized in enterprise-wide terms; company metrics emphasize corporate performance, such as top-line growth and profitability, rather than departmental goals or ROI.

An executive sponsor planning to follow this path must get the rest of the organization on board. The first step is to set a good example. Executives send a powerful message to the entire organization when they make decisions based on facts, not opinions. They must also demand that subordinates support their recommendations with analytically based insights. Second, they must articulate a clear and urgent need for change. It's always easier, of course, to move an organization in an entirely new direction when it is facing a dramatic crisis. Executives at highly successful companies confide that it is difficult to persuade (or compel) employees to become more analytical when no clear need to change is present.

Third, the CEO or executive sponsor must also be able to commit the necessary resources. Seriously ailing companies (though they have a clear mandate to do things differently in order to survive) may lack the resources needed for analytical competition. In such cases, pursuing an analytical strategy is like proposing "wellness sessions" to a patient undergoing cardiac arrest. Those organizations will have to revive themselves before pursuing the full-steam-ahead path to analytical competition.

An organization that makes competing on analytics its top priority can expect to make substantial strides in a year or two. While we are convinced that the full-steam-ahead path is ultimately faster, cheaper, and the way to the greatest benefits, we have found relatively few companies prepared to go down this road. If top management lacks the passion and commitment to pursue analytical competition with full force, it is necessary to prove the value of analytics through a series of smaller, localized projects.

Stage 2: Prove-It Detour

To those already convinced of the benefits of analytical competition, having to avoid the fast track feels like an unnecessary detour. Indeed, this path is much slower and circuitous, and there is a real risk that an organization can remain stalled indefinitely. We estimate that having to "prove-it" will add one to three years to the time needed to become an analytical competitor. But executives unwilling to make the leap should take a test-and-learn approach—trying out analytics in a series of small steps.

For organizations taking the detour, analytical sponsors can come from anywhere in the organization. For example, at one consumer packaged goods manufacturer, a new marketing vice president was shocked to discover that the analytical capabilities he took for granted at his former employer did not exist at his new company. Rather than try to garner support for a major enterprise-wide program, he logically chose to start small in his own department by adopting an analytically based model for planning retail trade promotions. In situations like this, initial applications should often be fairly tactical, small in scale, and limited in scope.

Despite its drawbacks, there are also important advantages to taking the slower path. Any true analytical competitor wants to have a series of experiments and evidence documenting the value of the approach, and the prove-it path helps the organization accumulate that empirical evidence. As managers get more experience using smaller, localized applications, they can gain valuable insights that can be translated into business benefits. Each incremental business insight builds momentum within the organization in favor of moving to higher stages of analytical competitiveness.

There are practical reasons for taking the prove-it road as well. By starting small, functional managers can take advantage of analytics to improve the efficiency and effectiveness of their own departments without having to get buy-in from others. This approach also requires a lower level of initial investment, since stand-alone analytical tools and data for a single business function cost less than any enterprise-wide program.

In stage 2, it is best to keep things simple and narrow in scope. The steps essentially boil down to:

1. Finding a sponsor and a business problem that can benefit from analytics

2. Implementing a small, localized project to add value and produce measurable benefits

3. Documenting the benefits and sharing the news with key stakeholders

4. Continuing to build a string of localized successes until the organization has acquired enough experience and sponsorship to progress to the next stage

An organization can linger in stage 2 indefinitely if executives don't see results, but most organizations are ready to move to the next stage in one to three years. By building a string of successes and carefully collecting data on the results, managers can attract top management attention and executive sponsorship for a broader application of analytics. At that point, they are ready to progress to stage 3.

Table 6-2 summarizes some of the major differences in scope, resources, and approach between the full-steam-ahead and the prove-it paths.

For an example of a company that chose the prove-it path, we will now look at the experiences of an organization that has begun to develop its analytical capabilities. (We have disguised the company and the names of the individuals.)

TABLE 6-2

Attributes of two paths to analytical competition

	Full steam ahead	Prove-it
Management sponsorship	Top general manager/CEO	Functional manager
Problem set	Strategic/distinctive capability	Local, tactical, wherever there's a sponsor
Measure/demonstrate value	Metrics of organizational performance to analytics (e.g., revenue growth, profitability, shareholder value)	Metrics of project benefits: ROI, productivity gains, cost savings
Technology	Enterprise-wide	Proliferation of analytics tools, integration challenges
People	Centralized, highly elite, skilled	Isolated pockets of excellence
Process	Embedded in process, opportunity through integration supply/demand	Stand-alone or in functional silo
Culture	Enterprise-wide, large-scale change	Departmental/functional, early adopters

PulpCo: Introducing Analytics
to Combat Competitive Pressure

PulpCo is a successful company engaged in the sale of pulp, paper, and lumber-based products, including consumer goods such as paper cups, industrial products like newsprint, and lumber-based products such as particleboard for residential construction. It has successfully sold these products in the United States and Europe for more than twenty years but has been facing increasing pressure from new entrants from developing economies, newly competitive European firms, and providers of substitute materials for construction and consumer products. The PulpCo management team has been with the company for years; most began their careers working at the mills. Traditionally, analytics have taken a back seat to PulpCo's more intuitive understanding of the industry and its dynamics.

Under increasing competitive pressure, the CEO, at a board member's urging, broke with long-standing tradition and hired a new CFO from outside the industry. Azmil Yatim, the new CFO, had been lured by PulpCo's scale of operations and major market position. But after a month on the job, he was wondering whether he had made a career mistake. The members of PulpCo's management team behaved as though they had limited awareness of the financial implications of their actions. Lacking accurate information about their customers and market competition, executives largely relied on feedback of the last customer they had visited. Major investment decisions were often made on the basis of inaccurate, untested assumptions. In operations, managers had grown used to having to make decisions without the right data. They had an incomplete understanding of their costs for major products such as particleboard, construction lumber, toilet paper, and newsprint. As a result, they made some costly mistakes, from unnecessary capital investments in plants and machinery to poor pricing.

The CFO resolved to improve the financial and decision-making capabilities of the organization. Sensing that the support of COO Daniel Ghani, a widely respected insider, would be critical to his efforts, Yatim initially sought his support for a bold and far-ranging change initiative to transform the organization. Ghani rejected it as too radical. But the COO was tired of constantly dealing with one crisis after another, and after talking with Yatim, he began to realize that many of these crises resulted from a lack of accurate financial and customer information, which in turn produced poor decisions. Ghani became convinced that the organization could not afford to continue to make decisions in an analytical vacuum. He urged Yatim to devise a new plan that would make effective use of financial data generated by the company's enterprise systems. Better financial information and control became a shared priority of the two executives.

Using a recent series of embarrassing missteps—including a major customer defection to a key competitor—as a rallying point, Yatim (together with the CIO, who reported to him) gained approval and funding for an initiative to improve financially based insights and decision making. He began by reviewing the skills in the finance function and at the mills and realized that operating managers needed help to leverage the new system. He arranged for formal training and also created a small group of analysts to help managers at the mills use and interpret the data. He also provided training to employees engaged in budgeting and forecasting.

As Yatim began to analyze the new data he was receiving, an unsettling picture emerged. PulpCo was actually losing money on some major accounts. Others that were deemed less strategically valuable were actually far more profitable. Armed with these insights, Yatim and his analysts worked with individual executives to interpret the data and understand the implications. As he did, the executive team became more convinced that they needed to instill more financial discipline and acumen in their management ranks.

A breakthrough occurred when detailed financial analysis revealed that a new plant, already in the early stages of construction, would be a costly mistake. Management realized that the company could add to capacity more cost-effectively by expanding and upgrading two existing plants, and the project was canceled. Managers across the company were shocked, since "everyone knew" that PulpCo needed the new plant and had already broken ground.

The executive team then declared that all major investments under way or planned in the next twelve months would be reviewed. Projects that were not supported by a business case and facts derived from the company's enterprise system would be shut down. New projects would not be approved without sufficient fact-based evidence. Managers scrambled to find data to support their projects. But it wasn't until a new managerial performance and bonus program was introduced that managers really began to take financial analysis seriously.

After a year of concerted effort, initial hiccups, and growing pains, PulpCo is a changed organization. Major financial decisions are aligned with strategic objectives and based on facts. Management is largely positive about the insights gained from better financial analysis and supportive of further analytical initiatives in other parts of the business. Forecasts are more accurate, and managers are better able to anticipate and avoid problems. The culture is no longer hostile to the use of data. Operational managers at the mills and at corporate headquarters have increased their financial acumen and are more comfortable interpreting financial analyses. The use of analytics has begun to spread as the organization's managers realize that better insight into costs and profitability can give them an edge in competitive situations. Inspired by analytical companies such as CEMEX, PulpCo has begun a test program to bypass the lumberyard and deliver products directly to the construction site. Not surprisingly, PulpCo is also enjoying better financial performance.

Initially, Yatim just wanted improved financial data for decision making. With limited sponsorship and inadequate systems, PulpCo's CFO realized that he needed to conduct some experiments and build credibility within the organization before attempting a broader change program. With each success, PulpCo's leadership team became more enthusiastic about using analytics and began to see their broader potential. PulpCo is not an analytical competitor and may never reach stage 5, but today management is enthusiastic about the benefits of analytics and is considering whether it should make the leap to stage 3.

Stage 3: Analytical Aspirations

Stage 3 is triggered when analytics gain executive sponsorship. The executive sponsor becomes an outspoken advocate of a more fact-based culture and builds sponsorship with others on the executive team.

Executive sponsorship is so vital to analytical competition that simply having the right sponsor is enough to move an organization to stage 3 without any improvement in its analytical capabilities. However, those organizations pursuing the prove-it path will have already established pockets of analytical expertise and will have some analytical tools in hand. The risk is that several small groups will have their own analytical fiefdoms, replete with hard-to-integrate software tools, data sets, and practices.

Whether an organization has many analytical groups or none at all, it needs to take a broader, more strategic perspective in stage 3. The first task, then, is to articulate a vision of the benefits expected from analytical competition. Bolstered by a series of smaller successes, management should set its sights on using analytics in the company's distinctive capability and addressing strategic business problems. For the first time, program benefits should be defined in terms of improved business performance and care should be taken to measure progress against broad business objectives. A critical element of stage 3 is defining a set of achievable performance metrics and putting the processes in place to monitor progress. To focus scarce resources appropriately, the organization may create a centralized "analytics hub" to foster and support analytical activities.

In stage 3, companies will launch their first major project to use analytics in their distinctive capability. The application of more sophisticated analytics may require specialized analytical expertise and adding new analytical technology. Management attention to change management is critical because significant changes to business processes, work roles, and responsibilities are necessary.

If it hasn't already done so, the IT organization must develop a vision and program plan (an analytical architecture) to support analytical competition. In particular, IT must work more aggressively to integrate and standardize enterprise data in anticipation of radically increased demand from users.

The length of stage 3 varies; it can be as short as a few months or as long as two years. Once executives have committed resources and set a timetable to build an enterprise-wide analytical capability, they are ready to move to the next stage.

BankCo (again, we have disguised the company and other names) is an example of an organization moving from stage 3 toward stage 4.

BankCo: Moving Beyond Functional Silos to Enterprise Analytics

Wealth management has been a hot topic within the banking industry over the last decade, and banks have traditionally been well positioned to offer this service. In-house trust departments have provided advice and services to generations of wealthy clients. But over the past several years, new competitors have emerged. Banks have moved away from using individual investment managers, taking a more efficient but less personalized approach. A trend toward greater regulatory oversight further transformed the industry. At the same time, customers are more open to alternatives to traditional money management. Robo-advisers such as Betterment and Wealthfront use algorithms to provide fully automated investment portfolio management at a lower cost than most retail banks charge their clients. This confluence of factors threatens bank trust departments' hold on the service of managing individuals' wealth.

At BankCo, the executive vice presidents of marketing, strategy, and relationship management were asked by the bank's senior management team to create a strategic response to this threat. They quickly concluded that significant changes were needed to improve the bank's relationships with its customers. BankCo's trust department assets had declined by 7 percent over two years, despite a positive market that had produced increased assets overall and good performance in individual trust accounts. The decline was attributed to discounting by more aggressive competition and to cannibalism of accounts by the bank's brokerage business. BankCo had tried introducing revamped products to retain customers but with limited success.

As in many banks, each department (retail, brokerage, trust) maintained its own customer data that was not available to outsiders. As a result, executives could not get a complete picture of their clients' relationships throughout the bank, and valuable relationships were jeopardized unnecessarily. For example, one client with a $100 million trust was charged $35 for bouncing a check. When he called his retail banker to complain, he was told initially that his savings account wasn't large enough for the bank to justify waiving the fee.

After analyzing these issues, the team concluded that an enterprise-wide focus on analytics would not only eliminate the majority of these problems but also uncover cross-selling opportunities. The team realized that a major obstacle to building an enterprise-level analytical capability would be resistance from department heads. Their performance measures were based on the assets of their departments, not on enterprise-wide metrics. The bank's senior management team responded by introducing new performance metrics that would assess overall enterprise performance (including measures related to asset size and profitability) and cross-departmental cooperation.

These changes cleared the path for an enterprise-wide initiative to improve BankCo's analytical orientation, beginning with the creation of an integrated and consistent customer database (to the extent permitted by law) as well as coordinated retail, trust, and brokerage marketing campaigns. At the same time, an enterprise-wide marketing analytics group was established to work with the marketing teams on understanding client values and behavior. The group began to identify new market segments and offerings, and to help prioritize and coordinate marketing efforts to high-net-worth individuals. It also began to develop a deeper understanding of family relationships and their impact on individual behavior. By bringing together statisticians and analysts scattered throughout the business, BankCo could deploy these scarce resources more efficiently. As demand quickly outstripped supply, it hired analytical specialists with industry expertise and arranged to use an offshore firm to further leverage its scarce analytical talent.

At first, there were occasional breakdowns in decision-making processes. When a competitor restructured its brokerage pricing, BankCo did not notice until several clients left. On another occasion, an analysis identified a new market segment, and management authorized changes to marketing, but the organization was slow to implement the changes. To overcome these hurdles, process changes were implemented to make sure that decisions were translated into action. Managers received training and tools so that they were equipped to make decisions analytically and understood how to develop hypotheses, interpret data, and make fact-based decisions. As the organization's analytical capabilities improved, these breakdowns became less frequent.

As more tangible benefits began to appear, the CEO's commitment to competing on analytics grew. In his letter to shareholders, he described the growing importance of analytics and a new growth initiative to "outsmart and outthink" the competition. A chief data officer was named to develop and implement the bank's data and analytics strategy. Analysts expanded their work to use propensity analysis and neural nets (an artificial intelligence technology incorporating nonlinear statistical modeling to identify patterns) to target and provide specialized services to clients with both personal and corporate relationships with the bank. They also began testing some analytically enabled new services for trust clients. Today, BankCo is well on its way to becoming an analytical competitor.

Stage 4: Analytical Companies

The primary focus in stage 4 is on building world-class analytical capabilities at the enterprise level. In this stage, organizations implement the plan developed in stage 3, making considerable progress toward building the sponsorship, culture, skills, strategic insights, data, and technology needed for analytical competition. Sponsorship grows from a handful of visionaries to a broad management consensus; similarly, an emphasis on experimentation and analytics pervades the corporate culture. As the organization learns more from each analysis, it obtains a rich vein of new insights and ideas to mine and exploit for competitive advantage. Building analytical capabilities is a major (although not the only) corporate priority.

While there are many challenges at this stage, the most critical one is allocating sufficient attention to managing cultural and organizational changes. We've witnessed many organizations whose analytical aspirations were squelched by open cultural warfare between the "quant jocks" and the old guard. A related challenge is extending executive sponsorship to the rest of the management team. If only one or two executives are committed to analytical competition, interest will immediately subside if they suddenly depart or retire. In one case, the CEO of a financial services firm saw analytical competition as his legacy to the organization he had devoted his life to build. But his successors did not share his enthusiasm, and the analytical systems developed under his leadership quickly fell into disuse.

As each analytical capability becomes more sophisticated, management will gain the confidence and expertise to build analytics into business processes. In some cases, they use their superior insight into customers and markets to automate key decision processes entirely.

In stage 4, many organizations realign their analysts and information workers to place them in assignments that are better suited to their skills. As a company becomes more serious about enterprise-wide analytics, it often draws together the most advanced analysts into a single group to focus on strategic issues. This provides the organization with a critical mass of analysts to focus on the most strategic issues, and provides the analysts with greater job satisfaction and opportunity to develop their skills.

Once an organization has an outstanding analytical capability combined with strategically differentiating analytics embedded into its most critical business processes and has achieved major improvements to its business performance and competitiveness, it has reached the final stage.

ConsumerCo: Everything but "Fire in the Belly"

At a large consumer products company, analytical competition is at stage 4. ConsumerCo has everything in place but a strong executive-level commitment to compete on this basis. It has high-quality data about virtually every aspect of its business, and a capable IT function. It has a group of analysts who are equal to any company's. The analysts have undertaken projects that have brought hundreds of millions of dollars in value to the company. Still, they have to justify their existence by selling individual projects to functional managers.

The CEO of ConsumerCo is a strong believer in product innovation and product-oriented research but not particularly in analytics. The primary advocate for analytics is the COO. Analytics are not discussed in annual reports and analyst calls, though the company does have a culture of fact-based decision making and uses a large amount of market research. ConsumerCo is doing well financially but has been growing primarily through acquisitions. In short, analytics are respected and widely practiced but are not driving the company's strategy. With only a bit more "fire in the belly" from senior executives, it could become a true analytical competitor in a short time.

Stage 5: Analytical Competitors

In stage 5, analytics move from being a very important capability for an organization to the key to its strategy and competitive advantage. Analytical competitors routinely reap the benefits of their enterprise-wide analytical capability. Proprietary metrics, analytics, processes, and data create a strong barrier to competitors, but these companies are always attempting to move the analytical bar further.

Executive commitment and passion for analytical competition in this stage is resolute and widespread. The organization's expertise in analytical competition is discussed in annual reports and in discussions with investment analysts. Internal performance measures and processes reinforce a commitment to scientific objectivity and analytical integrity. Analytics are used to drive innovation across the organization. And predictive and prescriptive analytics are an important and growing component of the enterprise's product offerings as well.

However, analytical competitors must avoid complacency if they are to sustain their competitive advantage. They need to build processes to continually monitor the external environment for signs of change. They must also remain vigilant in order to recognize when changing market conditions require them to modify their assumptions, analytical models, and rules.

We've described a large number of these companies already, so we won't give an example here. Each stage 5 company is different in terms of the strategic capability it emphasizes, the applications it employs, and the path it followed to success. But they have in common an absolute passion for analytics and a resulting strong financial performance.

Progressing Along the Road Map

As you can see from these examples, becoming an analytical competitor takes more than an enthusiasm for data analysis. Many executives seeking to build their analytical capabilities begin by purchasing software, hiring quantitative analysts, and piloting some kind of analytical initiative. While those actions can be a good start, they are just that—a beginning from which analytical leaders must build in order to truly develop their analytic capability. "Analytics is a muscle we build," according to Elpida Ormanidou, formerly vice president of global people analytics at Walmart and now vice president of advanced analytics and testing at retailer Chico's FAS, Inc. "You cannot buy yourself into an analytics capability."[3]

The path to success with analytics will contain speed bumps along the way. Managers not yet on the full-steam-ahead path may be tempted to either shift resources away from or shut down completely an analytics initiative if business conditions put pressure on the organization. Also, the shift to analytics will most likely require employees to change their decision-making processes. It takes time for the organization to adjust to new skills and behaviors, but without them, no real change can occur. As a result, the most important activity for the leadership team is to keep analytical initiatives on track and to monitor outcomes to ensure that anticipated benefits are achieved.

At every stage of development, companies need to manage outcomes to achieve desired benefits, setting priorities appropriately and avoiding common pitfalls.

As we described in chapter 2, the DELTA model provides guidance to executives seeking to create a road map for building their organization's analytical capabilities. DELTA, the Greek letter that signifies "change" in an equation, seemed like a fitting acronym to describe the elements and steps needed to implement an analytical capability. Unless you are blessed with analytical leadership and culture, becoming an analytical competitor means significant change for an organization. To recap, DELTA stands for:

- *Data:* Leveraging data to glean valuable insights

- *Enterprise:* Managing and coordinating resources at an enterprise level

- *Leadership:* Fostering an analytical leadership team and culture

- *Targets:* Focusing analytics investments on the best, high value areas

- *Analysts:* Developing and managing analytical talent

We'll briefly summarize each of these capability elements here.

Data. Data is, of course, a prerequisite for using analytics. On occasion, a single data point might be enough to make a difference.[4] But most of the time, having lots of data is better. Having high-quality, diverse, and dynamic data—easily accessible to users in a data warehouse, data mart, or data lake—generally yields better results too. Unique data is better still. Analytical competitors view data as a strategic asset, and like any other strategic asset, it must be managed to maximize its value to the organization. We will talk more about finding, organizing, and managing data in chapter 8.

Enterprise. As we explained in chapter 2, it is important to take an enterprise perspective. Lacking an enterprise perspective means having a fractured and incomplete understanding of the issues facing the organization, and the resources available to address them. Executives require a broad business perspective if they are to address the strategic issues at the core of business competitiveness and effectiveness. Only an enterprise orientation can properly answer important questions such as, "Which performance factors have the greatest impact on future growth and profitability?" "How should we optimize investments across our products, geographies and marketing channels?" Or "Are decisions aligned with company strategy, or just promoting someone's self-interest?" Similarly, since major analytics initiatives invariably touch multiple functions across the organization, it is important to avoid placing vital analytical resources (such as data, technology, or analysts) in functional silos. We discuss some of these organizational issues further in chapter 7.

Leadership. It is fitting that leadership is at the center of the DELTA model, because without committed analytical leadership, the potential for using analytics is quite limited. Analytical leaders are passionate advocates for analytics and fact-based, data-driven decision making. They set a hands-on example by being voracious consumers of data and analytics. These executives routinely challenge conventional wisdom and untested assumptions. Analytical leaders are also highly experimental and innovative. They continually seek innovative ways to get valuable insights. They explore ways to incorporate proprietary data and algorithms into new products and services. Analytical leaders prefer to surround themselves with smart, analytical people. And above all, they encourage a culture that views data as a strategic asset—that strives to be a meritocracy where the best data and ideas win. These types of leaders aren't found everywhere, but there definitely are some. We discuss more considerations of being an analytical leader in chapter 7.

Targets. All organizations have finite resources, and therefore it is critical to prioritize potential investments in analytics where they will have the most beneficial impact. Picking the right spots for investment is the core of an analytical road map. The right targets will depend on the organization's analytical maturity, industry, and business strategy. Targets should be achievable yet have the potential to make a significant impact by cutting costs, optimizing processes, improving customer engagement, expanding the business, or increasing profitability. As an enterprise's analytical maturity improves, targets should be focused on the organization's distinctive capabilities, leading to initiatives that are more strategic and game-changing for the organization and its customers. The number of targets can also grow with time and greater analytical maturity.

Analysts. Managing and developing analytical talent goes beyond hiring a few smart, analytical employees. Analytical professionals and data scientists build and maintain the models and algorithms used throughout the organization. Analytical talent also includes the executives who oversee analytical initiatives, decision makers who use the results of analyses, and analytical amateurs—the information workers who routinely use data in their jobs. We describe the roles of different types of analysts in chapter 7—senior executives (including the chief data and analytics officer), analysts, data scientists, and analytical amateurs—along with some organizational considerations for getting the most value from this valuable resource. Because technologies and quantitative techniques tend to become more sophisticated with growing maturity, we also will describe these factors.

In our first cut at the DELTA model, we felt that these five factors were sufficient to explain and predict how a company could succeed with analytics. But with the advent of big data and a variety of new analytical techniques (including artificial intelligence, for example), it may also be useful to add the following two capabilities to the model.

Technology. Technology for analytics has changed rapidly over the last decade. Providing the infrastructure, tools, and technologies to support analytics across the organization is no small task, and this responsibility should belong to the IT department (though it doesn't always). Most organizations have plenty of data, software, and processing power; the challenge is getting it all to work together with a minimum of fuss. Too much data is locked into organizational silos, and efforts to solve the problem by pulling data into warehouses or data lakes too often result in conflicting data repositories. Despite the proliferation of analytical software, statistical programming tools, data warehouses, visualization tools, and the like, relatively few organizations have a truly robust and well-integrated technical environment that fully supports enterprise-wide analytics and big data. The technologies underpinning big data and analytics are a rapidly evolving field and beyond the scope of any one book. In chapter 8, we describe (at a conceptual level) the required components and considerations for an analytic technical architecture.

Analytical Techniques. There are many different quantitative and analytical disciplines that contribute analytical techniques. They come from many diverse fields, such as computer science, statistics, econometrics, informatics, physics, actuarial science, artificial intelligence, operations research, and biostatistics. Organizations are wise to draw on many different types of analytical techniques drawn from these disciplines, ranging from simple descriptive statistics and probability, to machine learning and genetic algorithms. Determining the "best" or "right" technique depends on many different factors and will vary depending on the industry or function, the types of questions being addressed, data characteristics and the creativity of the analyst. Sometimes the best answers are obtained by combining techniques rather than relying on a single quantitative discipline. As organizations become more sophisticated in their application of analytics, they generally rely on more diverse and advanced analytical techniques too. We provided a sampling of these techniques and some appropriate situations in which to use them in chapters 4 and 5.

For a high-performing analytical capability, all the elements of the DELTA model need to be working together. If one element lags too far ahead or behind the others, it can be a roadblock to moving forward. Table 6-3 describes the typical conditions for each element of the DELTA framework at each maturity stage and table 6-4 does the same for *technologies* and *analytical techniques*. These can be used as a quick assessment tool or as a reference to help you understand where you need improvement. For a more detailed explanation of the assets and capabilities needed at every stage of analytical maturity, our book *Analytics at Work* provides much more guidance.[5]

Managing for Outcomes

Four types of outcomes are critical to measuring an initiative's performance: behaviors; processes and programs; products and services; and financial results. While financial results may be all that matter in the end, they probably won't be achieved without attention to intermediate outcomes.

Behaviors. To a large extent, improved financial outcomes depend on changing employee behaviors. Implementing new analytical insights into pricing, for example, can require thousands of individuals to change their behaviors. Salespeople may resist pricing recommendations. Sales managers may initially believe that their own pricing experience is better than that of any system. Managers have to monitor measures and work with employees who don't comply with policies. Executives have to send out frequent messages to reinforce the desired change of direction.

TABLE 6-3

The DELTA model of analytical capabilities by stage

	Stage 1: Analytically impaired	Stage 2: Localized analytics	Stage 3: Analytical aspirations	Stage 4: Analytical companies	Stage 5: Analytical competitors
Data	Inconsistent, poor-quality, and unstandardized data; difficult to do substantial analysis; no groups with strong data orientation	Standardized and structured data, mostly in functional or process silos; senior executives do not discuss data management	Key data domains identified and central data repositories created	Integrated, accurate, common data in central repositories; data still mainly an IT matter, little unique data	Relentless search for new data and metrics leveraging structured and unstructured data (e.g., text, video); data viewed as a strategic asset
Enterprise	No enterprise perspective on data or analytics; poorly integrated systems	Islands of data, technology, and expertise deliver local value	Process or business unit focus for analytics; infrastructure for analytics beginning to coalesce	Key data, technology, and analysts managed from an enterprise perspective	Key analytical resources focused on enterprise priorities and differentiation
Leadership	Little awareness of or interest in analytics	Local leaders emerge but have little connection	Senior leaders recognize importance of analytics and developing analytical capabilities	Senior leaders develop analytical plans and build analytical capabilities	Strong leaders behave analytically and show passion for analytical competition
Targets	No targeting of opportunities	Multiple disconnected targets, typically not of strategic importance	Analytical efforts coalesce behind a small set of important targets	Analytics centered on a few key business domains with explicit and ambitious outcomes	Analytics integral to the company's distinctive capability and strategy
Analysts	Few skills that are attached to specific functions	Unconnected pockets of analysts; unmanaged mix of skills	Analysts recognized as key talent and focused on important business areas	Highly capable analysts explicitly recruited, developed, deployed, and engaged	World-class professional analysts; cultivation of analytical amateurs across the enterprise

TABLE 6-4

Additional technical capabilities for advanced analytics

	Stage 1: Analytically impaired	Stage 2: Localized analytics	Stage 3: Analytical aspirations	Stage 4: Analytical companies	Stage 5: Analytical competitors
Technology	Desktop technology, standard office packages, poorly integrated systems	Individual analytical initiatives, statistical packages, descriptive analytics, database querying, tabulations	Enterprise analytical plan, tool and platforms; predictive analytical packages	Enterprise analytic plan and processes, cloud-based big data	Sophisticated, enterprise-wide big data and analytics architecture, cognitive technologies, prescriptive and autonomous analytics
Analytical techniques	Mostly ad hoc, simple math, extrapolation, trending	Basic statistics, segmentation, database querying, tabulations of key metrics are leveraged to gain insights	Simple predictive analytics, classification and clustering; dynamic forecasts	Advanced predictive methods deployed to discover insights; advanced optimization, sentiment analytics, text and image analytics	Neural nets and deep learning, genetic algorithms, advanced machine learning

Processes and Programs. Fact-based analyses often require process and program changes to yield results. For example, insights into the best way to persuade wireless customers not to defect to another carrier need to be translated into actions—such as developing a new program to train customer-facing employees.

One way to ensure that insights are incorporated into business processes is to integrate analytics into business applications and work processes. Incorporating analytical support applications into work processes helps employees accept the changes and improves standardization and use. For more advanced analytical competitors, automated decision-making applications can be a powerful way of leveraging strategic insights.

Products and Services. One of the best ways to add value with data is by creating innovative products and services that incorporate data and/or analytics; we described these in greater detail in chapter 3.

QUESTIONS TO ASK WHEN EVALUATING NEW ANALYTICAL INITIATIVES

- How will this investment make us more competitive?

- To what extent will this investment make us more agile to respond to changing market conditions?

- How does the initiative improve our enterprise-wide analytical capabilities?

- How will the investment foster greater innovation and growth opportunities?

- What complementary changes need to be made in order to take full advantage of new capabilities, such as developing new or enhanced skills; improving IT, training, and processes; or redesigning jobs?

- Does the right data exist? If not, can we get it or create it? Is the data timely, consistent, accurate, and complete?

- Is the technology reliable? Is it cost-effective? Is it scalable? Is this the right approach or tool for the right job?

For existing products and services, introducing smarter products and services can increase margins and be a powerful differentiator. Innovative analytically based products can open up entirely new customer markets and revenue streams.

Financial Results. It is important to specify the financial outcomes desired from an analytical initiative to help measure its success. Specific financial results may include improved profitability, higher revenues, lower costs, or improved market share or market value. Initially, cost savings are the most common justification for an analytical initiative because it is much easier to specify in advance how costs will be cut. Revenue increases are more difficult to predict and measure but can be modeled with analytical tools and extrapolated from small tests and pilot studies. As an organization's analytical maturity increases, it will be more willing to invest in initiatives targeted at exploiting growth opportunities and generating revenue.

Establishing Priorities

Assuming that an organization already has sufficient management support and an understanding of its desired outcomes, analytical orientation, and decision-making processes, its next step is to begin defining and prioritizing actions. See the box "Questions to Ask When Evaluating New Analytical Initiatives" for critical questions managers should use to assess the potential of an analytical initiative. Projects with the greatest potential benefit to the organization's distinctive capabilities and competitive differentiation should take precedence. Taking an analytical approach to investment decisions, requiring accountability, and monitoring outcomes will help reinforce the analytical culture and maximize investments where they are likely to have the greatest impact. A common error is to assume that merely having analytical technology is sufficient to transform an organization. The *Field of Dreams* approach—"If you build it, they will come"—usually disappoints. If you build a data warehouse or a full-blown analytical technical infrastructure without developing the other DELTA model components, the warehouse and the data contained in it will just sit there.

Avoiding the Potholes

Since every organization is different, we won't attempt to provide detailed instructions to navigate around all the potential hazards encountered along the road. Hazards can appear suddenly at any stage of development. However, we can provide guidelines to help make the planning and implementing efforts go as smoothly as possible.

First, some missteps are due primarily to ignorance. The most common errors of this kind are:

- Focusing excessively on one dimension of analytical capability (e.g., too much technology)

- Collecting data without any plans to use it

- Attempting to do everything at once

- Investing excessive resources on analytics that have minimal impact on the business

- Investing too much or too little in any analytical capability, compared with demand

- Choosing the wrong problem, not understanding the problem sufficiently, using the wrong analytical technique or the wrong analytical software

- Automating decision-based applications without carefully monitoring outcomes and external conditions to see whether assumptions need to be modified

Of greater concern to many executives is the intentional undermining of analytical competition. Many managers share Benjamin Disraeli's suspicion that there are "lies, damned lies, and statistics."[6] Data analysis has the potential for abuse when employed by the unscrupulous, since statistics, if tortured sufficiently, will confess to anything.[7] Applying objective criteria and data for decision making is highly threatening to any bureaucrat accustomed to making decisions based on his or her own self-interest. Analytical competition cannot thrive if information is hoarded and analytics manipulated. Executives must relentlessly root out self-serving, manipulated statistics and enforce a culture of objectivity.[8]

Conclusion

This chapter has explored the key attributes of an analytical capability and provided a directional guide to the steps that lead to enhanced analytical capabilities. We wish you rapid movement to the full-steam-ahead path to becoming an analytical competitor. In chapter 7, we will explore ways to successfully manage an organization's commitment to key people who are—or need to be—using analytics.

CHAPTER SEVEN

M ANAGING ANALYTICAL PEOPLE

CULTIVATING THE SCARCE INGREDIENT THAT MAKES ANALYTICS WORK

WHEN MOST PEOPLE VISUALIZE BUSINESS ANALYTICS, they think of computers, software, and printouts or screens full of numbers. What they should be envisioning, however, are their fellow human beings. It is people who make analytics work and who are the scarce ingredient in analytical competition.

Analytical Urban Legends

This assertion is contrary to some analytical urban legends, so let us dispel those now. Years ago, we began hearing extravagant tales of software that would eliminate the need for human analysts. The most popular story involved a data mining episode involving diapers and beer. The gist of the story was that some grocery retailer had turned loose its powerful data mining software on a sales database, and it had come up with an interesting finding. Male customers who came in to buy beer for the weekend also tended to remember that their wives had asked them to buy diapers (some versions of the story switched around the primary shopping intent), so they put both products in their shopping carts. The retailer quickly moved diapers over by the beer (or vice versa), and sales exploded.

We chased this one down, and the most credible version of the story happened at Osco, a drugstore chain. Some of the company's data analysts do dimly remember seeing a correlation between diaper and beer sales in their stores. But the analysts had told the software where and how to look for the relationship; it wasn't just stumbled on by an enterprising young computer. Most importantly, the finding was deemed an anomaly, and diapers and beer were never put in proximity in the Osco stores (not all of which could even sell beer).

The legend is worth discussing, however, for a few lessons it provides. While data mining software is a wonderful thing, a smart human still needs to interpret the patterns that are identified, decide which patterns merit validation or subsequent confirmation, and translate new insights into recommendations for action. Other smart humans need to actually take action. When we studied more than thirty firms with a strong analytical capability in 2000, we found that a heavy dose of human skills was present at each of the firms, and the analytical competitors we've studied over the years certainly have lots of smart analysts on board.[1]

The other key lesson of the diapers and beer legend is that analytics aren't enough, even when orchestrated by a human analyst. In order for analytics to be of any use, a decision maker has to make a decision and take action—that is, actually move the diapers and beer together. Since decision makers may not have the time or ability to perform analyses themselves, such interpersonal attributes as trust and credibility rear their ugly heads. If the decision maker doesn't trust the analyst or simply doesn't pay attention to the results of the analysis, nothing will happen and the statistics might as well never have been computed.

We found another good example of this problem in our previous study of analytical capability. We talked to analysts at a large New York bank who were studying branch profitability. The analysts went through a painstaking study in the New York area—identifying and collecting activity-based costs, allocating overheads, and even projecting current cost and revenue trends for each branch into the near future. They came up with a neat, clear, ordered list of all branches and their current and future profitability, with an even neater red line drawn to separate the branches that should be left open from those that should be closed.

What happened? Nary a branch was shut down. The retail banking executive who had asked for the list was mostly just curious about the profitability issue, and he hardly knew the analysts. He knew that there were many political considerations involved in, say, closing the branch in Brooklyn near where the borough president had grown up, even if it was well below the red line. Analytically based actions usually require a close, trusting relationship between analyst and decision maker, and that was missing at the bank. Because of the missing relationship, the analysts didn't ask the right questions, and the executive didn't frame the question for them correctly.

There are really three groups, then, whose analytical skills and orientations are at issue within organizations. One is the senior management team—and particularly the CEO—which sets the tone for the organization's analytical culture and makes the most important decisions. Then there are the professional analysts, who gather and analyze the data, interpret the results, and report them to decision makers. The third group is a diverse collection we will refer to as analytical amateurs, a very large group of "everybody else," whose use of the outputs of analytical processes is critical to their job performance. These could range from frontline manufacturing workers, who have to make multiple small decisions on quality and speed, to middle managers, who also have to make middle-sized decisions with respect to their functions and units. Middle managers in the business areas designated as distinctive capabilities by their organizations are particularly important, because they oversee the application of analytics to these strategic processes. IT employees who put in place the software and hardware for analytics also need some familiarity with the topic. We'll describe each of these groups in this chapter.

Before we go any further, however, it is important to point out that the role of humans in analytics is changing somewhat, and is likely to change more in the near future. One key development is that machine learning and other intelligent technologies are changing how analytical models are generated. A human analyst might be able to generate a few new models per week, but a machine learning system could easily generate tens of thousands of models per week. Thus far, however, machine learning models still need humans to kick them off, point them in the direction of the right data and the variables to be predicted, and ensure that the resulting models make sense. We don't think that machine learning models have inhibited employment for quantitative analysts and data scientists yet, but they may in the future.

The other technological factor that's driving change for humans in the world of analytics is automation of decisions and actions. While an autonomous system is unlikely to close a set of bank branches without human intervention, complex decisions and digital tasks can both be performed by machine. They can do things like approve insurance policies, authorize loans, reboot computer servers, and replace and mail a lost ATM card. It's likely that the decisions taken over by analytics and computers will be tactical and repetitive ones, but these probably constitute the bulk of decisions in many organizations. We don't think high-level managers will lose their jobs to autonomous systems, but it's likely that some employees will. The good news here is that an automated decision system is unlikely to ignore an analytical result. Humans who ignore analytics in the future will do so at their own peril.

Senior Executives and Analytical Competition

As if CEOs, presidents, COOs and other senior executives weren't busy enough already, it is their responsibility to build the analytical orientation and capabilities of their organizations. If the CEO or a significant fraction of the senior executive team doesn't understand or appreciate at least the outputs of quantitative analysis or the process of fact-based decision making, analysts are going to be relegated to the back office, and competition will be based on guesswork and gut feel, not analytics. Fact-based decision making doesn't always involve analytics—sometimes "facts" may be very simple pieces of evidence, such as a single piece of data or a customer survey result—but the desire to make decisions on the basis of what's really happening in the world is an important cultural attribute of analytical competitors.[2]

For an example, take Phil Knight, the founder and chairman emeritus of Nike. Knight has always been known as an inspirational but intuitive leader who closely guarded the mythical Nike brand. Perhaps needless to say, it didn't take a lot of analytics to come up with the famous "swoosh." At the beginning of 2005, however, Knight brought in William Perez, formerly head of S. C. Johnson & Son, as CEO of Nike. Perez, accustomed to the data-intensive world of Johnson's Wax, Windex, and Ziploc bags, attempted to bring a more analytical style of leadership into Nike. He notes about himself, "I am a data man—I like to know what the facts are. If you come from the world of packaged goods, where data is always valuable, Nike is very different. Judgment is very important. Feel is very important. You can't replace that with facts. But you can use data to guide you."[3]

Perez attempted, for example, to move Nike into middle-tier retail environments, where his data suggested that footwear growth was fastest. In response to arguments from Knight and other Nike executives that such a move would weaken the brand, Perez pointed to companies such as Apple that sell successfully in Walmart without diluting their brands. But these and other clashes eventually led Knight and the board of directors to remove Perez little more than a year later.

The good news is that Perez's departure only delayed the rise of analytics at Nike. Over the last several years, the company has become much more analytical. It uses data and analytics to influence shoe design, marketing programs, outlet store locations, logistics, and many other types of decisions. Nike has perhaps the world's largest analytics group that's focused on sustainability. The company may have gotten there faster if Perez had stayed, but it is definitely moving toward analytical competitor status.

The general lesson here, however, is that if a CEO can't move the culture in a more analytical direction, a middle or junior manager would have even less of a chance of doing so. In fact, we've seen several companies in which fairly senior functional managers—corporate heads of marketing or technology, for example—were trying to bring a more analytical orientation to their firms and faced substantial obstacles. One, for example, a senior vice president of sales and marketing at a technology company, was known as a true "data hound," bringing piles of statistical reports to meetings and having perfect command of his own (and other managers') statistics. The sales and marketing organizations slowly began to become more data focused, but for years the overall company culture continued to emphasize chutzpah and confidence more than correlations. Again, that company eventually embraced analytics (it helped that the "data hound" kept getting pro-moted, eventually becoming president), but a more receptive culture would have allowed it to happen faster.

While there's no doubt that almost any employee can move an orga-nization in a more analytical direction, it takes top management com-mitment for a company to become an analytical competitor. In fact, we didn't find a single stage 4 or 5 analytical competitor where either the CEO or a majority of the senior management team didn't believe strongly in analytics as a primary competitive resource. Senior exec-utive support is even important at stage 3, when organizations begin to aspire to analytical competition.

Characteristics of Analytical Leaders

What are the traits that senior executives and other analytical cham-pions in an analytical competitor should have? A few key ones are described next.

They should be passionate believers in analytical and fact-based decision making. You can't inspire others to change their behavior in a more analytical direction if you're not passionate about the goal. A truly committed executive would demonstrate fact-based and analytical deci-sion making in his or her own decisions and continually challenge the rest of the organization to do the same. For example, whenever Barry Beracha, previously CEO of the private-label baker Earthgrains (which was acquired by Sara Lee Bakery Group), needed to make a decision, he searched to turn up the right data. He insisted that the entire orga-nization needed better data, and led the company to implement a new ERP system to create it. After it was available, he pressed his employ-ees to use it when deciding what products to keep and what customers to serve. He was so passionate about data-based decisions that his em-ployees referred to him as a "data dog"—to his delight.

They should have some appreciation of analytical tools and meth-ods. The senior executives of analytical competitors don't necessarily have to be analytical experts (although it helps!). As Professor Xiao-Li Meng—formerly the chair of the statistics department at Harvard and now dean of the Graduate School of Arts and Sciences—points out, you don't need to become a winemaker to become a wine connoisseur.[4] Management users of data analytics do need to have an awareness of what kinds of tools make sense for particular business problems, and the limitations of those tools. Just as a politician analyzing polls should know something about confidence intervals, the CEO making a decision about a plant expansion should know something about the statistical and qualitative assumptions that went into predicting demand for the goods the plant will make.

They should be willing to act on the results of analyses. There is little point in commissioning detailed analytics if nothing different will be done based on the outcome. Many firms, for example, are able to segment their customers and determine which ones are most profitable or which are most likely to defect. However, they are reluctant to treat different customers differently—out of tradition or egalitarianism or whatever. With such compunctions, they will have a very difficult time becoming successful analytical competitors—yet it is surprising how often companies initiate analyses without ever acting on them. The "action" stage of any analytical effort is, of course, the only one that ultimately counts.

They should be willing to manage a meritocracy. With widespread use of analytics in a company, it usually becomes very apparent who is performing and who isn't. Those who perform well should be rewarded commensurately with their performance; those who don't perform shouldn't be strung along for long periods. As with customers, when the differences in performance among employees and managers are visible but not acted on, nothing good results—and better employees may well become disheartened. Of course, the leaders of such meritocratic firms have to live and die by this same analytical sword. It would be quite demoralizing for a CEO to preach the analytical gospel for everyone else but then to make excuses for his or her own performance as an executive.

How Does Analytical Leadership Emerge?

Some organizations' leaders had the desire to compete analytically from their beginning. Amazon was viewed by founder Jeff Bezos as competing on analytics from its start. Its concept of personalization was based on statistical algorithms and web transaction data, and it quickly moved into analytics on supply chain and marketing issues as well. Amazon used analytics to determine the timing and extent of its holiday advertising strategy, outspending Walmart in October and November 2016. Capital One, Netflix, and Google were also analytical from the beginning because their leaders wanted them so. The visions of the founders of these startup businesses led to analytical competition.

In other cases, the demand for analytical competition came from a new senior executive arriving at an established company. Gary Loveman at Caesars, and Tom Ricketts, the new owner of the Chicago Cubs, brought with them an entirely new analytical strategy.

Sometimes the change comes from a new generation of managers in a family business. At the winemaker E. & J. Gallo, when Joe Gallo, the son of one of the firm's founding brothers, became CEO, he focused much more than the previous generation of leaders on data and analysis—first in sales and later in other functions, including the assessment of customer taste. At the National Football League's New England Patriots, the involvement in the team by Jonathan Kraft, a former management consultant and the son of owner Bob Kraft, helped move the team in a more analytical direction in terms of both on-field issues like play selection and team composition and off-field issues affecting the fan experience.

The prime mover for analytical demand doesn't always have to be the CEO. At Procter & Gamble, for example, the primary impetus for more analytics at one point came from the firm's two vice chairmen. One of them, Bob McDonald, became CEO and accelerated P&G's analytical journey. And Jonathan Kraft is the president of the Patriots, not the CEO.

In addition to the general characteristics described earlier in the chapter (which are generally relevant for the CEO), there are specific roles that particular executives need to play in analytical competition. Three key roles are the chief financial officer (CFO), the chief information officer (CIO) and the chief data and analytics officer (CDAO).

Role of the CFO

The chief financial officer in most organizations will have responsibility for financial processes and information. Therefore, analytical efforts in these domains would also be the CFO's concern. Since most analytical projects should involve some sort of financial information or returns, the CFO is at least a partial player in virtually all of them.

We have found several companies in which the CFO was leading the analytical charge. In order to play that role effectively, however, a CFO would have to focus on analytical domains in addition to finance and accounting. For example, at a large insurance company, the CFO had taken responsibility for analytics related to cost control and management but also monitored and championed analytical initiatives in the claims, actuarial, and marketing areas of the company. He also made it his responsibility to try to establish in the company's employees the right overall balance of intuitive versus analytical thinking.

At Deloitte's US business, the person leading the charge on analytics (at least for internal consumption) is Frank Friedman, the CFO. He has assembled a group of data scientists and quantitative analysts within the Finance organization. They are working with him to address several initiatives, including optimized pricing, predictive models of performance, identifying services that help sell other services, and factors that drive receivables. They have also worked to predict which candidates will be successful recruits to the firm.

Another CFO (technically a senior vice president of finance) at a retail company made analytics his primary focus, and they weren't even closely connected to finance. The company had a strong focus on customers and customer orientation, and he played a very active role in developing measures, systems, and processes to advance that capability. The company already had good information and analytics on such drivers of its business as labor, space allocation, advertising, and product assortment. His goal was to add the customer relationship and customer segment information to those factors. Since his role also incorporated working with the external financial community (Wall Street analysts, for example), he was also working on making the company's analytical story well known to the outside world. He also viewed his role as including advocacy of a strong analytical orientation in a culture where it wasn't always emphasized. He noted, "I'm not the only advocate of analytics in the company—I have a number of allies. But I am trying to ensure that we tell our stories, both internally and externally, with numbers and analytics."

At Bank of America, CFO (2005–2006) Al de Molina viewed himself as a major instigator of analytical activity. The bank had tried—and largely failed with—a big data warehouse in the early 1990s, so managers were generally wary of gathering together and integrating data. But in his previous job as head of the treasury function, de Molina felt that in order to accurately assess the bank's risks, it needed to consolidate information about assets and rates across the bank. Since the bank was growing rapidly and was assimilating several acquisitions, integrating the information wasn't easy, but de Molina pushed it anyway. The CFO also took responsibility for analytics around US macroeconomic performance. Since it has a wealth of data on the spending habits of American consumers, Bank of America could make predictions on the monthly fluctuations in macroeconomic indicators that drive capital markets. This had obvious beneficial implications for the bank's risks. Both the interest rate risk and the macroeconomic analytics domains are obvious ones for a CFO's focus. De Molina largely deferred to other executives where, for example, marketing analytics were concerned. De Molina left Bank of America and eventually was named CEO of GMAC, now Ally Financial.

Role of the CIO

The CEO or another top operating executive will have the primary responsibility for changing the culture and the analytical behaviors of employees. But CIOs play a crucial role in this regard too. They can work with their executive peers to decide what behaviors are necessary and how to elicit them.

At the telecommunications firm Verizon, the CIO's objective is to create a similar change in analytical culture. Verizon and other firms arising out of the "Bell System" have long been analytically oriented, but decisions were generally made slowly and were pushed up the organizational hierarchy. While CIO at Verizon from 2000 to 2010 (he later became CEO of Juniper Networks and Coriant, another telecom equipment firm), Shaygan Kheradpir attempted to change this culture through continual exposure to information. He created a form of continuous scorecard in which hundreds of performance metrics of various types are broadcast to PCs around the company, each occupying the screen for fifteen seconds. The idea was to get everyone—not just senior executives—focused on information and what it means, and to encourage employees at all levels to address any issues that appear in the data. Kheradpir felt that the use of the scorecard changed Verizon's culture in a positive direction.

Of course, the most traditional approach to analytics for CIOs is through technology. The CIO must craft an enterprise information strategy that serves the needs of everyone in the organization. This includes much more than running the enterprise transaction applications, management reporting, and external websites. A technology infrastructure must be capable of delivering the data, analytics, and tools needed by employees across the organization. Chapter 8 discusses analytical technology, and it should certainly be apparent from reading that chapter that both an architect and a leader are necessary. Those roles may not have to be played by the CIO personally, but the person(s) playing them would in all likelihood at least report to the CIO.

The CIO may also provide a home and a reporting relationship for specialized analytical experts. Such analysts make extensive use of IT and online data, and they are similar in temperament to other IT people. Some of the analytical competitors where analytical groups report to the office of the CIO include Procter & Gamble, the trucking company Schneider National, Inc., and Marriott. Procter & Gamble, for example, consolidated its analytical organizations for operations and supply chain, marketing, and other functions. This allowed a critical mass of analytical expertise to be deployed to address P&G's most critical business issues by "embedded" analysts within functions and units. The group reported to the CIO and is part of an overall emphasis within the IT function on information and decision making (in fact, the IT function was renamed "information and decision solutions" at Procter & Gamble). Then-CIO Filippo Passerini worked closely with vice chairman, later CEO, Bob McDonald to architect a much more analytical approach to global decision-making at the company. They developed a series of innovations, including "business sphere" rooms for data-driven decision-making, and "decision cockpits" with real-time data for over fifty thousand employees.

CIOs wanting to play an even more valuable analytical role than simply overseeing the technology will focus on the *I* in their titles—the information. Analytical competition, of course, is all about information—do we have the right information, is it truly reflective of our performance, and how do we get people to make decisions based on information? These issues are more complex and multifaceted than buying and managing the right technology, but organizations wishing to compete on analytics will need to master them. Research from one important study suggests that companies focusing on their information orientations perform better than those that address technology alone.[5] The authors of the study argue that *information orientation* consists of information behaviors and values, information management practices, and information technology practices—whereas many CIOs address only the latter category. While that study was not primarily focused on analytics, it's a pretty safe bet that information orientation is highly correlated with analytical success.

Role of the CDAO (Chief Data and Analytics Officer)

As we mentioned in chapter 2, many analytical competitors have created a new role, the *chief data and analytics officer* (or sometimes only *chief analytics officer* or *chief data officer*, still with analytics responsibilities). The CDAO is responsible for ensuring that the enterprise has the data, organizational capabilities, and mindset needed to successfully compete on analytics. Gartner describes the role this way: "The CDO is a senior executive who bears responsibility for the firm's enterprise wide data and information strategy, governance, control, policy development, and effective exploitation. The CDO's role will combine accountability and responsibility for information protection and privacy, information governance, data quality and data life cycle management, along with the exploitation of data assets to create business value."[6]

The CDAO serves as the champion and passionate advocate for the adoption of big data analytics in the organization. The analysts and data scientists in a firm may report directly to the CDAO, or they may have a matrixed reporting relationship. At a minimum, the CDAO keeps data scientists and other analysts productively focused on important business objectives, clears bureaucratic obstacles, and establishes effective partnerships with business customers. Many CDAOs tell us that they spend half their time "evangelizing" for analytics with the business community.

Depending on the organization and its strategic priorities, the CDAO may report variously to the CEO, COO, CIO, chief risk officer, or the chief marketing officer. Since the CDAO does not directly own business processes, he or she must work closely with the rest of the management team to embed data analytics into decision making and operations. And this executive must ensure that analyst's insights are put into practice and produce measurable outcomes. If data management and analytics are combined into one CDAO role, it's important for the incumbents to carve out time for both defense—data security, privacy, governance, etc.—and offense, which includes the use of analytics to create business value.[7]

What If Executive Commitment Is Lacking?

The enemies of an analytical orientation are decisions based solely on intuition and gut feel. Yet these have always been popular approaches to decision making because of their ease and speed and a belief that gut-feel decisions may be better. As we noted in chapter 6, the presence of a committed, passionate CEO or other top executive can put the organization on the fast track to analytical competition. But for those organizations without sufficient demand for data and analysis in executive decision making, the obvious question is whether such demand can be stimulated. If there is no senior executive with a strong analytical orientation, must the organization wait for such a manager to be appointed?

If you don't have committed executives, it's going to be difficult to do much as an outright analytical competitor, but you can lay the groundwork for a more analytical future. If you're in a position to influence the IT infrastructure, you can make sure that your technical platforms, transaction systems, data, and business intelligence software are in good shape, which means that they reliably produce data and information that is timely and accurate. You can obtain and encourage the use of analytical software, programming languages, and data visualization tools. If you head a function or unit, you can make headway toward a smaller-scale analytical transformation of your part of the business. If you are really smart, influential, and politically astute, you might even plot an analytical coup and depose your nonanalytical rulers. But needless to say, that's a risky career strategy.

There are approaches that can be taken to stimulate demand for analytics by executives. These would generally be actions on the prove-it detour described in chapter 6. At one pharmaceutical firm where we interviewed several IT executives, there was generally little demand from senior executives for analytical decision making, particularly in marketing. IT managers didn't have access to the decisions marketers were trying to make, and the marketing executives didn't know what data or analysis might be available to support their decisions. However, two external events offered opportunities to build analytical demand. One marketing manager discovered a vendor who showed how sales data could be displayed graphically in terms of geography on an interactive map. The company's IT executives felt that the display technique was relatively simple, and they began to offer similar capabilities to the manager to try to build on his interest and nurture the demand for marketing analytics.

A second opportunity was offered by an external study from a consulting firm. One outcome of the study will be a new set of performance indicators. The IT group plans to seize on the indicators and will offer more analysis and related data to the management team. These IT managers refuse to wait until more analytically oriented senior executives happen to arrive at the company.

Analytical Professionals and Data Scientists

There is an old joke about analytical professionals. It goes this way:

Question: What did the math PhD say to the MBA graduate?

Answer: Would you like fries with that?

That joke is now totally obsolete, as demand for analytical talent has skyrocketed. Data science, math, and other analytical professionals are being avidly recruited to play key roles in helping companies compete on analytics.

In addition to committed executives, most of the analytical competitors we studied had a group of smart and hardworking analytical professionals within their ranks. It is the job of these professionals to design and carry out experiments and tests, to define and refine analytical algorithms, and to perform data mining and statistical analyses on key data. Analytical pros create the predictive and prescriptive analytics applications used in the organization. In most cases, such individuals would have advanced degrees—often PhDs—in such analytical fields as statistics, data science, econometrics, mathematics, operations research, logistics, physics, and marketing research. As they become more widely available, they are being joined by a new generation of analysts with master's degrees in applied analytics, informatics, and data science. In some cases, where the company's distinctive capabilities involve a specialized field (such as geology for an oil exploration firm), the advanced degree will be in that specialty.

One great example of this type of person we found in our research is Katrina Lane. We first encountered her as vice president of channel marketing at Caesars Entertainment. There, Lane had the job of figuring out which marketing initiatives to move through which channels, including direct mail, email, call centers, and so forth. This is a complex field of business that hasn't been taught in most business schools, so Lane had to figure a lot out on her own. Fortunately, her skills were up to the task. To start with, she has a PhD in experimental physics from Cornell. She was head of marketing for a business unit of the May Department Stores Company and a consultant with McKinsey & Company's marketing and sales practice. How common is such a combination of skills and experience? Not very, which is why assembling a capable group of analytical professionals is never easy. The rarity of her skills also explains why Lane was promoted to chief technology officer at Caesars, and then recruited to be an executive vice president and general manager of marketing and operations for Consumer Cards at American Express. Now she is the VP of Global Delivery Experience for Amazon. She clearly excels in highly analytical management roles in highly analytical companies.

With her PhD in experimental physics, Lane would today be hired as a "data scientist," a job that can bring structure to unstructured data, create sophisticated models to analyze it, and interpret the results for their implications for key decisions and business directions. Data scientists, whom Tom and his coauthor D. J. Patil (until recently, the chief data scientist in the White House) described as holding "the sexiest job of the 21st century," are in hot demand.[8] Some starting salaries for data scientists exceed $200,000. Their earliest employers were Silicon Valley startups, but now they're being hired by large traditional firms as well. Procter & Gamble, for example, went from one data scientist in 2013 to over thirty in 2017. GE hired a couple hundred of them for its GE Digital operation in the San Francisco Bay area. There simply aren't enough to go around.

Even Google, which is one of the most desired employers on the planet right now, has challenges getting this sort of talent. It offers generous salaries, stock options, and what is reputed to be the best cafeteria food anywhere. Yet UC Berkeley professor Hal Varian, who has worked with Google as a consultant since 2002, notes the difficulty of hiring analytical professionals and data scientists there: "One point that I think needs more emphasis is the difficulty of hiring in this area. Given the emphasis on data, data warehousing, data mining and the like you would think that this would be a popular career area for statisticians. Not so! The bright ones all want to go into biotech, alas. So it is quite hard to pull the talent together, even for Google."[9]

Assuming you can find them, how many of these people are necessary? Of course, the answer depends on what an organization is attempting to do with analytics. In the companies we studied, the numbers range from about a dozen analytical professionals and data scientists to several hundred. GE had a goal of hiring four hundred data scientists for its software and analytics business based in the San Francisco area. We're not sure of the exact amount the company hired, but there were at least two hundred in this central organization, and now other business units are hiring their own. Procter & Gamble has two hundred or so. Google has about five hundred people with the "quantitative analyst" title, and thousands who do some sort of analytical work.

How are they organized? Most companies have centralized them to some degree, although organizational structures fluctuate over time. Procter & Gamble, for example, took analytical groups that had been dispersed around the organization, and combined them to form a new global analytics group as part of the IT organization. Then it decentralized them a bit while retaining a dotted line to the chief data officer. AIG created a centralized sixty-person science office for advanced analytics, but then decentralized it for greater responsiveness to the business.

Another logical alternative as an organizational home for these high-powered analysts would be the business function that is the primary competitive thrust for the organization. For example, Caesars keeps most of its "rocket scientists" (including Katrina Lane at the time) in the marketing department, because customer loyalty programs and improved customer service are the primary orientation of its analytics.

One argument in favor of central coordination is that at the most advanced stages of analytics, extensive knowledge of specialized statistical methods is required. As a result of what we learned about the companies we studied, we believe it is impractical for these advanced skills to be broadly distributed throughout the organization. Most organizations will need to have groups that can perform more sophisticated analyses and set up detailed experiments, and we found them in most of the companies we interviewed. It's unlikely, for example, that a "single echelon, uncapacitated, nonstationary inventory management algorithm," employed by one analytical competitor we studied in the supply chain area, would be developed by an amateur analyst. You don't learn about that sort of thing in a typical MBA program.

Most analytical competitors we have studied are evolving toward a hub-and-spoke organization reporting to the CDAO. Analysts are allocated among business units, corporate, and functions so they can specialize and work closely with decision makers. The centralized hub is responsible for knowledge sharing, spreading best practices, analytics training, career path development, common standards and tools. Often, the most highly skilled analysts and data scientists are centralized in the hub so they can be strategically deployed to work on the enterprise's most pressing projects.

Regardless of where the professional analysts are located in their firms, many of the analytical competitors we interviewed stressed the importance of a close and trusting relationship between these analysts and the decision makers. As the head of one group put it, "We're not selling analytics, we're selling trust." The need is for analytical experts who also understand the business in general and the particular business need of a specific decision maker. One company referred to such individuals as "front room statisticians," distinguishing them from "backroom statisticians" who have analytical skills but who are not terribly business oriented and may also not have a high degree of interpersonal skills.

In order to facilitate this relationship, a consumer products firm with an IT-based analytical group hires what it calls "PhDs with personality"—individuals with heavy quantitative skills but also the ability to speak the language of the business and market their work to internal (and, in some cases, external) customers. One typical set of job requirements (listed on Monster.com for a data scientist in Amazon's Advertising Platform group) reads:

- PhD in CS [computer science] machine learning, operational research, statistics or in a highly quantitative field

- 8+ years of hands-on experience in predictive modeling and analysis

- Strong grasp of machine learning, data mining and data analytics techniques

- Strong problem solving ability

- Comfortable using Java or C++/C. Experience in using Perl or Python (or similar scripting language) for data processing and analytics

- Experience in using R, Weka, SAS, Matlab, or any other statistical software

- Communication and data presentation skill

Some of these skills overlap with those of traditional quantitative analysts, but some don't. Data scientists tend to have more computer science–oriented backgrounds, whereas analysts tend to have a more statistical focus. Data scientists are also more likely to be familiar with open-source software and machine learning, and perhaps more likely to have a PhD in a scientific discipline. There are also differences in culture and attitude to some degree. A table of typical differences between these two groups is provided in table 7-1, which is based on a survey Jeanne led in 2014. Over time (and with the popularity of the data scientist title), however, these categories have become somewhat intermingled, and the differences may be diminishing.

TABLE 7-1

Analysts and data scientists: not quite a different species

	Analysts	Data scientists
Data structure	Structured and semistructured, mostly numeric	All, predominantly unstructured
Data types	Mostly numeric	All, including images, sound, and text
Preferred tools	Statistical and modeling tools, on data usually residing in a repository such as a data warehouse	Mathematical languages (such as R and Python), machine learning, natural language processing, and open-source tools; data on multiple servers (such as Hadoop)
Nature of assignment	Report, predict, prescribe, optimize	Explore, discover, investigate, visualize
Educational background	Operations research, statistics, applied analytics	Computer science, data science, symbolic systems, cognitive science
Mindset:		
• Entrepreneurial	69%	96%
• Explore new area	58%	85%
• Insights outside of projects	54%	89%

Source: Jeanne G. Harris and Vijay Mehrotra, "Getting Value from Your Data Scientists," *MIT Sloan Management Review* (Fall 2014).

Whatever the role is called, business relationships are a critical component of it. At Wells Fargo, a manager of a customer analytics group described the relationships his group tries to maintain: "We are trying to build our people as part of the business team; we want them sitting at the business table, participating in a discussion of what the key issues are, determining what information the business people need to have, and recommending actions to the business partners. We want this [analytical group] to be more than a general utility, but rather an active and critical part of the business unit's success."[10]

Other executives who manage or have managed analytics groups described some of the critical success factors for them in our interviews:

- *Building a sustainable pipeline.* Analytical groups need a pipeline of projects, client relationships, and analytical technologies.

The key is not just to have a successful project or two but to create sustainability for the organization over time. It's no good to invest in all these capabilities and have the analytical initiative be in existence for only a few years. However, it takes time to build success stories and to have analytics become part of the mythology of the organization. The stories instill a mindset in the company so that decision makers have the confidence to act.

- *Relationship to IT.* Even if an analytical group isn't officially part of an IT organization, it needs to maintain a close relationship with it. Analytical competitors often need to "push the frontier" in terms of IT. One analytical group's manager in a consumer products firm said that his group had been early users of supercomputers and multiuser servers and had hosted the first website for a product (which got thousands of hits on the first day). Exploration of new information technologies wasn't an official mission for the group but one that the company appreciated. It also helped capture the attention and imagination of the company's senior management team.

- *Governance and funding.* How the group is directed and funded is very critical, according to the executives we interviewed. The key issue is to direct analytical groups at the most important problems of the business. This can be done either by mandate or advice from some form of steering committee, or through the funding process. When steering committees are made up of lower-level executives, the tendency seems to be to suboptimize the use of analytical resources. More senior and strategic members create more strategic priorities for analytical professionals. Funding can also lead to strategic or tactical targets. One group we interviewed was entirely paid for by corporate overhead, which meant that it didn't have to go "tin cupping" for funding and work on unimportant problems that somehow had a budget. Another group did have to seek funding for each project, and said they had to occasionally go to senior management to get permission to turn down lucrative but less important work.

- *Managing politics.* There are often tricky political issues involved in analytical professionals' work, ranging from whose
  projects the group works on to what the function is called. One
  company called its analytical group Decision Analysis, only to
  find that executives objected because they felt it was their job
  to make decisions. The group then changed its name to Options
  Analysis. It can also be politically difficult simply to employ
  analysts. As one head of an analytical group put it: "So I go to
  Market Research and say, 'I have a better way to evaluate advertising expenditures.' They don't necessarily react with joy.
  It's very threatening to them. It makes it particularly difficult
  if you are asking them to pay you to make them look bad!"[11]

  Heads of analytical groups have to be sensitive to political
  issues and try to avoid political minefields. The problem is that
  people who are good at analytics do not often have patience for
  corporate politics! Before any analysis, they should establish
  with the internal client that both client and analyst have no
  stake in any particular outcome, and they will let the analytical chips fall where they may. CEOs can help their analytical
  professionals by making it clear that the culture rewards those
  who make evidence-based decisions, even when they go against
  previously established policies.

- *Don't get ahead of users.* It's important for analytical professionals to keep in mind that their algorithms and processes
  must often be implemented by information workers, who may
  be analytically astute but are not expert statisticians. If the
  analytics and the resulting conclusions are too complex or laced
  with arcane statistical terminology, they will likely be ignored.
  One approach is to keep the analytics as simple as possible or
  to embed them into systems that hide their complexity. Another
  is to train users of analytical approaches as much as possible.
  Schneider National's analytics group has offered courses such
  as "Introduction to Data Analysis" and "Statistical Process
  Control" for users in various functions at the company. It's not a
  formal responsibility for the group, but the courses are popular,
  and the group feels it makes their job easier in the long run.

Offshore or Outsourced Analytical Professionals

With expert analytical professionals in short supply within US and European companies, many companies are considering the possibility of outsourcing them or even going to India or China to find them. It's certainly true that an increasing number of firms offer "knowledge process outsourcing" in analytical fields including data mining, algorithm development, and quantitative finance. In India, firms such as Mu Sigma, Evalueserve, and Genpact have substantial practices in these domains. Genpact did work in analytical credit analysis when it was a part of GE Capital, and now also offers services in marketing and sales analytics. Most major consulting firms, including Accenture, Deloitte, and IBM, have large analytics groups based in India.

However, it is difficult for analysts to develop a trusting relationship with decision makers from several thousand miles away. It is likely that the only successful business models for this type of work will combine onshore and offshore capabilities. Onshore analysts can work closely with decision makers, while offshore specialists can do back-office analytical work. If a particular analytical application can be clearly described by the business owner or sponsor before it is developed, there is a good chance that development of the relevant algorithms could be successfully outsourced or taken offshore.

Analytical Amateurs

Much of the daily work of an analytically focused strategy has to be implemented by people without PhDs in statistics or operations research. A key issue, then, is how much analytical sophistication frontline workers need in order to do their jobs. Of course, the nature and extent of needed skills will vary by the company and industry situations. Some firms, such as Capital One, hire a large number of amateur analysts—people with some analytical background (perhaps MBAs), but mostly not PhD types. At one point, when we looked at open jobs on Capital One's website, there were three times as many analyst openings as there were jobs in operations—hardly the usual ratio for a bank. According to its particular analytical orientation, a company simply needs to determine how many analytical amateurs it needs in what positions. Some may verge on being professionals (we call them *analytical semi-professionals*); others may have very limited analytical skills but still have to work in business processes that are heavily based on analytics.

The Boston Red Sox's situation in 2003, which we described in chapter 1, is an example of needing to spread analytical orientations throughout the organization. For more business-oriented examples, we'll describe two organizations that are attempting to compete on supply chain analytics. One, a beer manufacturer, put in new supply chain optimization software to ensure that it manufactured and shipped the right amount of beer at the right time. It even created a new position, "beer flow coordinator" (if only we had such a title on our business cards!) to use the system and oversee the optimization algorithms and process. Yet the company's managers admitted that the beer flow coordinators didn't have the skills to make the process work. No new people were hired, and no substantial training was done. The new system, at least in its early days, was not being used. The company was expecting, one might say, champagne skills on a beer-skills budget.

At a polymer chemicals company, many of the company's products had become commoditized. Executives believed that it was important to optimize the global supply chain to squeeze maximum value and cost out of it. The complexity of the unit's supply chain had significantly increased over the previous couple of years. Responding to the increased complexity, the organization created a global supply chain organization, members of which were responsible for the movement of products and supplies around the world. In the new organization, someone was responsible for the global supply chain, there were planning groups in the regions, and then planners in the different sites. The greatest challenge in the supply chain, however, involved the people who did the work. The new roles were more complex and required a higher degree of analytical sophistication. The company knew that the people performing the previous supply chain roles didn't have the skills to perform the new analytical jobs, but it kept them anyway. At some point, the company plans to develop an inventory of skills needed and an approach to developing or hiring for them, but thus far the lack of skills remains a bottleneck in the implementation of its new logistical process.

When a company is an analytical competitor, it will need to ensure that a wide variety of employees have some exposure to analytics. Managers and business analysts are increasingly being called on to conduct data-driven experiments, interpret data, and create innovative data-based products and services. Many companies have concluded that their employees require additional skills to thrive in a more analytical environment. An Avanade survey found that more than 63 percent of respondents said their employees need to develop new skills to translate big data analytics into insights and business value.[12] Anders Reinhardt, formerly head of Global Business Intelligence for the VELUX Group—an international manufacturer of skylights, solar panels, and other roof products based in Denmark—is convinced that "the standard way of training, where we simply explain to business users how to access data and reports, is not enough anymore. Big data is much more demanding on the user."[13]

To succeed at an analytical competitor, information workers and decision makers need to become adept at three core skills:[14]

- *Experimental:* Managers and business analysts must be able to apply the principles of scientific experimentation to their business. They must know how to construct intelligent hypotheses. They also need to understand the principles of experimental testing and design, including population selection and sampling, in order to evaluate the validity of data analyses. As randomized testing and experimentation become more commonplace in the financial services, retail, and telecommunications industries, a background in scientific experimental design will be particularly valued. Google's recruiters know that experimentation and testing are integral parts of their culture and business processes. So job applicants are asked questions such as "How many tennis balls would fit in a school bus?" or "How many sewer covers are there in Brooklyn?" The point isn't to find the right answer but to test the applicant's skills in experimental design, logic, and quantitative analysis.

- *Numerate:* Analytical leaders tell us that an increasingly critical skill for their workforce is to become more adept in the interpretation and use of numeric data. VELUX's Reinhardt explains that "Business users don't need to be statisticians, but they need to understand the proper usage of statistical methods. We want our business users to understand how to interpret data, metrics, and the results of statistical models." Some companies, out of necessity, make sure that their employees are already highly adept at mathematical reasoning when they are hired. Capital One's hiring practices are geared toward hiring highly analytical and numerate employees into every aspect of the business. Prospective employees, including senior executives, go through a rigorous interview process, including tests of their mathematical reasoning, logic, and problem-solving abilities.

- *Data literate:* Managers increasingly need to be adept at finding, manipulating, managing, and interpreting data, including not just numbers but also text and images. Data literacy is rapidly becoming an integral aspect of every business function and activity. Procter & Gamble's former chairman and CEO Bob McDonald is convinced that "data modeling, simulation, and other digital tools are reshaping how we innovate." And that changed the skills needed by his employees. To meet this challenge, P&G created "a baseline digital-skills inventory that's tailored to every level of advancement in the organization." The current CEO, David Taylor, also supports and has continued this policy. At VELUX, data literacy training for business users is a priority. Managers need to understand what data is available, and to use data visualization techniques to process and interpret it. "Perhaps most importantly, we need to help them to imagine how new types of data can lead to new insights," notes Reinhardt.[15]

Depending on the business function, additional expertise may be needed. Most IT people, for example, should have some sense of what analyses are being performed on data, so that they can ensure that IT applications and databases create and manage data in the right formats for analysis. HR people need to understand something about analytics so that they can hire people with the right kinds of analytical skills. Even the corporate legal staff may need to understand the implications of a firm's approach to analytical and automated decision making in case something goes awry in the process.

Firms that have upgraded the analytical skills of employees and managers are starting to see benefits. For example, at a consumer products firm with an analytical strategy, they're seeing a sea change in middle managers. Upper middle management has analytical expertise, either from mathematical backgrounds or from company experience. Two of the central analytical group's key clients have new managers who are more analytical. They were sought out for their analytical orientations and have been very supportive of analytical competition. The analytical managers are more challenging and drive the professional analyst group to higher levels of performance. The senior management team now has analytical discussions, not political ones.

Tools for Amateurs

One of the issues for amateur analysts is what IT tools they use to deal with analytics. There are three possible choices, and none seems ideal. One choice is to give them powerful statistical analysis tools so that they can mine data and create powerful algorithms (which they are unlikely to have the skills to do). A second choice is to have the prescriptive models simply spit out the right answer: the price that should be charged, the amount of inventory to be shipped, and so on. While we think this may be the best of the three options, it may sometimes limit the person's ability to use data and make decisions. The third option, which is by far the most common, is to have amateurs do their analytics on spreadsheets.

Spreadsheets (by which we really mean Microsoft Excel, of course) are still the predominant tool by which amateurs manipulate data and perform analytics. Spreadsheets have some strengths, or they wouldn't be so common. They are easy to use (at least the basic capabilities); the row-and-column format is widely understood; and they are inexpensive (since Excel comes bundled with widely used office productivity software). Yet as we point out in chapter 2, spreadsheets are a problematic tool for widespread analytical activity. It's very difficult to maintain a consistent, "one version of the truth" analytical environment across an enterprise with a large number of user-managed spreadsheets. And spreadsheets often have errors. Any firm that embraces spreadsheets as the primary tool for analytical amateurs must have a strong approach to data architecture and strong controls over analytics.

An intermediate approach would be to give amateur analysts the ability to view and analyze data, while still providing a structure for the analytical workflow. Vendors of business intelligence and data visualization software make such a workflow available. They allow the more analytically sophisticated users to do their own visual queries or create visual reports, while letting less sophisticated users observe and understand some of the analytical processes being followed. These tools are becoming increasingly popular and are leading to the democratization of analytics. At some point, we may even see the emergence of the "citizen data scientist," for whom most of the difficult data management and analysis tasks are done by intelligent machines.

Autonomous Decision Making

Another critical factor involving analytical amateurs that must be addressed is how highly automated a solution for a given problem should be.[16] As automating more and more decisions becomes possible, it is increasingly important for organizations to address which decisions have to be made by people and which can be computerized. Automated decision applications are typically triggered without human intervention: they sense online data or conditions, apply analytical algorithms or codified knowledge (usually in the form of rules), and make decisions—all with minimal human intervention.

Fully automated applications are configured to translate high volume or routine decisions into action quickly, accurately, and efficiently because they are embedded into the normal flow of work. Among analytical competitors, we found automated decision technologies being used for a variety of operational decisions, including extension of credit, pricing, yield management, and insurance underwriting. If experts can readily codify the decision rules and if high-quality data is available, the conditions are ripe for automating the decision.[17] Bank credit decisions are a good example; they are repetitive, are susceptible to uniform criteria, and can be made by drawing on the vast supply of consumer credit data that is available.

Still, some types of decisions, while infrequently made, lend themselves well to automation—particularly cases where decision speed is crucial. For example, in the electrical energy grid, quick and accurate shutoff decisions at the regional level are essential to avert a systemwide failure. The value of this rapid response capability has often been demonstrated in large power outages, when automated systems in regions of the United States have been able to respond quickly to power surges to their networks by shutting off or redirecting power to neighboring lines with spare capacity. It is also evident in some of today's most advanced emergency response systems, which can automatically decide how to coordinate ambulances and emergency rooms across a city in the event of a major disaster.

Autonomous decision-making applications have some limitations, however. Even when fully automating a decision process is possible, fiduciary, legal, or ethical issues may still require a responsible person to play an active role. Also, automated decisions create some challenges for the organization. Because automated decision systems can lead to the reduction of large staffs of information workers to just a handful of experts, management must focus on keeping the right people—those with the highest possible skills and effectiveness. This expert-only approach, however, raises the question of where tomorrow's experts will come from.

The Override Issue

A related issue is how amateurs should deal with automated decisions with which they don't agree. Some firms, such as Caesars, discourage employees from overriding their automated analytical systems, because they have evidence that the systems get better results than people do. A hotel manager, for example, is not allowed to override the company's revenue management system, which figures out the ideal price for a room based on availability trends and the loyalty level of the customer.

Marriott, as we've described in chapter 3, has similar revenue management systems for its hotels. Yet the company actually encourages its regional "revenue leaders" to override the system. It has devised ways for regional managers to introduce fast-breaking, anomalous information when local events unexpectedly affect normal operating data—such as when Houston was inundated with Hurricane Katrina evacuees. The revenue management system noticed that an unexpected number of people wanted Marriott rooms in Houston in August, and on its own it would have raised rates. But Marriott hardly wanted to discourage evacuees from staying in its Houston-area hotels, so revenue leaders overrode the system and lowered rates. Marriott executives say that such an approach to overriding automated systems is part of a general corporate philosophy. Otherwise, they argue, they wouldn't have bothered to hire and train analytically capable people who make good decisions.

Why these two different philosophies? There are different systems involved, different business processes, and different levels of skill. Companies with a high skill level among analytical amateurs may want to encourage overrides when people think they know more than the system. Partners HealthCare's physicians, who are often also professors at Harvard Medical School, are encouraged to override automated decision systems when doing so is in the best interest of the patient. With such highly trained experts involved in the process, the best result is probably from the combination of humans and automated decision rules.

Companies that feel they have most of the variables covered in their automated analytical models—and that have lower levels of analytical skills at the front line—may prefer to take a hard line on overrides. To some degree, the question can be decided empirically—if overrides usually result in better decisions, they should be encouraged. If not, they should be prohibited most of the time. If a company does decide to allow overrides, it should develop some systematic means of capturing the reasons for them so that the automated model might be improved through the input. At Partners, for example, physicians are asked to give a reason when they override the automated system, and physicians who constantly override a particular system recommendation are interviewed about their reasoning.

Whatever the decision on people versus automation, the key message of this chapter is that the human resource is perhaps the most important capability an analytical competitor can cultivate. When we asked analytical competitors what's hard about executing their strategies, most said it was getting the right kinds of analytical people in sufficient numbers. Hardware and software alone can't come close to creating the kinds of capabilities that analytical strategies require. Whether we're talking about senior executives, analytical professionals and data scientists, or frontline analytical amateurs, everyone has a job to do in making analytical competition successful.

CHAPTER EIGHT

THE ARCHITECTURE OF ANALYTICS AND BIG DATA

ALIGNING A ROBUST TECHNICAL ENVIRONMENT WITH BUSINESS STRATEGIES

OVER THE LAST DECADE OR SO, IT HAS BECOME TECHNIcally and economically feasible to capture and store huge quantities of data. The numbers are hard to absorb for all but the geekiest, as data volumes have grown from megabytes to gigabytes (billions of bytes) to terabytes (trillions of bytes) to petabytes (quadrillions of bytes). While low-end personal computers and servers lack the power and capacity to handle the volumes of data required for analytical applications, high-end 64-bit processors, specialty "data appliances," and cloud-based processing options can quickly churn through virtually unfathomable amounts of data.

However, while organizations have more data than ever at their disposal, they rarely know what to do with it. The data in their systems is often like the box of photos you keep in your attic, waiting for the "someday" when you impose meaning on the chaos. IDC estimated that only 0.5 percent of all data is ever analyzed, and we would guess that the amount of data is growing faster than the amount of it that's analyzed.

Further, the unpalatable truth is that most IT departments strain to meet minimal service demands and invest inordinate resources in the ongoing support and maintenance of basic transactional capabilities. Unlike the analytical vanguard, even companies with sound transaction systems struggle with relatively prosaic issues such as data cleansing when they try to integrate data into analytical applications. In short, while improvements in technology's ability to store data can be astonishing, most organizations' ability to manage, analyze, and apply data has not kept pace.

Companies that compete on analytics haven't solved all these problems entirely, but they are a lot better off than their competition. In this chapter, we identify the technology, data, and governance processes needed for analytical competition. We also lay out the components that make up the core of any organization's analytical architecture and forecast how these elements are likely to evolve in the future.

The Architecture of Analytical Technology

While business users of analytics often play an important role, companies have historically delegated the management of information technology for analytics and other applications to an information technology (IT) organization. For example, by capturing proprietary data or embedding proprietary analytics into business processes, the IT department helps develop and sustain an organization's competitive advantage.

But it is important to understand that this work cannot be delegated to IT alone. Most "small data" can be easily analyzed on a personal computer, and even the largest dataset can be sent to Amazon Web Services' or Microsoft Azure's clouds and analyzed by anyone with the requisite knowledge and a credit card. This can lead to uncontrolled proliferation of "versions of the truth," but it can also lead to insightful answers to business problems. Determining how to encourage the latter and prevent the former is a critical task in any analytical architecture.

Even when IT help is required, determining the technical capabilities needed for analytical competition requires a close collaboration between IT organizations and business managers. This is a principle that companies like Progressive Insurance understand fully. Glenn Renwick, formerly both CEO of Progressive Insurance and head of IT there, understands how critical it is to align IT with business strategy: "Here at Progressive we have technology leaders working arm in arm with business leaders who view their job as solving business problems. And we have business leaders who are held accountable for understanding the role of technology in their business. Our business plan and IT are inextricably linked because their job objectives are."[1]

Although Renwick has just retired, Progressive has a long history of IT/business alignment and focus on analytics, and we're sure they will continue. We found this same collaborative orientation at many analytical competitors.

Analytical competitors also establish a set of guiding principles to ensure that their technology investments reflect corporate priorities. The principles may include statements such as:

- We will be an industry leader in adopting new technologies for big data and machine learning.

- The risk associated with conflicting information sources must be reduced.

- Applications should be integrated, since analytics increasingly draw data that crosses organizational boundaries.

- Analytics must be enabled as part of the organization's strategy and distinctive capability.

Responsibility for getting the data, technology, and processes right for analytics across the enterprise is the job of the *IT architect* (or the chief data or technology officer, if there is one). This executive (working closely with the chief information officer) must determine how the components of the IT infrastructure (hardware, software, and networks, and external cloud resources) will work together to provide the data, technology, and support needed by the business. This task is easier for digital companies, such as Netflix or eBay, that can create their IT environment with analytical competition in mind from the outset. In large established organizations however, the IT infrastructure can sometimes appear to have been constructed in a series of

DATA AND IT CAPABILITY BY STAGE OF ANALYTICAL COMPETITION

Established companies typically follow an evolutionary process to develop their IT analytical capabilities:

- **Stage 1.** The organization is plagued by missing or poor-quality data, multiple definitions of its data, and poorly integrated systems.

- **Stage 2.** The organization collects transaction data efficiently but often lacks the right data for better decision making. Some successful analytical applications or pilot programs exist and they may even use some sophisticated statistics or technologies. But these are independent initiatives sponsored by functional executives.

- **Stage 3.** The organization has a proliferation of business intelligence and analytics tools and data repositories, but some

weekend handyman jobs. It does the job it was designed to do but is apt to create problems whenever it is applied to another purpose.

To make sure the IT environment fully addresses an organization's needs at each stage of analytical competition, companies must incorporate analytics and big data technologies into their overall IT architecture. (Refer to the box "Data and IT Capability by Stage of Analytical Competition.")

We're using the term *analytics and big data* in this context to encompass not only the analysis itself—the use of large and small data to analyze, forecast, predict, optimize, and so on—but also the processes and technologies used for collecting, structuring, managing, and reporting decision-oriented data. The *analytics and big data architecture* (a subset of the overall IT architecture) is an umbrella term for an enterprise-wide set of systems, applications, and governance processes that enable sophisticated analytics by allowing data, content, and analyses to flow to those who need it, when they need it. (Refer to the box "Signposts of Effective IT for Analytical Competition.")

non-transaction data remains unintegrated, nonstandardized, and inaccessible. IT and data architecture are updated to support enterprise-wide analytics.

- **Stage 4.** The organization has high-quality data, an enterprise-wide analytical plan, IT processes and governance principles, and some embedded or automated analytics. It is also working to some degree on big, less structured data.

- **Stage 5.** The organization has a full-fledged analytics architecture that is enterprise-wide, automated and integrated into processes, and highly sophisticated. The company makes effective and integrated use of big and small data from many internal and external sources, including highly unstructured data. The company begins to explore and use cognitive technologies and autonomous analytics.

"Those who need it" will include data scientists, statisticians of varying skills, analysts, information workers, functional heads, and top management. The analytics architecture must be able to quickly provide users with reliable, accurate information and help them make decisions of widely varying complexity. It also must make information available through a variety of distribution channels, including traditional reports, ad hoc analysis tools, corporate dashboards, spreadsheets, emails, and text message alerts—and even products and services built around data and analytics. This task is often daunting: Amazon, for example, spent more than ten years and over $1 billion building, organizing, and protecting its data warehouses.[2]

Complying with legal and regulatory reporting requirements is another activity that depends on a robust analytical architecture. The Sarbanes-Oxley Act of 2002, for example, requires executives, auditors, and other users of corporate data to demonstrate that their decisions are based on trustworthy, meaningful, authoritative, and accurate data. It also requires them to attest that the data provides a clear picture of the

SIGNPOSTS OF EFFECTIVE IT FOR ANALYTICAL COMPETITION

- Analysts have direct, nearly instantaneous access to data, some of it real-time.

- Information workers spend their time analyzing data and understanding its implications rather than collecting and formatting data.

- Managers focus on improving processes and business performance, not culling data from laptops, reports, and transaction systems.

- Analytics and data are incorporated into the company's products and services.

- Managers never argue over whose numbers are accurate.

- Data is managed from an enterprise-wide perspective throughout its life cycle, from its initial creation to archiving or destruction.

- A hypothesis can be quickly analyzed and tested without a lot of manual behind-the-scenes preparation beforehand—and

business, major trends, risks, and opportunities. The Dodd-Frank Act, a regulatory framework for financial services firms enacted in 2010, has equally rigorous requirements for that specific industry (although there are doubts that it will continue in its present form). Health care organizations have their own set of reporting requirements.

Conceptually, it's useful to break the analytics and big data architecture into its six elements (refer to figure 8-1):

- *Data management* that defines how the right data is acquired and managed

- *Transformation tools and processes* that describe how the data is extracted, cleaned, structured, transmitted, and loaded to "populate" databases and repositories

some analytical models are created without human hypotheses at all (i.e., with machine learning).

- Data is increasingly analyzed at the "edge" of the organization without needing to send it to a centralized repository.

- Both the supply and demand sides of the business rely on forecasts that are aligned and have been developed using a consistent set of data.

- High-volume, mission-critical decision-making processes are highly automated and integrated.

- Data is routinely and automatically shared between the company and its customers and suppliers.

- Reports and analyses seamlessly integrate and synthesize information from many sources, both internal and external.

- Rather than have data warehouse or analytics initiatives, companies manage data and analytics as strategic corporate resources in all business initiatives.

- *Repositories* that organize data and metadata (information about the data) and store it for use

- *Analytical tools and applications* used for analysis

- *Data visualization* tools and applications that address how information workers and non-IT analysts will access, display, visualize, and manipulate data

- *Deployment processes* that determine how important administrative activities such as security, error handling, "auditability," archiving, and privacy are addressed

We'll look at each element in turn, with particular attention to data since it drives all the other architectural decisions.

FIGURE 8-1

Analytics and big data architecture

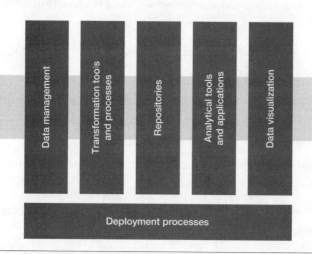

Data management

Transformation tools and processes

Repositories

Analytical tools and applications

Data visualization

Deployment processes

Data Management

The goal of a well-designed data management strategy is to ensure that the organization has the right information and uses it appropriately. Large companies invest millions of dollars in systems that snatch data from every conceivable source. Systems for enterprise resource planning, customer relationship management, and point-of-sale transactions, among others, ensure that no transaction or exchange occurs without leaving a mark. Many organizations also purchase externally gathered data from syndicated providers such as IRI and ACNielsen in consumer products and Quintiles IMS in pharmaceuticals. Additionally, data management strategies must determine how to handle big data from corporate websites, social media, internet clickstreams, Internet of Things data, and various other types of external data.

In this environment, data overload can be a real problem for time-stressed managers and professionals. But the greatest data challenge facing companies is "dirty" data: information that is inconsistent, fragmented, and out of context. Even the best companies often struggle to address their data issues. We found that companies that compete on analytics devote extraordinary attention to data management processes and governance. Capital One, for example, estimates that 25 percent of its IT organization works on data issues—an unusually high percentage compared with other firms.

There's a significant payoff for those who invest the effort to master data management. For example, GE addressed the problem of multiple overlapping sources of supplier data within the company. Many business units and functions had their own versions of supplier databases across hundreds of transaction systems, and the same suppliers were represented multiple times, often in slightly different ways. As a result, GE couldn't perform basic analytics to determine which suppliers sold to multiple business units, which suppliers were also customers, and how much overall business it did with a supplier. So it embarked on an effort to use new machine learning tools to curate and integrate the supplier data. After several months, it had created an integrated supplier database, and it could start pressing the most active suppliers for volume discounts. Overall, GE estimates that the work led to $80 million in benefits to the company in its first year, and it expects substantially higher benefits in the future. GE is also working on customer data and parts data using the same approach.

To achieve the benefits of analytical competition, IT and business experts must tackle their data issues by answering five questions:

- *Data relevance:* What data is needed to compete on analytics?

- *Data sourcing:* Where can this data be obtained?

- *Data quantity:* How much data is needed?

- *Data quality:* How can the data be made more accurate and valuable for analysis?

- *Data governance:* What rules and processes are needed to manage data from its creation through its retirement?

What Data Is Needed to Compete on Analytics?

The question behind this question is, what data is most valuable for competitive differentiation and business performance? To answer, executives must have a clear understanding of the organization's distinctive capability, the activities that support that capability, and the relationship between an organization's strategic and operational metrics and business performance. Many of the companies described in this book have demonstrated the creative insight needed to make those connections.

But ensuring that analysts have access to the right data can be difficult. Sometimes a new metric is needed: the advent of credit scores made the mortgage-lending business more efficient by replacing qualitative assessments of consumer creditworthiness with a single, comparative metric. But not everything is readily reducible to a number. An employee's performance rating doesn't give as complete a picture of his work over a year as a manager's written assessment. The situation is complicated when business and IT people blame each other when the wrong data is collected or the right data is not available. Studies repeatedly show that IT executives believe business managers do not understand what data they need.[3] And surveys of business managers reflect their belief that IT executives lack the business acumen to make meaningful data available. While there is no easy solution to this problem, the beginning of the solution is for business leaders and IT managers to pledge to work together on this question. This problem has been eased somewhat in companies like Intel and Procter & Gamble, where quantitative analysts work closely alongside business leaders. Without such cooperation, an organization's ability to gather the data it needs to compete analytically is doomed.

A related issue requiring business and IT collaboration is defining relationships among the data used in analysis. Considerable business expertise is required to help IT understand the potential relationships in the data for optimum organization. The importance of this activity can be seen in an example involving health care customers. From an insurance company's perspective, they have many different customers—their corporate customers that contract for policies on behalf of their employees, individual subscribers, and members of the subscribers' families. Each individual has a medical history and may have any number of medical conditions or diseases that require treatment. The insurance company and each person covered by a policy also have relationships with a variety of service providers such as hospitals, HMOs, and doctors. A doctor may be a general practitioner or a specialist. Some doctors will work with some hospitals or insurers but not others. Individuals can have insurance from multiple providers, including the government, that need to be coordinated. Without insight into the nature of these relationships, the data's usefulness for analytics is extremely limited.

Where Can This Data Be Obtained?

Data for analytics and business intelligence originates from many places, but the crucial point is that it needs to be managed through an enterprise-wide infrastructure. Only by this means will it be streamlined, consistent, and scalable throughout the organization. Having common applications and data across the enterprise is critical because it helps yield a "consistent version of the truth," an essential goal for everyone concerned with analytics. While it is possible to create such an environment by ex post facto integration and the transformation of data from many systems, companies are well advised to update and integrate their processes and transaction systems before embarking on this task.

For internal information, the organization's enterprise systems are a logical starting point. For example, an organization wishing to optimize its supply chain might begin with a demand-planning application. However, it can be difficult to analyze data from transaction systems (like inventory control) because it isn't defined or framed correctly for management decisions. Enterprise systems—integrated software applications that automate, connect, and manage information flows for business processes such as order fulfillment—often help companies move along the path toward analytical competition: they provide consistent, accurate, and timely data for such tasks as financial reporting and supply chain optimization. Vendors increasingly are embedding analytical capabilities into their enterprise systems so that users can develop sales forecasts and model alternative solutions to business problems. However, the data from such systems usually isn't very distinctive to a particular firm, so it must be combined with other types of data to have competitive differentiation.

In addition to corporate systems, an organization's personal computers and servers are loaded with data. Databases, spreadsheets, presentations, and reports are all sources of data. Sometimes these sources are stored in a common knowledge management application, but they are often not available across the entire organization.

Internal data also increasingly means data from Internet of Things (IoT) sensors and devices at the "edge" of the organization—in the oil-field drilling equipment, the retail point of sale device, or the aircraft engine, for example. The traditional model was to send all this data to a centralized repository to store and analyze it. But an alternative paradigm of *edge analytics* is growing in currency. The rapid growth of the IoT and other edge devices that generate data means that it is often unfeasible to send it all to headquarters or even to the cloud for analysis. In an oilfield, for example, operational data from drilling equipment (including drill-bit RPMs, cutting forces, vibration, temperature, and oil and water flows) can be used in real time to change drilling strategies. It's often not feasible to send all this data to a central repository. Some drilling operations already use microprocessor-based analytics to determine drilling strategies in real time. The IoT will make edge-based analytics approaches much more common in the future.

There has been an explosion of external data over the past decade, much of it coming from the internet, social media, and external data providers. There has also long been the opportunity to purchase data from firms that provide financial and market information, consumer credit data, and market measurement. Governments at all levels are some of the biggest information providers (more so since the "Open Data" movement over the past decade), and company websites to which customers and suppliers contribute are another powerful resource. Less structured data can also come from such sources as email, voice applications, images (maps and photos available through the internet), photographs (of people, products, and of course cats), and biometrics (fingerprints and iris identification). The further the data type is from standard numbers and letters, however, the harder it is to integrate with other data and analyze—although deep learning technologies are making image recognition much faster and more accurate.

It can be difficult and expensive to capture some highly valuable data. (In some cases, it might even be illegal—for example, sensitive customer information or competitor intelligence about new product plans or pricing strategies.) Analytical competitors adopt innovative approaches to gain permission to collect the data they need. As we described in chapter 3, Progressive's Snapshot program offers discounts to customers who agree to install a device that collects data about their driving behavior. Former CEO Peter Lewis sees this capability as the key to more accurate pricing and capturing the most valuable customers: "It's about being able to charge them for whatever happens instead of what they [customers] say is happening. So what will happen? We'll get all the people who hardly ever drive, and our competitors will get stuck with the higher risks."[4] Progressive has now gathered over 10 billion miles of customer driving data, and it has become the best source of insight about what insurance will cost the company.

How Much Data Is Needed?

In addition to gathering the right data, companies need to collect a lot of it in order to distill trends and predict customer behavior. What's "a lot"? In 2007, the largest data warehouse in the world was Walmart's, with about 600 terabytes. At roughly the same time, the size of the US Library of Congress's print collection was roughly 20 terabytes.[5]

Fortunately, the technology and techniques for mining and managing large volumes of data are making enormous strides. The largest databases are no longer enterprise warehouses, but Hadoop clusters storing data across multiple commodity servers. The 600 terabytes in Walmart's warehouse in 2007 grew a hundredfold by 2017 to 60 petabytes. Digital firms manage even bigger data: Yahoo!'s 600 petabytes are spread across forty thousand Hadoop servers. That's the equivalent of storing about 30 trillion pages. Yahoo! isn't the perfect example of an analytical competitor anymore, but it's likely that more successful firms like Google and Facebook have similar volumes in their data centers.

Two pitfalls must be balanced against this need for massive quantities of data. First, unless you are in the data business like the companies we've just described, it's a good idea to resist the temptation to collect all possible data "just in case." For one thing, if executives have to wade through digital mountains of irrelevant data, they'll give up and stop using the tools at hand. "Never throwing away data," which has been advocated by Amazon's Jeff Bezos, can be done, but the costs outweigh the benefits for most companies. The fundamental issue comes back, again, to knowing what drives value in an organization; this understanding will prevent companies from collecting data indiscriminately.

A related second pitfall: companies should avoid collecting data that is easy to capture but not necessarily important. Many IT executives advocate this low-hanging-fruit approach because it relieves them of responsibility for determining what information is valuable to the business. For example, many companies fall into the trap of providing managers with data that is a by-product of transaction systems, since that is what is most readily available. Others analyze social media data simply because it's possible, even when they don't have any actions in mind when sentiment trends down or up a bit. Perhaps emerging technologies will someday eliminate the need to separate the wheat from the chaff. But until they do, applying intelligence to the process is necessary to avoid data overload.

How Can We Make Data More Valuable?

Quantity without quality is a recipe for failure. Executives are aware of the problem: in a survey of the challenges organizations face in developing a business intelligence capability, data quality was second only to budget constraints.[6] Even analytical competitors struggle with data quality.

Organizations tend to store their data in hard-walled, functional silos. As a result, the data is generally a disorganized mess. For most organizations, differing definitions of key data elements such as *customer* or *product* add to the confusion. When Canadian Tire Corporation, for example, set out to create a structure for its data, it found that the company's data warehouse could yield as many as six different numbers for inventory levels. Other data was not available at all, such as comparison sales figures for certain products sold in its 450-plus stores throughout Canada. Over several years, the company created a plan to collect new data that fit the company's analytical needs.[7]

Several characteristics increase the value of data:

- *It is correct.* While some analyses can get by with ballpark figures and others need precision to several decimal points, all must be informed by data that passes the credibility tests of the people reviewing it.

- *It is complete.* The definition of *complete* will vary according to whether a company is selling cement, credit cards, season tickets, and so on, but completeness will always be closely tied to the organization's distinctive capability.

- *It is current.* Again, the definition of *current* may vary; for some business problems, such as a major medical emergency, data must be available instantly to deploy ambulances and emergency personnel in real time (also known as *zero latency*); for most other business decisions, such as a budget forecast, it just needs to be updated periodically—daily, weekly, or monthly.

- *It is consistent.* In order to help decision makers end arguments over whose data is correct, standardization and common definitions must be applied to it. Eliminating redundant data reduces the chances of using inconsistent or out-of-date data.

- *It is in context.* When data is enriched with *metadata* (usually defined as structured data about data), its meaning and how it should be used become clear.

- *It is controlled.* In order to comply with business, legal, and regulatory requirements for safety, security, privacy, and "auditability," it must be strictly overseen.

- *It is analyzed.* Analytics are a primary means of adding value to data, and even creating products from and monetizing it.[8] Insights are always more valuable than raw data, which is a primary theme of this book.

What Rules and Processes Are Needed to Manage the Data from Its Acquisition Through Its Retirement?

Each stage of the data management life cycle presents distinctive technical and management challenges that can have a significant impact on an organization's ability to compete on analytics.[9] Note that this is a traditional data management process; an organization seeking to create analytics "at the edge" will have to do highly abbreviated versions of these tasks.

- *Data acquisition.* Creating or acquiring data is the first step. For internal information, IT managers should work closely with business process leaders. The goals include determining what data is needed and how to best integrate IT systems with business processes to capture good data at the source.

- *Data cleansing.* Detecting and removing data that is out-of-date, incorrect, incomplete, or redundant is one of the most important, costly, and time-consuming activities in any business intelligence technology initiative. We estimate that between 25 percent and 30 percent of an analytics initiative typically goes toward initial data cleansing. IT's role is to establish methods and systems to collect, organize, process, and maintain information, but data cleansing is the responsibility of everyone who generates or uses data. Data cleansing, integration, and curation can increasingly be aided by new tools including machine learning and crowdsourcing.[10]

- *Data organization and storage.* Once data has been acquired and cleansed, processes to systematically extract, integrate, and synthesize it must be established. The data must then be put into the right repository and format so that it is ready to use (see the discussion of repositories later in the chapter). Some storage technologies require substantially more organization than others.

- *Data maintenance.* After a repository is created and populated with data, managers must decide how and when the data will be updated. They must create procedures to ensure data privacy, security, and integrity (protection from corruption or loss via human error, software virus, or hardware crash). And policies and processes must also be developed to determine when and how data that is no longer needed will be saved, archived, or retired. Some analytical competitors have estimated that they spend $500,000 in ongoing maintenance for every

$1 million spent on developing new analytics-oriented technical capabilities. We believe, however, that this cost is declining with newer technologies such as Hadoop and data lakes.

Once an organization has addressed data management issues, the next step is to determine the technologies and processes needed to capture, transform, and load data into a data warehouse, Hadoop cluster, or data lake.

Transformation Tools and Processes

Historically, for data to become usable by managers in a data warehouse, it had to first go through a process known in IT-speak as ETL, for *extract, transform, and load*. It had to be put into a relational format, which stores data in structured tables of rows and columns. Now, however, new storage technologies like Hadoop allow storage in virtually any data format. *Data lakes* may be based on Hadoop or other underlying technologies, and the concept formalizes the idea of storing data in its original format. These are particularly useful for storing data before the organization knows what it will do with it. To analyze data statistically, however, it must eventually be put in a more structured format—typically rows and columns. The task of putting data into this format, whether for a data warehouse or a statistics program, can be challenging for unstructured data.

While extracting data from its source and loading it into a repository are fairly straightforward tasks, cleaning and transforming data is a bigger issue. In order to make the data in a warehouse decision-ready, it is necessary to first clean and validate it using business rules that use data cleansing or scrubbing tools such as Trillium or Talend, which are also available from large vendors like IBM, Oracle, or SAS. For example, a simple rule might be to have a full nine-digit ZIP code for all US addresses. Transformation procedures define the business logic that maps data from its source to its destination. Both business and IT managers must expend significant effort in order to transform data into usable information. While automated tools from vendors such as Informatica Corporation, Ab Initio Software Corporation, and Ascential Software can ease this process, considerable manual effort is still required. Informatica's former CEO Sohaib Abbasi estimates that "for every dollar spent on integration technology, around seven to eight dollars is spent on labor [for manual data coding]."[11]

Transformation also entails standardizing data definitions to make certain that business concepts have consistent, comparable definitions across the organization. For example, a "customer" may be defined as a company in one system but as an individual placing an order in another. It also requires managers to decide what to do about data that is missing. Sometimes it is possible to fill in the blanks using inferred data or projections based on available data; at other times, it simply remains missing and can't be used for analysis. These mundane but critical tasks require an ongoing effort, because new issues seem to constantly arise.

Some of these standardization and integration tasks can increasingly be done by automated machine learning systems. Companies such as Tamr (where Tom is an adviser) and Trifacta work with data to identify likely overlaps and redundancies. Tamr, for example, worked with GE on the example we described earlier in this chapter to create a single version of supplier data from what was originally many different overlapping sources across business units. The project was accomplished over a few months—much faster than with traditional, labor-intensive approaches. GE is now working with the same tools on consolidating customer and product data.

For unstructured big data, transformation is typically performed using open-source tools like Pig, Hive, and Python. These tools require the substantial coding abilities of data scientists, but may be more flexible than packaged transformation solutions.

Repositories

Organizations have several options for organizing and storing their analytical data:

- *Data warehouses* are databases that contain integrated data from different sources and are regularly updated. They may contain, for example, time series (historical) data to facilitate the analysis of business performance over time. They may also contain prepackaged "data cubes" allowing easy—but limited—analysis by nonprofessional analysts. A data warehouse may be a module of an enterprise system or an independent database. Some companies also employ a staging database that is used to get data from many different sources ready for the data warehouse.

- *A data mart* can refer to a separate repository or to a partitioned section of the overall data warehouse. Data marts are generally used to support a single business function or process and usually contain some predetermined analyses so that managers can independently slice and dice some data without having statistical expertise. Some companies that did not initially see the need for a separate data warehouse created a series of independent data marts or analytical models that directly tapped into source data. One large chemical firm, for example, had sixteen data marts. This approach is rarely used today, because it results in balkanization of data and creates maintenance problems for the IT department. Data marts, then, should be used only if the designers are confident that no broader set of data will ever be needed for analysis.

- *A metadata repository* contains technical information and a data definition, including information about the source, how it is calculated, bibliographic information, and the unit of measurement. It may include information about data reliability, accuracy, and instructions on how the data should be applied. A common metadata repository used by all analytical applications is critical to ensure data consistency. Consolidating all the information needed for data cleansing into a single repository significantly reduces the time needed for maintenance.

- *Open-source distributed data frameworks* like Hadoop and Spark (both distributed by the Apache Foundation) allow storage of data in any format and typically at substantially lower cost than a traditional warehouse or mart. However, they may lack some of the security and simultaneous user controls that an enterprise warehouse employs, and they often require a higher level of technical and programming expertise to use. One company, TrueCar, Inc., stores a lot of data (several petabytes) on vehicles for sale and their attributes and pricing. In converting its storage architecture, it did a comparison of costs between Hadoop and an enterprise data warehouse. It found that its previous cost for storing a gigabyte of data (including hardware, software, and support) for a month in a data warehouse was $19. Using Hadoop, TrueCar pays 23 cents a month per gigabyte for hardware, software, and support. That two-orders-of-magnitude cost differential has been appealing to many organizations. There can be performance improvements as well with these tools, although they tend to be less dramatic than the cost differential.

- *A data lake* employs Apache Hadoop, Apache Spark, or some other technology (usually open source) to store data in its original format. The data is then structured as it is accessed in the lake and analyzed. It is a more formalized concept of the use of these open-source tools. Traditional data management vendors like Informatica, as well as startups like Podium Data, have begun to supply data lake management tools.

Once the data is organized and ready, it is time to determine the analytic technologies and applications needed.

Analytical Tools and Applications

Choosing the right software tools or applications for a given decision depends on several factors. The first task is to determine how thoroughly decision making should be embedded into business processes and operational systems. Should there be a human who reviews the data and analytics and makes a decision, or should the decision be automated and something that happens in the natural process workflow? With the rise of *cognitive computing*, or artificial intelligence, over the last decade, there are several technologies that can analyze the data, structure the workflow, reach into multiple computer systems, make decisions, take action, and even learn over time.[12] Some of these are analytical and statistics-based; others rely on previous technologies like rule engines, event-streaming technology, and process workflow support. We addressed this issue from a human perspective in chapter 7.

The next decision is whether to use a third-party application or create a custom solution. A growing number of functionally or industry-specific business applications, such as capital budgeting, mortgage pricing, and anti–money laundering models, now exist. These solutions are a big chunk of the business for analytics software companies like SAS. Enterprise systems vendors such as Oracle, SAP, and Microsoft are building more (and more sophisticated) analytical applications into their products. There is a strong economic argument for using such solutions. According to IDC, projects that implement a packaged analytical application yield a median ROI of 140 percent, while custom development using analytical tools yields a median ROI of 104 percent. The "make or buy" decision hinges on whether a packaged solution exists and whether the level of skill required exists within the organization.[13] Some other research organizations have found even greater returns from analytics applications; Nucleus Research, for example, argued in 2014 that analytics projects yielded $13.01 for every dollar spent.[14]

But there are also many powerful tools for data analysis that allow organizations to develop their own analyses (see the boxes "Analytical Technologies" and "Equifax Evolves Its Analytics Architecture"). Major players such as SAS, IBM, and SAP offer product suites consisting of integrated tools and applications, as well as many industry- or function-specific solutions. Open-source tools R and RapidMiner have been the fastest-growing analytical packages over the past several years.[15] Some tools are designed to slice and dice or to drill down to predetermined views of the data, while others are more statistically sophisticated. Some tools can accommodate a variety of data types, while others are more limited (to highly structured data or textual analysis, for example). Some tools extrapolate from historical data, while others are intended to seek out new trends or relationships. Some programming languages like Python are increasingly used for statistical analysis and allow a lot of flexibility while typically requiring more expertise and effort of the analyst.

Whether a custom solution or off-the-shelf application is used, the business IT organization must accommodate a variety of tools for

ANALYTICAL TECHNOLOGIES

Executives in organizations that are planning to become analytical competitors should be familiar with the key categories of analytical software tools:

- **Spreadsheets** such as Microsoft Excel are the most commonly used analytical tools because they are easy to use and reflect the mental models of the user. Managers and analysts use them for "the last mile" of analytics—the stage right before the data is presented in report or graphical form for decision makers. But too many users attempt to use spreadsheets for tasks for which they are ill suited, leading to errors or incorrect conclusions. Even when used properly, spreadsheets are prone to human error; more than 20 percent of spreadsheets have errors, and as many as 5 percent of all calculated cells are incorrect.[16] To minimize these failings, managers have to insist on always starting with accurate, validated data and that spreadsheet developers have the proper skills and expertise to develop models.

- **Online analytical processors** are generally known by their abbreviation, OLAP, and are used for semistructured decisions and analyses on relational data. While a *relational database* (or RDBMS)—in which data is stored in related tables—is a highly efficient way to organize data for transaction systems, it is not particularly efficient when it comes to analyzing array-based data (data that is arranged in cells like a spreadsheet), such as time series. OLAP tools are specifically designed for multidimensional, array-based problems. They organize data into "data cubes" to enable analysis across time, geography, product lines, and so on. Data cubes are simply collections of data in three variables or more that are prepackaged for reporting and analysis; they can be thought of as multidimensional spreadsheets. While spreadsheet programs like Excel have a maximum of three dimensions (down, across, and worksheet pages), OLAP models can have seven or more. As a result, they require specialized skills to develop, although they can be created by "power users" familiar with their capabilities. Unlike traditional spreadsheets, OLAP tools must deal with data proliferation, or the models quickly become unwieldy. SAP's BusinessObjects and IBM's Cognos are among the leading vendors in this category.

- **Data visualization.** OLAP tools were once the primary way to create data visualizations and reports, but a newer generation of easier-to-use tools that can operate on an entire dataset (not just a data cube) have emerged and gained substantial popularity. Tableau and QlikView are the most popular tools in this category; older vendors like Microsoft, MicroStrategy, and SAS also compete in it.

- **Statistical or quantitative algorithms** enable analytically so-phisticated managers or statisticians to analyze data. The algo-rithms process quantitative data to arrive at an optimal target such as a price or a loan amount. In the 1970s, companies such as SAS and SPSS (now part of IBM) introduced packaged com-puter applications that made statistics much more accessible. Statistical algorithms also encompass predictive modeling applications, optimization, and simulations. SAS remains the proprietary analytics software market leader; R and RapidMiner have emerged as open-source market leaders.

- **Rule engines** process a series of business rules that use condi-tional statements to address logical questions—for example, "If the applicant for a motorcycle insurance policy is male and under twenty-five, and does not either own his own home or have a graduate degree, do not issue a policy." Rules engines can be part of a larger automated application or provide recommenda-tions to users who need to make a particular type of decision. FICO, IBM's Operational Decision Manager, and Pegasystems, Inc. are some of the major providers of rule engines for businesses.

(continued)

- **Machine learning** and other cognitive technologies that can learn from data over time have superseded rule engines somewhat in popularity. These include various technologies, including machine learning, neural networks, and deep learning (the latter a more complex form of the former, with more layers of explanatory variables), natural language processing and generation, and combinations of these like IBM's Watson. They are both more complex to develop and less transparent to understand than rule-based systems, but the ability to learn from new data and improve their analytical performance over time is a powerful advantage.

- **Data mining tools** (some of which use machine learning) draw on techniques ranging from straightforward arithmetic computation to artificial intelligence, statistics, decision trees, neural networks, and Bayesian network theory. Their objective is to identify patterns in complex and ill-defined data sets. Sprint and other wireless carriers, for example, use neural analytical technology to predict which customers are likely to switch wireless carriers and take their existing phone numbers with them. SAS and IBM offer both data and text mining capabilities and are major vendors in both categories; R and Rapid-Miner offer open-source alternatives.

- **Text mining** tools can help managers quickly identify emerging trends in near-real time. Spiders, or *data crawlers*, which identify and count words and phrases on websites, are a simple example of text mining. Text mining tools can be invaluable in sniffing out new trends or relationships. For example, by monitoring technical-user blogs, a vendor can recognize that a new product has a defect within hours of being shipped instead of waiting for complaints to arrive from customers. Other text mining products can recognize references to people, places, things, or topics and use this information to draw inferences about competitor behavior.

- **Text categorization** is the process of using statistical models or rules to rate a document's relevance to a certain topic. For example, text categorization can be used to dynamically evaluate competitors' product assortments on their websites.

- **Natural language processing tools** go beyond text mining and categorization to make sense of language and even answer human questions; they may employ semantic analysis, statistical analysis, or some combination of the two. *Natural language generation* creates text for contexts such as sports reporting, business earnings reports, and investment reports in financial services.

- **Event streaming** isn't, strictly speaking, an analytical technology, but it is increasingly being combined with analytics to support real-time smart processes. The idea is to analyze data as it comes in—typically from voluminous and fast-flowing applications like the Internet of Things. The goal isn't normally to perform advanced analytics on the data, but rather to "curate" it—which may involve filtering, combining, transforming, or redirecting it. This approach has also been employed for a decade or longer in fast-moving data in the financial services industry.

- **Simulation tools** model business processes with a set of symbolic, mathematical, scientific, engineering, and financial functions. Much as computer-aided design (CAD) systems are used by engineers to model the design of a new product, simulation tools are used in engineering, R&D, and a surprising number of other applications. For example, simulations can be used as a training device to help users understand the implications of a change to a business process. They can also be used to help streamline the flow of information or products—for example, they can help employees of health care organizations decide where to send donated organs according to criteria ranging from blood type to geographic limitations.

(continued)

- **Web or digital analytics** is a category of analytical tools specifically for managing and analyzing online and e-commerce data. The bulk of web analytics are descriptive—telling managers of websites how many unique visitors came to a site, how long they spent on it, what percentage of visits led to conversions, and so forth. Some web analytics tools allow *A/B testing*—statistical comparisons of which version of a website gets more clicks or conversions. Web analytics has largely been a world unto itself in the organizational analytics landscape, but is slowly being integrated into the larger group of quantitative analysts.[17] Another related category of analytical tools is focused on *social media analytics*—not only counting social activities, but also assessing the positive or negative sentiment associated with them.

different types of data analysis (see the box "Analytical Technologies" for current and emerging analytical tools). Employees naturally tend to prefer familiar products, such as a spreadsheet, even if it is ill suited for the analysis to be done.

Another problem is that without an overall architecture to guide tool selection, excessive technological proliferation can result. In a 2015 survey, respondents from large organizations reported that their marketing organizations averaged more than twelve analytics and data management tools for data-driven marketing.[18] And there are presumably many other tools being used by other business functions within these firms. Even well-managed analytical competitors often have a large number of software tools. In the past, this was probably necessary, because different vendors had different capabilities—one might focus on financial reporting, another on ad hoc query, and yet another on statistical analysis. While there is still variation among vendors, the leading providers have begun to offer business intelligence suites with stronger, more integrated capabilities.

There is also the question of whether to build and host the analytical application onsite or use an "analytics as a service" application in the cloud. As with other types of IT, the answer is increasingly the latter. Leading software vendors are embracing this trend by disaggregating their analytics tools into "micro-analytics services" that perform a particular analytical technique. SAS executives, for example, report that a growing way to access the vendor's algorithms and statistical techniques is through open application program interfaces, or APIs. This makes it possible to combine analytics with other types of transactional and data management services in an integrated application.

Data Visualization

Since an analysis is only valuable if it is acted on, analytic competitors must empower their people to impart their insights to others through business intelligence software suites, data visualization tools, scorecards, and portals. Business intelligence software allows users to create ad hoc reports, interactively visualize complex data, be alerted to exceptions through a variety of communication tools (such as email, texts, or pagers), and collaboratively share data. (Vendors such as SAP, IBM, SAS, Microsoft, and Oracle sell product suites that include data visualization, business intelligence, and reporting solutions.) Commercially purchased analytical applications usually have an interface to be used by information workers, managers, and analysts. But for proprietary analyses, these tools determine how different classes of individuals can use the data. For example, a statistician could directly access a statistical model, but most managers would hesitate to do so.

The current generation of visual analytical tools from vendors such as Tableau and Qlik and from traditional analytics providers such as SAS—allow the manipulation of data and analyses through an intuitive visual interface. A manager, for example, could look at a plot of data, exclude outlier values, and compute a regression line that fits the data—all without any statistical skills.

Because they permit exploration of the data without the risk of accidentally modifying the underlying model, visual analytics tools significantly increase the population of users who can employ sophisticated analyses. Over the past several years they have made "analytics for the masses" much more of a reality than a slogan. At Vertex

EQUIFAX EVOLVES ITS ANALYTICS ARCHITECTURE

In 2010 Tom consulted at Equifax, a leading provider of consumer credit and financial information, on an assessment of the company's analytical capabilities. The company's then and current CEO, Rick Smith, an advocate of competing on analytics, wasn't sure the needed capabilities were present in the firm. The assessment found that a key barrier to success for Equifax was that analytics activities took too long to complete due to organizational and data-related issues. The company had the SAS statistical package, but the absence of an enterprise data warehouse made it difficult to assemble different types of data in the necessary time frame. There were pockets of strong analytical capability, but the company didn't address analytics as an enterprise resource. The assessment also recommended the creation of a chief analytics officer role.

Now, seven years later, the climate and capability for analytics have changed dramatically. Prasanna Dhore is the company's chief data and analytics officer (he participated in our 2006 "Competing on Analytics" study at a different company). Peter Maynard, who arrived at Equifax from Capital One (another early analytical competitor) is the SVP of Global Analytics. He told us that both the technology and the speed with which analytics are conducted have undergone major change under Prasanna's leadership and Equifax's infrastructure investment.

A big component of the change is the shift to a Hadoop-based data lake, which allows Equifax to store and assemble multiple types of data with ease and at low cost. The company leverages the SAS High-Performance Analytics platform to get maximum value out of the data that resides in Hadoop.

Maynard notes that this in-memory architecture has dramatically accelerated the speed of analytics at Equifax:

> We have moved from building a model using a month of consumer credit data to two years' worth, and we are always analyzing the trended data across time. We have a neural network model that looks at all the data and identifies trends in the consumer's credit history. Whenever we introduce new data and variables into the model, we need to determine how they affect the trend. It used to take about a month to evaluate a new data source, but now it's just a few days because of our much faster analytics environment.

Maynard said that the neural network model was developed using SAS's Enterprise Miner offering. It's a complex model, because it requires a set of "reason codes" that help explain specific credit decisions to consumers.

The Equifax analytics technology architecture also makes room for open-source tools like R and Python. Recent graduates in their data science group like them, Maynard notes, but he says that Equifax has a lot of existing SAS models and code, and many of its data scientists and quantitative analysts are comfortable with it. Maynard is also considering moving to SAS streaming analytics for even more speed and to employ SAS Model Risk Management for ongoing assessment and governance of models.

Maynard and his colleagues regularly attend SAS events and visit the company's headquarters in Cary, North Carolina, for briefings and discussions. Equifax's analytical leaders have made major changes in their approaches to analytics, and they are satisfied that SAS's offerings are changing along with them.

Pharmaceuticals, for example, longtime CIO Steve Schmidt (now a medical device analytics entrepreneur) estimated several years ago that only 5 percent of his users could make effective use of algorithmic tools, but another 15 percent could manipulate visual analytics. Our guess is that the percentage of potential visual analytics users has increased dramatically with the availability of these new tools.

Deployment Processes

This element of the analytics architecture answers questions about how the organization creates, manages, implements, and maintains data and applications. Great algorithms are of little value unless they are deployed effectively. Deployment processes may also focus on how a standard set of approved tools and technologies are used to ensure the reliability, scalability, and security of the IT environment. Standards, policies, and processes must also be defined and enforced across the entire organization. There may be times when a particular function or business unit will need its own analytics technology, but in general it's a sign of analytical maturity for the technology to be centrally managed and coordinated. Some firms are beginning to use structured "platforms" to manage deployment process. One firm, FICO, has a deployment platform and discusses the deployment issue as managing "the analytics supply chain."[19]

Latter-stage deployment issues such as privacy and security as well as the ability to archive and audit the data are of critical importance to ensure the integrity of the data and analytical applications. This is a business as well as a technical concern, because lapses in privacy and security (for example, if customer credit card data is stolen or breached) can have dire consequences. One consequence of evolving regulatory and legal requirements is that executives can be found criminally negligent if they fail to establish procedures to document and demonstrate the validity of data used for business decisions.

Conclusion

For most organizations, an enterprise-wide approach to managing data and analytics will be a major departure from current practice; it's often been viewed as a "renegade" activity. But centralized analytical roles—a chief data and analytics officer, for example—and some degree of central coordination are signs of a company having its analytics act together. Top management can help the IT architecture team plan a robust technical environment by helping to establish guiding principles for analytical architecture. Those principles can help to ensure that architectural decisions are aligned with business strategy, corporate culture, and management style.[20] To make that happen, senior management must be committed to the process. Working with IT, senior managers must establish and rigorously enforce comprehensive data management policies, including data standards and consistency in data definitions. They must be committed to the creation and use of high-quality data—both big and small—that is scalable, integrated, well documented, consistent, and standards-based. And they must emphasize that the analytics architecture should be flexible and able to adapt to changing business needs and objectives. A rigid architecture won't serve the needs of the business in a fast-changing environment. Given how much the world of analytics technology has changed in the last decade, it's likely that the domain won't be static over the next one.

CHAPTER NINE

THE FUTURE OF ANALYTICAL COMPETITION

APPROACHES DRIVEN BY TECHNOLOGY, HUMAN FACTORS, AND BUSINESS STRATEGY

THROUGHOUT THIS BOOK, WE HAVE LARGELY DESCRIBED the present state of analytical competition. In many cases, the analytical competitors we have identified are ahead of their industries in sophistication and progressive practices and are hence bellwethers leading their peers into the future. In this concluding chapter, we speculate broadly on what analytical competitors of the future will be doing differently.

As William Gibson once noted, the future is already here but unevenly distributed. We've already observed leading companies beginning to adopt the approaches described later in this chapter, and we believe they'll simply become more common and more refined. Like most prognosticators of the future, we predict more of what we are writing about: more companies choosing to compete on analytics as their distinctive capability, more companies learning from these analytical competitors to become more analytical themselves, and analytical firms employing analytics in more parts of their businesses. In other cases, we don't know of anybody using a particular practice yet, but logic and trends would dictate that the approach will be employed before long.

We hesitate to be pinned down as to when these elements of the future will transpire, but we estimate that five years is the approximate horizon for when many of these ideas will come to fruition. It's possible that things could accelerate at a faster rate than we predict if the world continues to discover analytical competition. For the first thirty or so years of the history of analytics and decision support, actual advances have been relatively slow. But over the past decade, we've seen them accelerate dramatically, as the introduction to this book describes.

We divide the analytical world of the future into three categories: approaches driven by technology, those involving human capabilities, and those involving changes in business strategy. Technology probably changes the most quickly of these three domains and often forces changes in the other areas.

Technology-Driven Changes

A series of technological capabilities are already used on a small scale within organizations, and we expect they will only expand in the near future. These extrapolations of existing practice include:

- *Pervasive data.* Arguably the biggest change in analytics over the past decade—and probably the next as well—is the availability of massive quantities of data. The internet and social media applications are already streaming massive quantities of it—more than 25 terabytes of data streamed by fans at the 2017 Super Bowl, for example. Internet of Things sensors (one estimate suggests 8.4 billion of them will be in use in 2017) in cars, factories, hospitals, and many other settings will provide much more data. At an individual level, smartphones, activity trackers, and other personal devices both generate and receive massive amounts of data.

  We will of course need analytics to make sense of all this data, and at the moment we are only scratching the surface of how pervasive data and analytics can change our work and our lives. Pervasive data is changing the technologies we use to analyze it and the locations for the analysis; more analytics are being performed at the edge. Pervasive data also implies a strong need for better tools—including the machine learning tools we described in chapter 8—for "curating" (cleaning, integrating, matching, and so forth) data. And data is also playing a more important role in creating and improving models (see the next trend); that's really what machine learning is all about.

- *More autonomous analytics and decision making,* as opposed to relying on humans to look at data and make decisions. The resource that's already most in short supply with analytics is the human attention to look at them, interpret them, and make decisions on the basis of them. Cognitive technologies, AI, machine learning, deep learning—all of these will increase the ability of smart machines to do automated analysis, make automated decisions, and take automated actions. Machine learning already helps many organizations to dramatically increase the productivity of human analysts by creating thousands of models in the time previously required for one. Quantitative analysts and data scientists' jobs aren't threatened yet, but they do need to learn how to work with these new tools. At the moment, machine-created models can be difficult to interpret, but in the future we may see machines that can not only find the best-fitting model for data, but also make sense of it for humans who want an explanation.

- *The democratization of analytics software.* The ability to analyze and report on data is already very common from a software standpoint. Vendors such as Microsoft embed analytical capabilities in business versions (particularly Office 365, the cloud version) of Microsoft Office, even including web analytics and personal productivity analytics. Many traditional applications systems, such as Salesforce.com for sales, marketing, service, and e-commerce applications, include various forms of analytics and even artificial intelligence capabilities. Smaller companies that can't afford expensive analytics software packages have available free or inexpensive open-source tools such as R and RapidMiner. And plenty of big, rich companies are using these free tools as well. At one point, the most advanced analytical capabilities were expensive, but the pace of development for open-source software is such that they are now more likely to be free. Of course, lower costs for software are sometimes canceled out by higher costs of people capable of using it—the data scientists who are expert at open-source tools may be more expensive than traditional quantitative analysts with proprietary software skills.

- *Increasing use of in-memory processing* for analytics that can dramatically speed the response and calculation time for typical analyses. Instead of storing the data and algorithms on disk, they're loaded into the computer's memory. These are available from vendors like SAP (Hana), SAS, Tableau, Qlik, and several more. In the future, we may see even greater speed from in-chip analytics. We're already also seeing edge analytics in which some analytics and decision making are performed by small, smart devices at the edge of a network.

- *Increasing use of real-time (or at least "right-time") analytics.* It has historically taken some time—from days to weeks—for firms to extract data from transaction systems, load it into analytical applications, and make sense of it through analysis. Increasingly, however, managers need to make more rapid decisions, and firms are attempting to implement analytics in real time for at least some decisions. Of course, some real-time systems make use of autonomous decision making in order to take humans out of the loop altogether. The granddaddy of real-time applications with human users is UPS's ORION, the project we've mentioned throughout this book, to provide routing to UPS drivers. Before they started to use this application, UPS drivers drove the same route every day. Today, they get a new route every morning that optimizes their deliveries and pickups based on the packages and requests that came in last night. Tomorrow (or at least within the next few years), their routes will change in real time based on such factors as traffic, weather, and new requests from customers for package pickups.

Most organizations should adopt a *right-time* approach, in which the decision time frame for a class of decisions is determined within an organization, and the necessary data and analytical processes are put in place to deliver it by that time. In an *InformationWeek* survey, 59 percent of the IT executive respondents said they were trying to support real-time business information.[1] But research that Tom did with SAP suggests that many managers care about real-time information much more in some areas than others.[2] Companies shouldn't waste their efforts on delivering real-time information when there isn't a need.

- *Going beyond alerts to preserve management attention.* Alerts have been a useful strategy for organizations seeking to preserve management attention. They say, "Look at this number— you said you wanted to hear about it if it went this high!" More organizations are beginning to make use of automated alerts to notify managers when key indicators are at undesirable levels. Intel, for example, uses alerts to let supply chain commodity managers know when they should act on purchasing and pricing data.[3] The concern with alerts, however, is that too many of them will lead to "alert fatigue" on the part of the alerted individuals. Of course, if a system can take an automated action, that prevents humans from needing to be in the loop at all.

- *More explanatory analytics,* as opposed to numbers and programming languages. This trend has been taking place for a while, simply because many managers prefer to see and digest analytics in visual formats. Of course, different people have different learning styles. Those who prefer verbal narratives can increasingly have a visual analytic converted into a story that summarizes the result. The new trend will be for software to deliver the best format for you as an individual, your data, and your decision or question. Let's hope that all these developments mean the end of the pie chart, which visual analytics experts have noted for years is rarely a useful format.

- *More prediction and prescription* (and less reporting). It's obviously more useful to predict what's going to happen than to
  explain what's already happened. Prediction, however, generally requires more sophisticated analysis and data than reporting or explanation. Prescriptive analytics require enough
  context about the task and the situation to make an informed
  recommendation. Despite these challenges, predictive and prescriptive analytics are extending into more and more business
  domains—from predicting the behavior of customers to telling
  them what to buy; from predicting disease to recommending
  treatment strategies. In a discussion with Salesforce.com users,
  for example, Tom heard many of them say that they wanted to
  move beyond descriptive analytics. One commented, "We don't
  have time for people to look at bar charts and figure out what to
  do." They prefer the idea (which Salesforce and other companies
  have begun to implement) of "smart data discovery" in which
  smart tools identify trends and anomalies in data—with no
  need for a human hypothesis—and point out their implications
  to users. Before long, managers may simply be able to converse
  with their automated assistants, who will be able to help interpret their financial reports, point out the weaknesses in their
  demand planning forecast, and predict that inventory is likely
  to run out two quarters from now. In addition to rapid data discovery, another benefit of this approach is that it's less subject
  to biased human interpretation than traditional descriptive
  and predictive analytics. If a machine is finding patterns in
  data, it's somewhat more difficult to "torture the data until it
  confesses."

- *More mining of text, speech, images, and other less structured
  forms of data.* The mining or detailed analysis of structured
  data is by now quite advanced, but the mining of text, speech,
  images, and even video are clearly in their early stages and are
  likely to expand considerably over the next few years. Technological capabilities to categorize and discern meaning in the
  lab are already better than humans in many cases, but they
  have yet to penetrate many business applications. Consumer

applications, such as Apple's Siri and Amazon's Echo/Alexa, are further along, and businesses are beginning to employ them within products and applications. Deep learning algorithms based on neural networks are able to learn how to categorize and make decisions on unstructured data—at least when given enough data to learn from. The availability of labeled training data—for example, the 14 million ImageNet images, or the 8 million labeled YouTube videos, will dramatically improve the performance of these algorithms over the next several years.

- *Model management finally comes of age.* The other major advance lies at the opposite end of the analytical process and involves the capture of models, learning, and insights from analytical and experimental results. In cultures with a broad-scale analytical or experimental orientation, there are likely to be many models created by many people, each with its own assumptions, variables, and results. Experiments have designs, test and control groups, and results. How do you keep track of such models and experiments without a repository? The answer, of course, is that you can't. Capital One, one of the earliest firms to embrace experimental design for business, had a repository of findings from its many experiments, but it was extremely unwieldy for users to search through and learn from. What the company decided to do, then, was to take a just-in-time approach to providing experimental knowledge to its analysts. The company built a system to guide the analyst through the process of designing a new credit card offering for a specified class of customers. It uses knowledge from the company's experiments to make suggestions at each stage of the design process about what options might work best. It might suggest everything from the optimal interest rate for balance transfers to the best color for the envelope to be used in the direct mail offer to the customer.

  Such systems for maintaining information about models are called *model management* systems, and they are currently widely used only in financial institutions (Capital One was an early adopter of these too). They are used in that industry primarily because regulators insist on them. However, as analytics become an enterprise resource—the source of competitive advantage and considerable value—we expect to see more model management tools employed, even when they aren't imposed by regulators. They will provide not only backup when a quantitative analyst leaves the firm, but also can prevent the need for new analyses when a similar one has already been performed elsewhere in an organization.

Human-Driven Changes

While humans don't change as rapidly as information technologies, there are changes in analytical competition that will be driven by the capabilities and configurations of analytical people within organizations. We expect, first of all, that the growth of analytical competition will lead to a need for substantially greater numbers of analytically oriented people—some number of analytical professionals and data scientists, and a much larger group of analytical amateurs, as we have called them. If many more decisions are to be made based on detailed analysis, many more people will have to have some understanding of how those analyses were performed and when they should be overridden. In short, analytics, and the use of them in decisions and actions, will be increasingly extended to the frontline analytical amateurs within organizations.

From where will these professional and frontline analysts come? Some of these, we believe, will come from business schools and other parts of universities, which have always offered some courses in statistics and data analysis. Over the last five years, literally hundreds of universities have added degree programs, certificates, and courses in analytics and data science. We expect that perceptive schools and their students will focus even more on analytical training in the future. The most advanced data scientists, who come from more diverse backgrounds like computer science and physics PhD programs, will continue to be sourced from relatively nonconventional academic sources. As yet, there are very few PhD programs in data science.

Corporations may also need to offer internal programs to educate their people on various forms of analytics and data science. Cisco Systems, for example, created a distance education program on data science for interested and qualified employees, partnering with two universities. The program lasts nine months and concludes with a certificate in data science from the university. More than two hundred data scientists have been trained and certified, and are now based in a variety of different functions and business units at Cisco. Cisco also created a two-day executive program led by business school professors on what analytics and data science are and how they are typically applied to business problems. The program also covers how to manage a workforce that includes data scientists, and how to know whether their products are any good.

Of course, not all workers will need to be involved in all analytical activities. It is likely that analytical professionals will have to become expert not only in quantitative analysis but also in job and process design for frontline analysts. They may also have to design information environments for frontline workers that provide just enough analytics and information for them to perform their jobs effectively. As one analyst (who refers to the concept as "pervasive business intelligence") put it, "It's the ability to take relevant information that is usually reported up to management and push it down to users. At the various organizational levels, the data is presented so that people see only what is most relevant to their day-to-day tasks . . . with expectations and performance clearly identified."[4]

We also expect substantially increased use of outsourced and off-shore analytical resources. Some of that has already emerged in the form of "math factories" like Mu Sigma in India. We noted in chapter 7 that it's difficult to establish the close, trusting relationships between analysts and executives that are necessary for widespread analytical decision making. However, there are certainly analytical tasks that can be accomplished without close interactions with executives. Back-office development and refinement of algorithms, cleaning and integration of data, and the design of small-scale experiments can often be done remotely. Substantial numbers of analytically trained workers in India, Russia, and China will undoubtedly be doing more analytical work in the future. Offshore companies in the outsourcing business are beginning to specialize in such services. However, if an analytical task can be outsourced, there is a growing likelihood that it can be automated with tools like machine learning. This may reduce the growth of analytics outsourcing over time.

We also anticipate that increasing numbers of firms will develop strong analytical capabilities within their IT organizations. We've already described Gartner surveys from 2006 to 2016 finding that business intelligence or analytics was the number-one technology priority of corporations.[5] As we have also pointed out in previous chapters, "better management decision making" is the number-one objective of large companies that have installed enterprise resource planning systems. With these priorities and objectives, it's only natural that CIOs and other IT executives will want to increase the IT function's ability to support analytics. This means that they'll be hiring quantitative analysts, specialists in analytics software, and IT professionals with expertise in data warehouses and marts. Some, like Procter & Gamble, will make this capability a primary focus of the in-house IT function, while outsourcing less critical capabilities to external suppliers. The business functions that IT supports—logistics and supply chain management, marketing, and even HR—will also be hiring analytical experts with a strong IT orientation. It will become increasingly difficult to distinguish analytical people in IT from those in the rest of the business. If you're trying to decide on a technical specialization, analytics are a good bet.

With the rise of analytical people across the entire organization, we can expect a greater need for structure and guidance in the management of their activities—either provided by humans or by the technology itself. As we've noted earlier, there will be no shortage of analytical tools, whether they're spreadsheets, visual analytical systems, machine learning, or some other form of software. However, if corporate strategies depend on the results of analytics, they have to be done with accuracy and professionalism.

How will companies provide greater structure and human capability for strategically important analyses? There will be no single method but rather a variety of tools and approaches. One way is to have the software guide the analysis process—letting a human analyst know what assumptions about the data are being made, what statistical analysis approach to employ, or what visual display to best summarize the data. Analytical software applications can guide an analyst through a decision process, either making the decision itself (perhaps with a human override option) or ensuring that a human decision maker has all needed information. Another answer would be substantial education. We believe that most organizations would benefit from education to create more capable analysts and improve the skills of existing ones. A third would be a group of "coaches" to help amateur analysts and certify their work as well done. For analytical work that substantially affects financial performance, internal and external auditors may need to get involved. There is no doubt that audits are becoming increasingly analytical.[6] Whatever the means, companies will need to both build analytical capability in their employees and ensure that they're doing a good job. As we've already described, some leading companies are beginning to employ these approaches for building human analytical capability through some sort of centralized analytics hub.

This attention to human capabilities won't stop at the analysis stage. Many organizations will begin to automate decisions and actions, which will have a considerable impact on the humans that previously performed those tasks. Tom and coauthor Julia Kirby have already written a book on how humans can add value to smart machines, so we won't go into detail on that topic here.[7] But determining the relationships between humans and machines, and how human work and business processes need to be modified to take advantage of machine intelligence, is clearly going to be an important topic in the near and distant future.

Strategy-Driven Changes

We anticipate that a number of changes in the analytical environment will be driven by business strategies. As more firms become aware of the possibilities for analytical competition, they will push the boundaries of analytics in their products, services, and business models. Virtually every provider of data and information services, for example, will probably offer analytics to its customers as a value-added service. Data itself has become something of a commodity, and customers for data often can't find the time or people to analyze it themselves. Software, once primarily focused on business transactions, increasingly includes analytics.

We also expect to see more analytics embedded in or augmenting products and services—describing, for example, the optimum way to make use of those offerings within the customer's business processes. The golf club sensor we described in chapter 3 that tells you how well you are swinging your club is a good example. We are already seeing automobiles (or at least insurance companies) that tell you how safely you are driving, health care and fitness trackers that analyze how healthily you are eating and living, and industrial machinery that tells you how well you are using it. Even industrial companies like GE and Monsanto are now selling products or services that tell their customers how to use their offerings more effectively. Of course, we may tire of all this advice, but it is potentially very useful.

This trend will be only a part of a broader one involving supplying analytics to customers and suppliers. We've already mentioned some firms, such as Walmart, that furnish analytical information to their customers or channel partners. There are others we haven't mentioned that are beginning to do this to some degree. Marriott shares analytical information with both channel partners—online and traditional travel agencies, for example—and major corporate customers. Channel partners get analyses involving pricing, joint promotions, and inventory; customers receive data and analysis that helps them with their own travel management. We expect that most firms will begin to view the internal audience for analytics as only one of several potential recipients, and that relationships with suppliers and customers will increasingly include the provision of analytics.

Another strategic trend involves the content of analytics. Thus far, most quantitative analyses are about internal business entities: inventory units, dollars, customers, and so forth. Most organizations realize, however, that internal information, no matter how well it's analyzed, gives a limited window on the world. Peter Drucker commented in 1998 that management has a tendency to "focus inward on costs and efforts, rather than outward on opportunities, changes, and threats."[8] Drucker said that outside information didn't exist then, but it does now. Data and analytics are increasingly available on what customers and non-customers are saying about our company, on trends and concerns in our industries, and on economic and sociopolitical movements that could affect our futures. Any firm that wishes to control—or at least react quickly to—outside forces must be applying analytics to this external information.

Thus far external information, when accessed at all, has not been put into a structure for easy, ongoing access. And it has been the subject of descriptive analytics at best—very little predictive or prescriptive analytics, at least outside of financial services. But such structured information systems—they might be called *situational awareness systems*, as they are in the military and intelligence communities—are beginning to be found in organizations. Several cities (e.g., Chicago's WindyGrid) and police forces (the NYPD's Domain Awareness System [DAS] is the best one we've seen) are using them. Deloitte has created one (actually, multiple tailored versions) for its senior executives, and it builds them for clients too. Recorded Future, a company Tom advises, scans and analyzes internet text to better understand what people are saying and doing around the world, particularly with regard to intelligence and cybersecurity. Many companies are using similar approaches to understand customer perceptions about products and brands.

Finally, we expect that strategic concerns will also drive firms to pay substantial attention to new metrics and their interrelationships in analyses and scorecards. We heard from a number of analytical competitors that they start with metrics in thinking about applying analysis to a distinctive capability. They either invent a new metric from their own proprietary data or refine an existing one. As metrics become commonplace (e.g., as we have discussed, the FICO score in consumer credit or the batting average in baseball), companies and organizations go beyond them to new measurement frontiers. We anticipate particularly high levels of activity in the domain of human resources and talent management, since these have been relatively unmeasured in the past. Once developed, of course, metrics must be incorporated into established scorecards and measurement processes, and the relationships between different measures must be explored and understood. Most importantly, these metrics must be incorporated into business and management decision-making processes. Just developing a measure, and just using it in some analyses, is never enough.

The Future of Analytical Competition

We'll end this book by discussing broadly what will happen to analytical competitors in the future. This will serve as both a summary of the key attributes of analytical competitors and a prediction of the future, because analytical competitors will continue to do more of what made them successful in the first place.

Analytical competitors will continue to examine their strategies and their business capabilities to understand where they can get an analytical edge. That's more and more important as more companies jump into analytics, at least at a surface level. But the best companies will focus on what makes their organizations distinctive and how analytics can support or drive a distinctive capability. After they address the most distinctive areas, analytics will eventually be applied to most other parts of their businesses—their motto will be, "If it's worth doing, it's worth doing analytically." These companies will identify measures of the distinctive capability that other organizations don't yet employ. After they identify a measure, they'll collect data on it and embed decisions based on the measures into their daily work processes.

Take Google, for example. The company is perhaps the most analytical firm on the planet today. But the presence of other analytical companies in its markets hasn't made it retreat at all. Instead, it's doubled down on such capabilities as artificial intelligence software, proprietary mapping data, analyzing the data from its autonomous vehicles, analyzing YouTube videos, and so forth. It started with its PageRank algorithm and then advertising algorithms, but has since moved on to being the leader in analytics for human resources, attribution of digital ads, venture capital, and many others. And not surprisingly, the company continues to perform extremely well.

In order to continue refining their analytical capabilities, companies will focus on both their human and technological dimensions. On the human side, they'll try to further embed an analytical orientation into the culture and to test as many hypotheses as they can. A 2017 survey of executives in fifty large companies by NewVantage Partners on big data suggests that while companies have found big data efforts successful and financially rewarding, the creation of a data-driven culture has been problematic.[9] Of those who responded, 86 percent said their companies have tried to create a data-driven culture, but only 37 percent said they've been successful at it.

The best analytical competitors will keep trying to achieve that type of culture, however. Their executives will argue for analytical strategies and decisions with passion and personal example. Their managers will constantly press subordinates for data or analytics before they take major actions. Employees at every level will use data and analytics to make decisions and take actions. And data and analytics will be employed to seek out truth, not to advance some executive's private objectives.

The managers of analytical competitors of the future will not be narrow "quant jocks." They'll always be thinking broadly about whether their analytical models and data are still relevant to their businesses. They'll constantly be reexamining the assumptions behind their analytical models. If a particular type of analysis becomes commoditized throughout their industries, they'll find some new basis for analytical competition. They'll use intuition sparingly but strategically when it isn't possible to test an assertion or gather data for an analysis. They'll be able to be more experimental and innovative. They'll advocate for new methods and new technologies like machine learning and cognitive technologies. They'll be looking for how they can employ these intelligent machines for new business strategies and models, and how to extract more productivity from every activity.

As a result of their efforts, they'll undoubtedly be hotly pursued by other firms that also want to be analytical competitors. If their employers are smart, these analytical heat-seeking missiles will find their jobs stimulating and satisfying and will stay put as long as they're recognized and promoted.

There will continue to be people in these organizations whose job primarily involves developing and refining analytics—analytical professionals and data scientists. They will either work in a central group or be highly networked, and they'll share approaches and ideas. They will also work to educate and partner with the analytical amateurs of the organizations, who need to understand how analytical models and tools support them in their jobs. The analytical competitor of the future will also supplement internal analytical resources with outsourced or offshore expertise. And these firms won't be shy about thinking of ways that machines themselves can do the difficult, time-consuming work of analytics. They'll focus particularly on how to automate the really labor-intensive part of analytics: preparing the data for analysis.

Analytical competitors will continue to have lots of data that is generated from enterprise systems, point-of-sale systems, and web transactions, as well as external data of various types from customers and suppliers. They'll organize it and put it aside for analysis in warehouses and Hadoop-based data lakes. They will ensure that data is integrated and common in the areas of their business where it really matters. They'll have integrated analytics suites or platforms that support reporting and analytics—both proprietary and open source. In domains where decisions must be made very rapidly or very often, they'll embed analysis into automated decision systems, allowing human overrides only under specified conditions.

Perhaps most importantly, analytical competitors will continue to find ways to outperform their competitors. They'll get the best customers and charge them exactly the price that the customer is willing to pay for their product and service. They'll have the most efficient and effective marketing campaigns and promotions. Their customer service will excel, and their customers will be loyal in return. Their supply chains will be ultra-efficient, and they'll have neither excess inventory nor stock-outs. They will embed data and analytics into new innovative products. They'll have the best people in the industry, and the employees will be evaluated and compensated based on their specific contributions. They'll understand both their internal and their external business environments, and they'll be able to predict, identify, and diagnose problems before they become too problematic. They will make a lot of money, win a lot of games, or help solve the world's most pressing problems. They will continue to lead us into the future.

NOTES

Introduction

1. Thomas H. Davenport and D. J. Patil, "Data Scientist: The Sexiest Job of the 21st Century," *Harvard Business Review*, October 2012, https://hbr.org/2012/10/datascientist-the-sexiest-job-of-the-21st-century.

2. NewVantage Partners, *Big Data Executive Survey 2017: Executive Summary of Findings*, http://newvantage.com/wp-content/uploads/2017/01/Big-Data-Executive-Survey-2017-Executive-Summary.pdf.

3. Thomas H. Davenport, Jeanne G. Harris, David W. Delong, and Alvin L. Jacobson, "Data to Knowledge to Results: Building an Analytic Capability," *California Management Review* 43, no. 2 (Winter 2001): 117–138; Thomas H. Davenport, "Competing on Analytics," *Harvard Business Review*, January 2006; Thomas H. Davenport, "Analyze This," *CIO*, October 1, 2005, http://www.cio.com/archive/100105/comp_advantage.html; and Thomas H. Davenport and Jeanne G. Harris, "Automated Decision Making Comes of Age," *MIT Sloan Management Review* (Summer 2005).

Chapter One

1. Netflix quotation from Jena McGregor, "At Netflix, the Secret Sauce Is Software," *Fast Company*, October 2005, 50. Other Netflix information comes from the company website (http://www.netflix.com); Mark Hall, "Web Analytics Get Real," *Computerworld*, April 1, 2002; Timothy J. Mullaney, "Netflix: The Mail-Order Movie House That Clobbered Blockbuster," *BusinessWeek Online*, May 25, 2006, http://www.businessweek.com/smallbiz/content/may2006/sb20060525_268860.htm?campaign_id=search; and a telephone interview with chief product officer Neil Hunt on July 7, 2006.

2. The "long tail" concept has been popularized by Chris Anderson in *The Long Tail: Why the Future of Business Is Selling Less of More* (New York: Hyperion, 2006).

3. Neil Hunt, interview with Tom Davenport, July 7, 2006.

4. Timothy J. Mullaney, "Netflix," *Bloomberg*, May 25, 2006, https://www.bloomberg.com/news/articles/2006-05-24/netflix.

5. We define *distinctive capabilities* as the integrated business processes and capabilities that together serve customers in ways that are differentiated from competitors and that create an organization's formula for business success.

6. David Darlington, "The Chemistry of a 90+ Wine," *New York Times Sunday Magazine*, August 7, 2005.

7. One of the first books written on the subject of decision support was by Peter G. W. Keen and Michael S. Scott Morton, *Decision Support Systems: An Organizational Perspective* (Reading, MA: Addison-Wesley, 1978). A subsequent book written on the topic is by John W. Rockart and David W. De Long, *Executive Support Systems: The Emergence of Top Management Computer Use* (Homewood, IL: Dow Jones-Irwin, 1988). Also note Tom Gerrity Jr.'s 1971 article, "The Design of Man-Machine Decision Systems: An Application to Portfolio Management," *MIT Sloan Management Review* 12, no. 2 (1971): 59–75; and Charles Stabell's 1974 work, "On the Development of Decision Support Systems on a Marketing Problem," *Information Processing*, as formative research in the field of DSS.

8. Rockart and De Long, *Executive Support Systems*.

9. Peter J. Denning, "The Science of Computing: Saving All the Bits," *American Scientist* 78, no. 5 (September–October 1990): 402–405, http://den ninginstitute.com/pjd/PUBS/AmSci-1990-5-savingbits.pdf.

10. Timothy King, "Gartner: BI & Analytics Top Priority for CIOs in 2016" (orig. posted March 11, 2016, in *Best Practices*), *Business Intelligence Solutions Review*, http://solutionsreview.com/business-intelligence /gartner-bi-analytics-top-priority-for-cios-in-2016/.

11. For example, refer to Jeffrey Pfeffer and Robert Sutton's article "Evidence-Based Management," *Harvard Business Review*, January 2006; and Eric Bonabeau's article "Don't Trust Your Gut," *Harvard Business Review*, May 2003.

12. Malcolm Gladwell, *Blink: The Power of Thinking Without Thinking* (New York: Little, Brown, 2005).

13. Gary Klein, *Sources of Power: How People Make Decisions* (Cambridge, MA: MIT Press, 1999).

14. Alan Deutschman, "Inside the Mind of Jeff Bezos," *Fast Company*, August 2004, 52.

15. Sujeet Indap, "IBM Bets on Mergers and Algorithms for Growth," *Financial Times*, January 12, 2016, https://www.ft.com/content /11010eea-ae5f-11e5-993b-c425a3d2b65a.

16. Seth Fiegerman, "Amazon Opens a Grocery Store with No Checkout Line," *Money*, December 5, 2016, http://money.cnn.com/2016/12/05/technology /amazon-go-store/.

17. Michael Lewis, *Moneyball: The Art of Winning an Unfair Game* (New York: W. W. Norton & Company, 2004).

18. Alan Schwartz, *The Numbers Game: Baseball's Lifelong Fascination with Statistics* (New York: St. Martin's Griffin, 2005).

19. Ben Lindbergh and Rob Arthur, "Statheads Are the Best Free Agent Bargains in Baseball," *fivethirtyeight*, April 26, 2016, https://fivethirtyeight .com/features/statheads-are-the-best-free-agent-bargains-in-baseball/.

20. For those not familiar with the Curse of the Billy Goat: https://en.wiki pedia.org/wiki/Curse_of_the_Billy_Goat.

21. "Cubs Brass Finalizes 'The Cubs' Way' Guide," *MLB.com*, February 18, 2012, http://m.mlb.com/news/article/26749684/.

22. Andy Wasynczuk, then chief operating officer, New England Patriots, telephone interview with Tom Davenport, January 11, 2005.

23. From "Interview with Packers Director of Research and Development Mike Eayrs," *Football Outsiders*, June 22, 2004, http://www.football-outsid ers.com/ramblings.php?p=226&cat=8.

24. Chris Ballard, "Measure of Success," *Sports Illustrated*, October 24, 2005.

25. Graham Ruthven, "When the Nerds Take Over," *Sports on Earth* (blog), December 13, 2013, http://www.sportsonearth.com/article/64603094.

26. Uta Spinger, "World Cup in Brazil: Cheat Sheets Make Way for Apps," SAP.com, June 17, 2014, http://news.sap.com/world-cup-brazil -cheat-sheets-make-way-apps/.

27. "The Great Analytics Rankings," ESPN.com, http://www.espn.com /espn/feature/story/_/id/12331388/the-great-analytics-rankings.

Chapter Two

1. David Alles and John Burshek, "Ranking Analytics Maturity by In- dustry," International Institute for Analytics report, June 2016, http://iiana lytics.com/analytics-resources/ranking-analytics-maturity-by-industry.

2. Professor Mark Oleson of the University of Missouri, quoted in Pat Curry, "The Future of FICO," Bankrate.com, November 1, 2005, http://www .bankrate.com/smrtpg/news/debt/debtcreditguide/fico-future1.asp.

3. Rajiv Lal and Patricia Matrone Carrolo, "Harrah's Entertainment, Inc.," Case 9-502-011 (Boston: Harvard Business School, 2002), 6.

4. Data from a BetterManagement survey and described in Gloria J. Miller, Dagmar Brautigam, and Stefanie V. Gerlach, *Business Intelligence Competency Centers: A Team Approach to Maximizing Competitive Advantage* (Hoboken, NJ: Wiley, 2006).

5. For more information on spreadsheet errors, see Raymond Panko's article, "What We Know About Spreadsheet Errors," *Journal of End User Computing* 10, no. 2 (Spring 1998): 15–21.

6. "Gartner Estimates That 90 Percent of Large Organizations Will Have a Chief Data Officer by 2019," press release, January 26, 2016, http://www .gartner.com/newsroom/id/3190117.

7. A. Charles Thomas, LinkedIn profile, https://www.linkedin.com/in /acharlesthomas, accessed April 20, 2017.

8. Christopher H. Paige, "Capital One Financial Corporation," Case 9-700-124 (Boston: Harvard Business School, 2001).

9. Victoria Chang and Jeffrey Pfeffer, "Gary Loveman and Harrah's En- tertainment," Case OB45 (Stanford, CA: Stanford Graduate School of Busi- ness, November 2003), 7.

10. Keith Coulter, managing director, U.K. cards and loans, Barclay, tele- phone interview with Tom Davenport, October 11, 2005.

11. ORION example taken from several interviews with Tom Davenport and Jeanne Harris in 2014 through 2016 with project leader Jack Levis and other UPS executives; some of the example is described in Thomas H. Davenport, "Prescriptive Analytics Project Delivering Big Benefits at UPS," *DataInformed*, April 19, 2016, http://data-informed.com/prescriptive -analytics-project-delivering-big-dividends-at-ups/.

12. Barry C. Smith, Dirk P. Gunther, B. Venkateshwara Rao, and Richard M. Ratliff, "E-Commerce and Operations Research in Airline Planning, Marketing, and Distribution," *Interfaces*, March–April 2001, 37–55.

13. Tallys H. Yunes, Dominic Napolitano, et al., "Building Efficient Product Portfolios at John Deere," working paper, Carnegie Mellon University, Pittsburgh, PA, April 2004.

14. Gary H. Anthes, "Modeling Magic," *Computerworld*, February 7, 2005.

15. Gary Loveman, CEO of Harrah's, from presentations and interviews with Tom Davenport, January 2005–June 2006.

16. The American Medical Informatics Association defines *informatics* as "data, information, and knowledge to improve human health and the delivery of health care services." See https://www.amia.org/sites/default/files/files_2 /What-is-Informatics-Fact-sheet-04-08-11.pdf.

Chapter Three

1. Ben Clarke, "Why These Tech Companies Keep Running Thousands of Failed Experiments," *Fast Company*, September 21, 2016, https://www .fastcompany.com /3063846/why-these-tech-companies-keep-running -thousands-of-failed.

2. Ibid.

3. Susan Nunziata, "Capital One: Think Like a Designer, Work Like a Startup," *InformationWeek*, May 2, 2016, http://www.informationweek.com /strategic-cio/capital-one-think-like-a-designer-work-like-a-startup/d/d-id /1325353?_mc=RSS_IWK_EDT&page_number=2.

4. Joanne Kelley, "Risky Business," *Context*, July–August 1999.

5. See http://www.progressive.com.

6. Clarke, "Why These Tech Companies Keep Running Thousands of Failed Experiments." Clarke quotes Jeff Bezos from Peter Diamandis, "Culture & Experimentation—with Uber's Chief Product Office," *Abundance Insights*, April 10, 2016, https://medium.com/abundance-insights/culture-experimentation-with-uber-s-chief-product-officer-520dc22cfcb4#.i9bh5xdie; and Jeffrey H. Dyer, Hal B. Gregersen, and Clayton M. Christensen, *The Innovator's DNA* (Boston: Harvard Business Review Press, 2011), 136.

7. Jim Collins, *Good to Great: Why Some Companies Make the Leap . . . and Others Don't* (New York: HarperCollins, 2001), 69.

8. Henry Morris, Stephen Graham, Per Andersen, Karen Moser, Robert Blumstein, Dan Velssel, Nathaniel Martinez, and Marilyn Carr, *The Financial Impact of Business Analytics: Distribution of Results by ROI Category*, IDC #28689 (Framingham, MA: International Data Corporation, January 2003).

9. Henry Morris, *Predictive Analytics and ROI: Lessons from IDC's Financial Impact Study*, IDC #30080 (Framingham, MA: International Data Corporation, September 2003).

10. "Analytics Pays Back $13.01 for Every Dollar Spent," Nucleus Research, September 2014, http://nucleusresearch.com/research/single/analytics-pays -back-13-01-for-every-dollar-spent/.

11. Rasmus Wegener and Velu Sinha, "The Value of Big Data: How Analytics Differentiates Winners," Bain Brief, September 17, 2013, http://www .bain.com/publications/articles/the-value-of-big-data.aspx.

12. Kendall's tau_b - coefficient: .194, error: .107 (one-tailed test); Spearman's rho - coefficient: .272, error: .094 (one-tailed test). The small sample size of publicly reporting firms (N=20) explains the relatively low significance levels.

13. For this study, we defined an *enterprise system* as an integrated software package (from vendors such as SAP and Oracle) that addresses most of an organization's day-to-day transactional data processing needs.

14. For more details, see Jeanne G. Harris and Thomas H. Davenport, *New Growth from Enterprise Systems* (Wellesley, MA: Accenture Institute for High Performance Business, May 2006).

15. Thomas H. Davenport, Jeanne G. Harris, and Susan Cantrell, *The Return of Enterprise Solutions: The Director's Cut* (Wellesley, MA: Accenture Institute for High Performance Business, 2002).

16. Using Pearson's product-moment coefficient of correlation, profit has a significant positive correlation with analytical orientation at r=.136 (p=.011), revenue growth is significantly correlated at r=.124 (p=.020), and shareholder return is correlated at r=.122 (p=.022).

17. For the purposes of this study, top and low performers were defined by asking respondents to assess their standing—on a scale of 1 to 5— in the industry relative to profit, shareholder return, and revenue growth. Top performers scored 14 or higher (out of a possible 15 points); 13 percent of the sample scored at this level. Low performers scored 8 or fewer points and represented 16 percent of the sample. We found these scores to be highly correlated with publicly reported business performance. We excluded government respondents because government agencies could not be evaluated using these criteria.

18. Steve LaValle, Eric Lesser, Rebecca Shockley, Michael S. Hopkins and Nina Kruschwitz, "Big Data, Analytics and the Path from Insights to Value," *MIT Sloan Management Review*, Winter 2011, http://sloanreview.mit.edu /article/big-data-analytics-and-the-path-from-insights-to-value/.

19. Accenture and MIT, *Winning with Analytics* (Executive Summary), 2015. https://www.accenture.com/t20170219T213328__w__/us-en/_acnmedia /Accenture/next-gen/hp-analytics/pdf/Accenture-Linking-Analytics-to-High -Performance-Executive-Summary.pdf#zoom=50.

20. Michael Lewis in a speech at Accenture, San Francisco, June 16, 2006.

21. CompStat is described in detail on Wikipedia—see http://en.wikipedia .org/wiki/CompStat. Steven Levitt has questioned the crime reductions due to CompStat in "Understanding Why Crime Fell in the 1990s: Four Factors That Explain the Decline and Six That Do Not," *Journal of Economic Perspectives* 18, no. 1 (Winter 2004): 163–190.

22. Thomas H. Davenport, "How Big Data Is Helping the NYPD Solve Crimes Faster," *Fortune*, July 17, 2016, http://fortune.com/2016/07/17 /big-data-nypd-situational-awareness/.

23. "Recent examples of crime reduction," predpol.com/results/, accessed April 21, 2017.

24. "LAPD Using Big Data to Fight Crime," *Dataconomy*, April 24, 2014, http://dataconomy.com/2014/04/lapd-using-big-data-fight-crime-2/.

25. Cindy Blanthorne and Kristen Selvey Yance, "The Tax Gap: Measuring the IRS's Bottom Line," *CPA Journal Online* (New York State Society of CPAs), April 2006,

26. Catherine Arnst, "The Best Medical Care in the U.S.," *BusinessWeek*, July 17, 2006, 51.

27. "Smart Nation Big on Big Data," Infocomm Media Development Authority website, https://www.imda.gov.sg/infocomm-and-media-news/buzz-central/2016/6/smart-nation-big-on-big-data, accessed April 21, 2017.

28. Duncan Cleary, "Using Analytics to predict fraud," SAS website, https://www.sas.com/sv_se/customers/irish-tax-and-customers.html, accessed April 21, 2017.

29. For examples of analytics use by police, see PredPol website: http://www.predpol.com/in-the-press/.

30. Stephen Russo, "Improved Crisis Preparedness with Smarter Emergency Response Planning," IBM Big Data & Analytics Hub blog, April 28, 2015, http://www.ibmbigdatahub.com/blog/improved-crisis-preparedness-smarter-emergency-response-planning.

31. Marco Iansiti and Karim Lakhani, "Data Ubiquity: How Connections, Sensors and Data Are Revolutionizing Business," *Harvard Business Review*, November 2014, https://hbr.org/2014/11/digital-ubiquity-how-connections-sensors-and-data-are-revolutionizing-business.

32. Julianne Pepitone, "What Your Wireless Carrier Knows About You," *CNN Money*, December 16, 2013, http://money.cnn.com/2013/12/16/technology/mobile/wireless-carrier-sell-data/.

33. Nathan Vardi, "The Quants Are Taking Over Wall Street," *Forbes*, August 17, 2016, http://www.forbes.com/sites/nathanvardi/2016/08/17/the-quants-are-taking-over-wall-street/.

34. Doug Henschen, "Catalina Marketing Aims for the Cutting Edge of 'Big Data,'" *Informationweek*, September 6, 2011, http://www.informationweek.com/big-data/big-data-analytics/catalina-marketing-aims-for-the-cutting-edge-of-big-data/d/d-id/1099971.

35. See http://www.catalinamarketing.com.

36. Sunil Garga, president of IRI's Analytical Insights group, telephone interview with Jeanne Harris, October 2, 2006.

Chapter Four

1. Abhishek Menon and Anupam Jain, *Overcoming Challenges in Data Integration, Stakeholder Collaboration, and Talent/Technology Investment to Operationalize Analytics in Pharma and Life Science*, 2014, http://www.genpact.com/docs/default-source/resource-/analytics-in-pharma-and-life-sciences.

2. Jerry Z. Shan et al., "Dynamic Modeling and Forecasting on Enterprise Revenue with Derived Granularities," Hewlett-Packard Laboratories, May 2005, http://www.hpl.hp.com/techreports/2005/HPL-2005-90.pdf.

3. Ibid., 6.

4. David Larcker and Chris Ittner, "Coming Up Short on Nonfinancial Measurement," *Harvard Business Review*, November 2003.

5. Mark Leon, "Ad Game Analytics," *Intelligent Enterprise*, January 21, 2005.

6. John Ballow, Robert Thomas, and Goran Roos, "Future Value: The $7 Trillion Challenge," *Accenture Outlook*, no. 1, 2004, http://www.accenture.com/xd/xd.asp?it=enweb&xd=ideas\outlook\1_2004\manage.xml.

7. For example, see Peter D. Easton, Travis S. Harris, and James A. Ohlson, "Aggregate Accounting Returns Can Explain Most of Security Returns," *Journal of Accounting and Economics* (1992); Gary C. Biddle, Robert M. Bowen, and James S. Wallace, "Does EVA(c) Beat Earnings? Evidence

on Associations with Stock Returns and Firm Values," *Journal of Accounting and Economics* (1997); and Stephen O'Byrne, "EVA and Its Critics," *Journal of Applied Corporate Finance* (1997).

8. The Microsoft example comes from Jennifer Warnick, "88 Acres: How Microsoft Quietly Built the City of the Future," Microsoft News Center, https://www.microsoft.com/en-us/stories/88acres/.

9. Coalition Against Insurance Fraud, "By the Numbers: Fraud Statistics," http://www.insurancefraud.org/statistics.htm, accessed April 21, 2017.

10. William Dibble, Infinity Property & Casualty Builds a Smarter System for Fraud, *InformationWeek Insurance and Technology*, November 30, 2011, http://www.insurancetech.com/infinity-property-and-casualty-builds-a-smarter-system-for-fraud/a/d-id/1313275?.

11. Ibid.

12. Symantec Corporation, "2016 Internet Security Threat Report," vol. 21, April 2016, https://www.symantec.com/security-center/threat-report, accessed April 21, 2017.

13. "Detecting Attacks before They Happen: Advanced Technologies for Better Cyber Attack Defense, FICO white paper, http://www.fico.com/en/latest-thinking/white-papers/detecting-attacks-before-they-happen.

14. Tom Davenport, "The Future of Cybersecurity," LinkedIn, November 4, 2016, https://www.linkedin.com/pulse/future-cybersecurity-tom-davenport.

15. "Deloitte M&A Focus On: Analytics Survey Findings," February 25, 2016, http://www.slideshare.net/DeloitteUS/deloitte-ma-focus-on-analytics-survey-findings.

16. Sujeet Indap, "IBM Bets on Mergers and Acquisitions for Growth," January 12, 2016 , https://www.ft.com/content/11010eea-ae5f-11e5-993b-c425a3d2b65a.

17. "NX CAD Technology Drives Custom Surfboard Design," Siemens case study, https://www.plm.automation.siemens.com/en_us/about_us/success/case_study.cfm?Component=123472.

18. Bill Brougher, interview with Tom Davenport, July 18, 2006.

19. International Institute for Analytics, "The Excellence in Analytics Award—'The Anny,'" http://www.iianalytics.com/analytics-resources/the-excellence-in-analytics-award, accessed April 21, 2017.

20. Shigeru Komatsu of Toshiba Semiconductor, interview with Tom Davenport, April 10, 2006.

21. "Toshiba Taps AI to Boost Productivity at Memory Plant *Nikkei Asian Review*, June 29, 2016. http://asia.nikkei.com/Spotlight/Toshiba-in-Turmoil/Toshiba-taps-AI-to-boost-productivity-at-memory-plant.

22. Rod Doerr, Union Pacific Railroad, 2016 Grain Safety and Quality Conference, Omaha, NE, August 3, 2016, https://www.youtube.com/watch?v=sJDNa-AWzJY, minute 16:35.

23. ORION example taken from several interviews in 2015 and 2016 with project leader Jack Levis and other UPS executives; some of the example is described in Thomas H. Davenport, "Prescriptive Analytics Project Delivering Big Benefits at UPS," DataInformed website, April 19, 2016, http://data-informed.com/prescriptive-analytics-project-delivering-big-dividends-at-ups/.

24. A factorial (represented in mathematical equations as an exclamation point) is calculated as the product of an integer (n) and every integer below it: $n! = n\,(n-1)(n-2)(n-3)\ldots$ In this case, $120! = 120*119*118\ldots*1$.

25. IIA––International Institute for Analytics, "CATERPILLAR 3000K," YouTube video, September 28, 2016, https://www.youtube.com /watch?v=JeS5SPyvHmA.

26. "13 Innovations Highlighted in Oberhelman's Remarks at the 2015 Annual Stockholders Meeting," press release, June 10, 2015, http://www .caterpillar.com/en/news/caterpillarNews/innovation/13-innovations -highlighted-in-oberhelmans-remarks-at-the-2015-annual-stockholders -meeting.html.

27. Barry Werth, *The Billion Dollar Molecule: One Company's Quest for the Perfect Drug* (New York: Simon & Schuster, 1995), 135.

28. Steven Schmidt of Vertex Pharmaceuticals, interview with Tom Davenport, April 5, 2006.

29. Alex Bangs, "Predictive Biosimulation and Virtual Patients in Pharmaceutical R&D," in *Medicine Meets Virtual Reality 13: The Magical Next Becomes the Medical Now*, eds. James D. Westwood et al., vol. 111, Studies in Health Technology and Informatics (Amsterdam, Netherlands: IOS Press, 2005), 41.

30. Information about American Healthways obtained from a presentation by Dr. Carter Coberly at the Health Information Technology Summit, Washington, DC, 2004, http://www.ehcca.com/presentations/cahealthit2/2_03_1.pdf.

31. Bill Belichick, "Quotes from New England Patriots Media Day," February 1, 2005, cited in James Lavin, *Management Secrets of the New England Patriots*, vol. 2 (Stamford, CT: Pointer Press, 2005), 159.

32. "The Right Profile Helps Super Bowl Champion New England Patriots Identify and Develop Mentally Tough Athletes," PRWeb, February 8, 2017, http://www.prweb.com/releases/therightprofile/athletetypes/prweb14053056.htm.

33. Quotation from Michelle Thompson, Asia Pacific vice president for HR at American Express, in "Mastering HR Analytics with Technology," *Human Resources (Australia),* March 27, 2006.

34. Kim S. Nash, "How Analytics Helped eBay Tackle Worker Retention," *Wall Street Journal,* February 3, 2017, http://blogs.wsj.com/cio/2017/02/03/ how-analytics-helped-ebay-tackle-worker-retention/?mod=WSJBlog.

35. Dr. John Sullivan, "Revealing the 'HR Professional of the Decade': Laszlo Bock of Google," ERE case study, March 30, 2015, https://www.eremedia.com/ere/revealing-the-hr-professional-of-the-decade-laszlo-bock-of-google/.

36. Thomas H. Davenport, Jeanne G. Harris, and Jeremy Shapiro, "Competing on Talent Analytics," *Harvard Business Review,* October 2010, http://hbr.org/2010/10/competing-on-talent-analytics/ar/1.

37. Joanne Kelly, "Getting All the Credit," *Context Magazine,* http:// www.contextmag.com/setFrameRedirect.asp?src=/archives/200202 /Feature2GettingalltheCredit.asp.

38. Owain Thomas, "What Has Walmart Learned from HR Analytics?" *HRD Connect,* April 27, 2016, https://www.hrdconnect.com/2016/04/27 /what-walmart-learned-from-hr-analytics/.

Chapter Five

1. In our survey of about four hundred organizations with enterprise systems, there was a relationship between analytics and supply chain integration. The correlation (Pearson product-moment correlation, one-tailed test) between strong analytical orientation and integration with suppliers was .23.

2. Tony Kontzer, "Big Bet on Customer Loyalty," *InformationWeek*, February 9, 2004.

3. American Customer Satisfaction Index, University of Michigan, 2005, fourth-quarter rankings, updated February 21, 2006, http://www.theacsi.org/fourth_quarter.htm.

4. Aaron O. Patrick, "Econometrics Buzzes Ad World as a Way of Measuring Results," *Wall Street Journal*, August 16, 2005.

5. Jim Ericson, "Coming to Account," *Business Intelligence Review*, April 2005.

6. The Target pregnancy marketing story was first reported by Charles Duhigg, "How Companies Learn Your Secrets," *New York Times*, February 16, 2012, http://www.nytimes.com/2012/02/19/magazine/shopping-habits.html.

7. Clive Humby and Terry Hunt, *Scoring Points: How Tesco Is Winning Customer Loyalty* (Philadelphia: Kogan Page, Ltd., 2003).

8. Yankee Group research report from 2005, quoted in Gary Anthes, "The Price Point," *Computerworld*, July 24, 2006, 34.

9. Gary Loveman, "Foreword," in Thomas H. Davenport and Jeanne G. Harris, *Competing on Analytics*, 1st edition (Boston: Harvard Business Review Press, 2007).

10. The MyMagic+ system has been described in interviews with Disney executives and these articles: Brooks Barnes, "At Disney Parks, A Bracelet Meant to Build Loyalty (and Sales)," *New York Times*, January 7, 2013, http://www.nytimes.com/2013/01/07/business/media/at-disney-parks-a-bracelet-meant-to-build-loyalty-and-sales.html; Brooks Barnes, "A Billion-Dollar Bracelet Is the Key to a Disney Park," *New York Times*, April 1, 2014, https://www.nytimes.com/2014/04/02/business/billion-dollar-bracelet-is-key-to-magical-kingdom.html; Austin Carr, "The Messy Business of Reinventing Happiness," *Fast Company*, April 15, 2015, https://www.fastcompany.com/3044283/the-messy-business-of-reinventing-happiness.

11. Information about HMH comes from interviews with company executives and a presentation by Zachary Monroe at the Oracle Cloud Marketing User Group, Chicago, May 19, 2016.

12. "Which Customers Are Worth Keeping and Which Ones Aren't? Managerial Uses of CLV," *Knowledge@Wharton*, July 30, 2003, http://www.whartonsp.com/articles/article.asp?p=328189&rl=1.

13. Peggy Anne Salz, "High Performance—Intelligent Use of Information Is a Powerful Corporate Tool," *Wall Street Journal*, April 27, 2006.

14. Adam Bloom, "20 Examples of ROI and Results with Big Data," Pivotal website, May 26, 2015, https://content.pivotal.io/blog/20-examples-of-roi-and-results-with-big-data.

15. Information about Skillsoft comes from http://www.skillsoft.com/about/press_room/press_releases/april_02_14_ibm.asp, accessed April 21, 2017; and Bloom. "20 Examples of ROI and Results with Big Data."

16. Pankaj Ghemawat, Stephen P. Bradley, and Ken Mark, "Wal-Mart Stores in 2003," Case 9-704-430 (Boston: Harvard Business School, September 2003).

17. Figures on Walmart are from a presentation given by chief information officer Linda Dillman, quoted by Dan Briody in *BizBytes*, April 2006.

18. "Software Development Engineer—Global Supply Chain Optimization," Amazon Fulfillment Services, https://www.amazon.jobs/en/jobs/384389, accessed February 14, 2017.

19. Spencer Soper, "Amazon Is Building Global Delivery Business to Take On Alibaba," Bloomberg Technology, February 9, 2016, https://www .bloomberg.com/news/articles/2016-02-09/amazon-is-building-global-delivery -business-to-take-on-alibaba-ikfhpyes.

20. Len Kennedy, vice president of UPS, in "What Can Brown Do for You?" *Location Intelligence*, December 5, 2002.

21. Taken from 1954 UPS annual report.

22. Beth Bacheldor, "Breakthrough," *InformationWeek*, February 9, 2004, http://www.informationweek.com/industries/showArticle.jhtml?articleID =17602194&pgno=1&queryText=.

23. Norbert Turek, "FedEx and UPS Lead the Logistics Pack," *InformationWeek*, January 11, 2001.

24. Richard Tomkins, "The Art of Keeping Customers Happy," *Financial Times* (London), June 17, 2005.

25. Alejandro Ruelas-Gossi and Donald Sull, "The Art of Innovating on a Shoestring," *Financial Times* (London), September 24, 2004.

Chapter Six

1. For more on effective decision-making processes, see Jeanne G. Harris, *The Insight-to-Action Loop: Transforming Information into Business Performance* (Wellesley, MA: Accenture Institute for High Performance Business, February 2005), http://www.accenture.com/Global/Research_and_Insights/ Institute_For_High_Performance_Business/By_Publication_Type/Research_ Notes/InsightToPractice.htm; and Glover Ferguson, Sanjay Mathur, and Baiju Singh, "Evolving from Information to Insight," *MIT Sloan Management Review* 46, no. 2 (2005): 51–58.

2. Vivienne Jupp and Elisabeth Astall, "Technology in Government: Riding the Waves of Change," Accenture Government Executive Series report, 2002, http://www.ebusinessforum.gr/content/downloads/gove_waves.pdf.

3. Elpida Ormanidou, telephone interview with Jeanne Harris, April 29, 2015.

4. The "Monty Hall problem" demonstrates the power of a single data point. Hall was the original host of the TV game show *Let's Make a Deal*. A contestant is offered one of three different doors. Only one has a valuable prize and the other two have a "zonk." Once the contestant chooses a door, Hall reveals a "zonk" behind one of the remaining doors. He then gives the contestant a choice. She can stay her original selection or switch. Statistics demonstrate that by switching doors the contestant doubles her odds of winning from 33 percent to 66 percent.

5. Thomas H. Davenport, Jeanne G. Harris, and Bob Morison, *Analytics at Work: Smarter Decisions, Better Results* (Boston: Harvard Business Review Press, 2010).

6. Mark Twain attributes this quote to Disraeli; see Charles Neider, ed., *The Autobiography of Mark Twain* (New York: HarperCollins, 2000), 195.

7. For more on this topic, see Darrell Huff, *How to Lie with Statistics* (New York: W. W. Norton & Company, 1954).

8. For more on preventing statistical abuse, see "The Use and Misuse of Statistics," *Harvard Management Update* 11, no. 3 (March 2006).

Chapter Seven

1. Thomas H. Davenport, Jeanne G. Harris, David W. De Long, and Alvin L. Jacobson, "Data to Knowledge to Results: Building an Analytic Capability," *California Management Review* 43, no. 2, 117–138.

2. For more on evidence-based management, see Jeffrey Pfeffer and Robert I. Sutton, *Hard Facts, Dangerous Half-Truths, and Total Nonsense: Profiting from Evidence-Based Management* (Boston: Harvard Business School Press, 2006).

3. Interview of William Perez by Michael Barbaro, "A Not-so-Nice Nike Divorce Came Down to Data vs. Feel," *The New York Times*, January 28, 2006, National edition, B4.

4. Tom Davenport, "Data Is Worthless If You Don't Communicate It," *Harvard Business Review*, June 2013, https://hbr.org/2013/06/data-is-worthless -if-you-don't.

5. Donald A. Marchand, William J. Kettinger, and John D. Rollins, *Information Orientation: The Link to Business Performance* (New York: Oxford University Press, 2002).

6. Tom McCall, "Understanding the Chief Data Officer Role," *Smarter with Gartner*, February 18, 2015, http://www.gartner.com/smarterwithgartner /understanding-the-chief-data-officer-role/.

7. Jeanne G. Harris and Vijay Mehrotra. "Getting Value from Your Data Scientists" *MIT Sloan Management Review* 56, no. 1 (Fall 2014).

8. Thomas H. Davenport and D. J. Patil, "Data Scientist: The Sexiest Job of the 21st Century," *Harvard Business Review*, October 2012, https://hbr .org/2012/10/data-scientist-the-sexiest-job-of-the-21st-century.

9. Hal Varian, email correspondence with Tom Davenport, December 6, 2005.

10. Bob Deangelis, telephone interview with Tom Davenport, February 8, 2005.

11. Head of an analytical group at a consumer products firm who wished to remain anonymous, telephone interview with Tom Davenport, May 24, 2005.

12. Tyson Hartman, "Is Big Data Producing Big Returns?" Avanade Insights, June 5, 2012, http://blog.avanade.com/avanade-insights/data -analytics/is-big-data-producing-big-returns/.

13. Anders Reinhardt, telephone interview with Jeanne Harris, September 2012. Originally published in Jeanne Harris, "Data Is Useless Without the Skills to Analyze It, *Harvard Business Review*, September 13, 2012, https://hbr.org/2012/09/data-is-useless-without-the-skills.

14. The three core skills needed for analytical managers is adapted research originally published in Harris, "Data Is Useless Without the Skills to Analyze It."

15. Reinhardt telephone interview with Jeanne Harris.

16. For more on this topic, see Thomas H. Davenport and Jeanne G. Harris, "Automated Decision Making Comes of Age," *MIT Sloan Management Review* (Summer 2005): 83–89.

17. For a description of business rules technology, see Barbara von Halle, *Business Rules Applied: Building Better Systems Using the Business Rule Approach* (New York: Wiley, 2001).

Chapter Eight

1. Julie Gallagher, "Business-Savvy CIO Turns Tech-Savvy CEO," *FinanceTech*, May 31, 2001, http://www.financetech.com/showArticle.jhtml? articleID=14706275.

2. Erick Schonfeld, "The Great Giveaway," Business 2.0, CNNMoney.com, April 1, 2005, http://money.cnn.com/magazines/business2/business2_ archive/2005/04/01/8256058/.

3. M. McDonald and M. Blosch, *Gartner's 2006 EXP CIO Survey* (Stamford, CT: Gartner, Inc., January 2006).

4. Marcia Stepanek, "Q&A with Progressive's Peter Lewis," *Business-Week*, September 12, 2000.

5. Charles Babcock, "Data, Data Everywhere," *InformationWeek*, January 9, 2006.

6. International Data Corporation, *Business Analytics Implementation Challenges: Top Ten Considerations for 2003 and Beyond*, IDC Report 28728 (Framingham, MA: International Data Corporation, January 2003).

7. Nicole Haggerty and Darren Meister, "Business Intelligence Strategy at Canadian Tire," Case 903E19 (London, Ontario: Ivey School of Business 2003).

8. Thomas H. Davenport and Stephan Kudyba, "Designing and Developing Analytics-Based Data Products," *MIT Sloan Management Review* (Fall 2016), http://sloanreview.mit.edu/article/designing-and-developing -analytics-based-data-products/.

9. Donald Marchand, William Kettinger, and John Rollins, *Making the Invisible Visible: How Companies Win with the Right Information, People and IT* (New York: Wiley, 2001).

10. Michael Stonebraker, "The Solution: Data Curation at Scale," in *Getting Data Right: Tackling the Challenges of Big Data Volume and Variety* (O'Reilly Publications, 2015), http://www.oreilly.com/data/free/getting-data -right.csp.

11. Madan Sheina, "Refocused: Back to the Future," *Computer Business Review*, September 2005.

12. Thomas H. Davenport and Julia Kirby, "Just How Smart Are Smart Machines?" *MIT Sloan Management Review* (Spring 2016), http://sloanreview .mit.edu/article/just-how-smart-are-smart-machines/.

13. Henry Morris et al., *The Financial Impact of Business Analytics: Distribution of Results by ROI Category*, IDC #28689 (Framingham, MA: International Data Corporation, January 2003).

14. Nucleus Research, "Analytics Pays Back $13.01 for Every Dollar Spent," Research Report 0204, September 2014, http://nucleusresearch.com /research/single/analytics-pays-back-13-01-for-every-dollar-spent/.

15. Gregory Piatetsky, "R Leads Rapid Miner, Python Catches Up, Spark Ignites," *KDNuggets*, May 27, 2015, http://www.kdnuggets.com/2015/05/poll -r-rapidminer-python-big-data-spark.html.

16. For more information on spreadsheet errors, see Raymond Panko's paper "What We Know About Spreadsheet Errors," January 2005, http:// panko.cba.hawaii.edu/ssr/Mypapers/whatknow.htm.

17. See, for example, Judah Phillips, *Building a Digital Analytics Organization* (Upper Saddle River, NJ: Pearson FT Press, 2013).

18. Jamie Oetting, "Too Many Tools? New Data on the Complexity of Marketing Technology," Hubspot blog post, February 17, 2015, https://blog.hubspot.com/agency/tools-data-complexity-marketing-technology#sm.001eqysc218dxdwmqld2nqeau3z8n.

19. Thomas H. Davenport and Zahir Balaporia, "The Analytics Supply Chain," *DataInformed*, February 20, 2017, http://data-informed.com/the-analytics-supply-chain/.

20. The principles-based approach to IT architecture is described in Thomas H. Davenport, Michael Hammer, and Tauno Metsisto, "How Executives Can Shape Their Company's Information Systems," *Harvard Business Review*, March–April 1989, 130–134.

Chapter Nine

1. Data from Outlook 2006 Survey, *InformationWeek*, January 2, 2006.

2. Thomas H. Davenport and Jim Hagemann Snabe, "How Fast and Flexible Do You Want Your Information, Really?" *MIT Sloan Management Review* (Spring 2011), http://sloanreview.mit.edu/article/how-fast-and-flexible-do-you-want-your-information-really/.

3. Charles P. Seeley and Thomas H. Davenport, "Integrating Business Intelligence and Knowledge Management at Intel," *Knowledge Management Review* 8, no. 6 (January–February 2006): 10–15.

4. Dave Mittereder, "Pervasive Business Intelligence: Enhancing Key Performance Indicators," *DM Review*, April 2005, http://www.dmreview.com/article_sub.cfm?articleID=1023894.

5. M. McDonald and M. Blosch, *Gartner's 2006 EXP CIO Survey* (Stamford, CT: Gartner, Inc., January 2006).

6. Thomas H. Davenport, "Innovation in Audit Takes the Analytics, AI Route," Deloitte University Press online essay, February 24, 2016, https://dupress.deloitte.com/dup-us-en/focus/cognitive-technologies/audit-analytics-artificial-intelligence.html.

7. Thomas H. Davenport and Julia Kirby, *Only Humans Need Apply: Winners and Losers in the Age of Smart Machines* (New York: Harper Business, 2016).

8. Peter Drucker, "The Next Information Revolution," *Forbes ASAP*, August 24, 1998.

9. NewVantage Partners, *Big Data Executive Survey 2017: Executive Summary of Findings*, http://newvantage.com/wp-content/uploads/2017/01/Big-Data-Executive-Survey-2017-Executive-Summary.pdf.

INDEX

Abbasi, Sohaib, 234
Ab Initio Software Corporation, 233
A/B testing, 242
Accenture, 77, 78, 85, 208
AC Milan, 42
ACNielsen, 131
action, designing decision making
    for, 163
activity-based costing (ABC), 92
actuarial and risk management
    103–105
AdSense, 136–137
advertising, digital, 133, 136–137
AIG, 202
airlines, 59, 78, 88–89
Alderson, Sandy, 37–38
alerts, 253
Alexander, Rob, 70–71
algorithmic trading, 85
Amazon
    analytical decision making at,
        33–34
    analytical leadership at, 193–194
    analytics-based competition at,
        24–25
    Analytics Maturity Assessment
        of, 47
    Echo/Alexa, 255
    experiments at, 73
    pricing optimization at, 141
    senior management commitment
        at, 55, 56
    supply chain management at,
        149–151
ambition, 58–61
Ambrose, John, 147
American Airlines, 59, 78, 88
American Express, 103, 123–124
analysts
    amateur, 208–216, 259

in culture wars, 174–175
data access for, 225–226
data scientists, 5, 6, 13
data scientists vs. quantitative, 5,
    204–205
in DELTA model, 17, 46–47, 178,
    179–180
DELTA model on, 47
future of, 256–259
managing, 200–208, 258–259
organization of, 202–203
outsourcing, 86, 208
quantitative, 5, 13–14
software as replacement for,
    187–190
analytical capabilities
    assessing, 160–163
    choosing a path for, 164–165
    DELTA model on, 177–181
    key elements in, 161
    managing for outcomes and,
        181–185
    maturity model on, 61
    road map to, 36, 157–186
    urban legends about, 187–190
analytical companies, 63–64,
    174, 176
    executives' roles in, 194–199
analytical competition, 21–44
    advantages of, 27–30
    analytical companies in, 174–176
    analytical decision making in,
        33–36
    aspirations to, 170–174
    assessing the degree of, 61–67
    choosing strategic focus, 161–162
    data and IT capabilities in,
        220–221
    definition of, 26
    differentiation via, 27–28

analytical competition (*continued*)
  in every industry, 25, 29–30
  four pillars of, 60
  full-steam-ahead vs. prove-it path
    to, 164–170
  future of, 249–264
  human element in, 36, 43–44
  the leading edge in, 36
  at Netflix, 21–24
  origins of, 30–33
  prerequisites to, 159–165
  progress toward, 176–186
  prove-it detour toward, 165–170
  road map for, 36, 157–186
  senior executives and, 190–200
  in sports, 37–43
  stages of, 61–67
analytical competitors, 176
  definition of, 45
  enterprise-level approach by, 51–54
  external processes in, 130
  four pillars of, 60
  key attributes of, 45–67
  large-scale ambition in, 58–61
  senior management commitment
    at, 54–58, 60–61
  strategic, distinctive capability at,
    48–51
analytical consulting, 85–87
analytical eras. *See* four eras of
  business analytics
analytical maturity model.
  See DELTA model
analytically impaired organizations,
  65–67
analytical techniques
  additional technical capabilities,
    180–181, 183
  for amateurs, 212–213
  for customer relationship
    management, 134–135
  for internal processes, 92–94
  leaders' knowledge of, 192–193
  for marketing, 134–135
  for supply chain management,
    148–149
Analytics 1.0–4.0. *See* four eras of
  business analytics
analytics
  commitment to, 75–77

definition of, 25–27
definitions of terms in, 26
DELTA model for capability
  building in, 17, 46–47
enterprise-level approach to, 51–54
in government, 81–83 (*see also*
  government)
localized, 65
Analytics at Work (Davenport,
  Harris, and Morison), 17, 46
analytics experts
  machine learning and, 10–11
  skills for, 13–14
analytics hubs, 54
Analytics Maturity Assessment,
  46–47
Apex Systems, 124
Apple, 255
architecture, 217–247
  of analytical technology, 217–224
  analytical tools/applications and,
    236–245
  data management, 222, 224–233
  data repositories, 223, 234–236
  data transformation, 233–234
  deployment processes and, 246
  at Equifax, 244–245
artificial intelligence, 8–11, 118
artisanal analytics, 10, 11–12
Ascential Software, 233
aspirations, 58–61
  analytical, 170–174
  competitive, 65
assumptions in quantitative
  analysis, 34
attribute analysis, 23
autonomous analytics, 8–12, 25, 26,
  251
autonomous decision-making
  applications, 213–214

Bain & Company, 74
Bank of America, 52, 106, 196
Barclays, 56–57, 59, 79
barriers, 88–89
Barton, Richard N., 24
baseball, 37–40, 122, 141, 208
basketball, 41–42
Bayesian inference, 92, 97

Beane, Billy, 37–38
Beech, Roland, 42
behaviors, managing, 181
Belichick, Bill, 41, 123
Bell, David, 145
Beracha, Barry, 55, 192
Betterment, 172
Beyene, Saba, 128
Bezos, Jeff, 33–34, 55, 56, 73,
    193–194, 229
Bierhoff, Oliver, 42
big data, 4–6
    architecture of, 222–223
    definition of, 31
    mainstream use of, 6–7
    origins of, 31
big data analytics, 32
Big Data @ Work (Davenport), 47
"black box" problem in machine
    learning, 10–11
Blink (Gladwell), 33
Blockbuster, 21
Bloomberg Technology, 151
Bock, Laszlo, 125, 126–127
Boger, Joshua, 118
Boston Celtics, 42
Boston Red Sox, 38–39,
    208–209
brand management, 142–143
Bridgewater Associates, 85
Brougher, Bill, 109
business environments, changing,
    99–100
business intelligence, 2–3, 25, 31
business intelligence and advanced
    analytics, 32
business models
    digital industrial, 7
    management skills for, 14–15
    obsolete, 88
BusinessWeek, 24, 83
buy-in, 57–58

Caesars Entertainment, 24
    analytical leadership at, 194
    analytical professionals at, 201
    analytical strategy at, 161–162
    distinctive capabilities at, 29
    enterprise-level approach at, 51

external processes analytics at,
    132–133
market share at, 59
pricing optimization at, 141
sales creation at, 144–145
senior management commitment
    at, 55, 56
strategic, distinctive capability of,
    48
unique strategy of, 79
Cafarella, Mike, 4
campaign management software,
    131–132
Canadian Tire Corporation, 230
capability maturity model, 61
capacity planning, 148
Capital One, 12–13
    amateur analysts in, 208
    ambition at, 58
    analytical decision making at, 34
    analytical leadership at, 194
    creation of, 69–71
    data issues at, 225
    duplication of strategy at, 79
    information-based strategy at, 29
    metrics at, 50–51
    model management at, 255–256
    outperformance of competitors by,
        80
    results at, 59
    senior management commitment
        at, 55
    subprime customers at, 139
    talent management at, 125,
        127–128
Capital One Health Care, 143–144
CareSage, 85
Carnegie Tech, 30–31
Catalina, 86
Caterpillar, 116–117
cement business, 29, 152–153
CEMEX, 29, 152–153
CHAID (chi-square automatic
    interaction detection), 134
change management, 115
Chicago Cubs, 39–40, 194
Chico, 177
chief analytics officers, 53–54
chief data and analytics officers
    (CDAOs), 53–54, 198–199

chief data officers (CDOs), 53–54
chief financial officers (CFOs),
    94–95, 194–196
chief information officers (CIOs),
    196–198
Cinematch, 22
Cisco Systems, 12, 96, 257
city planning, 83
Clark, Ben, 73
clickstream data, 4–6
Climate Pro, 7
clinical trial design, 119
closed loops of analytics, 142–143
cloud, the, 9, 35–36, 242–243
Coalition Against Insurance Fraud,
    103–104
cognitive technologies, 8–11,
    236–237, 240
collaborative filtering analytics,
    150–151
Collins, Jim, 73
combinatorial optimization, 92–93
combinatorics, 148
company value, 99
competitive advantage
    analytics as, 78–80
    internal processes in, 91–92
complacency, 176
CompStat, 81
computer-aided design (CAD),
    108–109, 241
configuration problem, 110–111
conflicts of interest, 96–97
conjoint analysis, 134
constraint analysis, 93
consulting, analytical, 85–87
content personalization, 146–147
cost management, 100–103
credit card industry, 69–70, 103–104
credit scores, 49–51
Credit Suisse, 98
crime statistics analysis, 81–82, 83,
    163
cross-selling, 137
Cuban, Mark, 43
culture
    in Analytics 1.0, 3
    in Analytics 2.0, 6
    in Analytics 4.0, 10–11
    changing, 14–15, 55–56

data-driven, 262–263
of data scientists, 204–205
executive commitment to, 55–56
executives in changing, 190–192,
    196–198
at Marriott, 71–72
at Netflix, 23–24
wars, 174–175
customer experience life cycle model,
    79
customer loyalty, 59
customer relationship management,
    99, 129–147
analytical techniques in, 134–135
attracting/retaining customers,
    133–139
brand management and, 142–143
connecting suppliers with
    customers and, 147–151
content personalization and,
    146–147
creating sales and, 143–145
life cycle management and, 145
pricing optimization and, 135,
    140–141
Cutting, Doug, 4
cybersecurity, 104–105

dashboards, 99
data
    acquisition of, 232
    capabilities by analytical
        competition stage, 220–221
    cleansing, 232
    in DELTA model, 17, 46–47, 177,
        178
    dirty, 224–225
    getting, cleaning, and loading, 3
    governance, 225, 231–232
    increasing amounts of, 34–35
    labeled training, 255
    maintenance of, 232–233
    management, 27
    organization and storage, 232
    pervasive, 250–251
    quality, 225, 230–231
    quantities, 225, 229–230
    relevance of, 225–227
    sourcing, 225, 227–229

structuring, 13
transformation, 233–234
value extraction from, 1–2,
    230–231
data analytics
    Analytics 1.0, 2–4
    Analytics 2.0, 4–6
    Analytics 3.0, 6–7
    Analytics 4.0, 8–12
    eras in, 1–17
    organizational implications of, 12–15
    pace of change in, 1
    skills for, 13–14
data cubes, 235
data lakes, 233, 236, 244
data literacy, 211
data management, 33, 222, 224–233
data marts, 31, 235
data mining, 31, 240
data products, 5
data repositories, 223, 234–236
DataRobot, 9
data scientists, 5
    culture and attitude of, 204–205
    education of, 6
    experimentation skills for, 13
    future of, 256–259
    job requirements for, 204
    managing, 200–208
"Data Scientist: The Sexiest Job of
    the 21st Century" (Davenport
    and Patil), 5
data visualization, 239–242
data warehousing, 31, 229–230,
    234–235
Davenport, Thomas H., 5, 17, 46, 259
decision making
    analytical, 33–36
    in analytical competition, 28
    automating without monitoring, 186
    autonomous, 213–214, 251
    designing into processes, 163
    enterprise systems and, 75
    fact-based, 33
    at Netflix, 23–24
    override issue in, 214–216
    performance and, 73–74
decision support, 91
    in Analytics 1.0, 3
    in Analytics 2.0, 5

in Analytics 3.0, 6–7
    external reporting/scorecards and,
        96–98
decision support systems (DSS),
    30–31
deep learning, 8, 14
Deere & Company, 59
Dell, 97–98, 110
Deloitte, 49, 85, 105, 195, 208, 261
DELTA model, 17, 46–47, 177–183
DELTTA model, 47
demand-supply matching, 148
de Molina, Al, 196
Department of Veterans Affairs, 83
deployment processes, 223, 246
descriptive analytics, 25
    in Analytics 1.0, 2–3
    definition of, 26
    external reporting/scorecards and,
        96–98
    localized analytics and, 65
    tools, 243
    See also business intelligence
Dhore, Prasanna, 244
diapers and beer urban legend,
    187–188
Dibble, Bill, 104
differentiation, 27–28
digital analytics, 242
digital industrial business model, 7
Disney's Parks and Resorts, 142–143
Disraeli, Benjamin, 186
distinctive capabilities
    of analytical competitors, 45, 48–51
    in analytics, 28–29
    based on analytics, 21–44
    competitive advantage and, 78–80
DnB NOR, 137
Dodd-Frank Act, 223
Domain Awareness System, 81–82
Dow Chemical, 159
Drucker, Peter, 260–261
Dunnhumby, 86, 138
dynamic pricing, 140

Earthgrains, 192
eBay, 122
econometric analysis, 133, 136–137
econometric modeling, 134, 142

edge analytics, 228
Einstein, 9
E. & J. Gallo, 30, 60–61, 194
embedded analytics, 77, 260
employee experience life cycle model, 79
employee learning and innovation, 99
employees
 core skills for, 210–211
 culture wars between, 174–175
 human resource analytics and, 122–128
 managing analytical, 187–216
 override issue and, 214–216
energy cost management, 101–103
Entelos, Inc., 120
enterprise-level approach, 17, 46–47, 51–54, 177, 178
 amateur analysts and, 208–216
 to data sourcing, 227–229
enterprise performance management, 98–100
enterprise resource planning (ERP) systems, 30, 31
enterprise systems
 analytical tools in, 237
 as data source, 227
 decision making and, 75
Epstein, Theo, 38, 40
Equifax, 244–245
eras, analytics. *See* four eras of business analytics
Eskew, Mike, 152
ESPN, 40
Evalueserve, 208
event streaming, 241
event triggers, 137–138, 253
Everest Group, 96–97
executives
 analytical, characteristics of, 192–193
 CFOs, 94–95, 194–196
 commitment of, 54–58, 60–61, 176, 199–200
 in culture change, 14–15, 55–56
 fact-based decision making and, 160
 in full-steam-ahead approach, 164–165

 managing analytical people and, 190–200
 passion for analytics in, 55–56
 roles of, 194–199
 sponsorship by, 36
executive support systems, 31
experimental design, 93
experimentation, 73
 external processes and, 130
 at Google, 109
 in marketing, 134
 skills in, 13
 worker skills in, 210
explanatory analytics, 253
external processes, 129–153
 customer-based, 133–147
 supply-based, 147–153
extract, transform, and load (ETL), 3, 233–234
eye tracking, 109

Facebook, 5, 6, 9
Fairbank, Rich, 55, 56, 69–70
fashion industry, 29
Fast Company, 73
FedEx, 152
FICO Corporation, 35, 246
FICO scores, 49–51, 80
Field of Dreams approach, 185
financial analytics, 94–105
 cost management, 100–103
 enterprise performance management/scorecards, 98–100
 external reporting, 96–98
 risk management, 103–105
financial results, 184–185
financial services
 analytical products/services in, 85
 Analytics Maturity Assessment of, 47
 credit cards, 69–70
 metrics development in, 49–51
 risk management in, 103–105
 senior management commitment in, 56–57
 wealth management, 171–174
Fincher, David, 23
Firewire Surfboards, 108, 110
First Analytics, 112–113

fivethirtyeight.com, 39, 40–41
Fleet Bank, 106
flexibility, 12–13, 58, 79
focus, choosing strategic, 162
football, 41, 61, 122–123
four eras of business analytics, 1–15
　　Analytics 1.0, 2–4
　　Analytics 2.0, 4–6
　　Analytics 3.0, 6–7
　　Analytics 4.0, 8–12
four pillars of analytical competition,
　　60
Ford, 110–111
Foxwoods Resort Casino, 79
Franks, Bill, 6
fraud
　　financial services, 103–105
　　tax, 82, 83
　　welfare, 82
Friedman, Frank, 195
full-steam-ahead approach, 164–165
funding of analytical groups, 206
future-value analysis, 93

Gallo, Joe, 60–61, 194
Garga, Sunil, 86–87
Garmin TruSwing, 87
Gartner, 32, 258
GE, 7, 84–85
　　data management at, 225
　　differentiation at, 29
GE Capital, 208
General Motors, 110–111
genetic algorithms, 93
Gennact, 208
Gibson, William, 249
Gillette, 34, 106
Gladwell, Malcolm, 33
Golden State Warriors, 41–42
golf club sensors, 87, 260
Good to Great (Collins), 73
Google, 5
　　analytical leadership at, 194
　　Analytics, 84, 87
　　analytics-based competition at,
　　　24–25
　　artificial intelligence software, 262
　　digital advertising at, 133,
　　　136–137

experimentation at, 109
experiments at, 73
human resource management at,
　　43
human resources analytics, 122
machine cognition at, 9
PageRank algorithm, 5
People and Innovation Lab
　　(PiLab), 126
Project Oxygen, 126
talent management at, 125–127,
　　202, 210
governance, 206, 225, 231–232
government
　　analytics in, 81–83
　　as data source, 228
　　Internal Revenue Service (IRS)
　　　programs, 82
　　New York City's CompStat
　　　program, 81
　　Singapore's "Smart Nation"
　　　program, 83
　　UK police analytics insights, 163
graphics processing units (GPUs), 9
Green Bay Packers, 41
Griffiths, Hugh, 146
Grove, Jonathan, 103

H2O, 13
Hadoop, 4, 229, 235, 244
Harrah's Entertainment. See
　　Caesars
Harris, Jeanne G., 17, 46
Hastings, Reed, 21, 22, 24, 55, 56
health care, 82–83
　　cost management, 101
　　insurance and credit scores in, 50
　　research and development
　　　analytics, 120–121
Healthways, 121
Henry, John, 38
Hewlett-Packard, 97
Hive, 4
Holland, Chuck, 57
HOLT, 98
Honda, 111–112
Houghton Mifflin Harcourt, 144
House of Cards, 23
Houston Rockets, 42, 43

Hoyer, Jed, 38, 40
human element in analytics, 36, 43–44
  change driven by, 256–259
  urban legends on, 187–190
  See also data scientists;
    quantitative analysts
human resource information systems
    (HRIS), 122
human resources analytics, 122–128
human resources management,
    187–216
  of analytical amateurs, 208–216
  of analytical professionals and
    data scientists, 200–208
  executives' roles in, 194–199
  in sports, 40–43
  urban legends about, 187–190
Hunt, Neil, 23–24

IBM, 208
  analytical tools, 35
  Cognos, 239
  Global Services, 85
  merger and acquisition algorithms,
    34, 106
  on performance and analytics use,
    77
  SPSS, 31
  Watson, 9
image mining, 254–255
ImageNet, 8, 255
industrial internet, 84–85
Infinity Property & Casualty, 104
Informatica Corporation, 233, 234, 236
information distribution, 221
information management, 27, 206
information orientation, 198
Information Resources Inc., 86–87,
    131
information technology
  in architecture of analytical
    technology, 218–224
  cybersecurity in, 104–105
  industry, 97
  signposts of effective, 222–223
  vision for, 171
InformationWeek, 70–71, 253
information workers, core skills for,
    210–211

initiatives, evaluating, 184
in-memory processing, 252
innovation, 117–121
in silico research, 120
insurance fraud, 103–104
integer programming, 92–93
Intel, 95
Intermountain Healthcare, 121
internal processes, 91–128.
  analytical techniques for, 92–94
  financial analytics, 94–105
  human resources analytics,
    122–128
  operational analytics, 106–117
  mergers and acquisition analytics,
    105
  research and development
    analytics, 117–121
  See also processes
Internal Revenue Service (IRS), 82
  National Research Program, 82
  Taxpayer Compliance
    Measurement Program, 82
International Data Corporation
    (IDC), 74, 217, 237
International Institute for Analytics,
    6, 46–47, 63
Internet of Things, 15, 34–35, 228,
    250–251
Intuit, 73
intuitive decision making, 29–30
  evidence on, 33
  executive commitment and,
    199–200
  on pricing, 140
inventory optimization, 59
Irish Tax and Customs Authority, 83
Ittner, Chris, 99

Jagex Games Studio, 146
James, Bill, 38–39, 42
James, Brent, 121
JetBlue, 88
Johnson & Johnson, 120

kaizen, 131
Keen, Peter, 30
Kheradpir, Shaygan, 196–197

Kirby, Julia, 259
Kizer, Kenneth W., 83
Klein, Gary, 33
Knight, Phil, 190–191
knowledge discovery, 31
Komatsu, Shigeru, 112
Korn Ferry, 49
Kraft, Bob, 61, 194
Kraft, Jonathan, 56, 61, 194
Kroger, 59, 86, 139

Lane, Katrina, 201
Larcker, David, 99
law enforcement analytics.
    See government
leadership, 177, 178–179
    analytical, characteristics of,
        192–193
    in building analytics capability, 17,
        46–47
    in DELTA model, 17, 46–47, 166,
        178–179
    emergence of analytical, 193–194
    See also executives
Leahy, Terry, 138, 139
Lever Brothers, 136
Leverhulme, Lord, 136
Levis, Jack, 57–58, 114–116
Lewis, Michael, 37, 80, 122
Lewis, Peter, 229
Liberson, Dennis, 127
lifetime value analysis, 134
LinkedIn, 5
Little, Grady, 39
localized analytics, 65
location analysis, 148
Lofgren, Chris, 56
logistics analytics, 114–117
logistics management, 151–153
Loop AI Labs, 9
Loveman, Gary, 51, 55, 56, 141, 194
loyalty programs, 72, 86, 138–139

machine learning, 8–11, 14, 240
    banking industry, 70–71
    models for, 10–11
Macy's, 140–141
management

alerts, 253
in analytical competition
    development, 36
by analytical competitors, 45
of analytical people, 187–216,
    258–259
commitment of senior, 54–58
enterprise-level approach to
    analytics and, 51–54
fact-based, 25
managing for outcomes and,
    181–185
of models, 255–256
skills across analytics eras,
    13–15
management consulting, 49
manufacturing analytics, 106–111
market experiments, 134
marketing
analytical techniques in,
    134–135
brand management and,
    142–143
price optimization and, 135,
    140–141
real-time, 132–133
market share, 59
Marriott, J. Willard, 71
Marriott International, 71–72, 197
data sharing at, 260
distinctive capability at, 51
overrides in, 214–215
strategic, distinctive capability at,
    48
Mars, 25
Massachusetts Institute of
    Technology (MIT), 77, 70
Maynard, Peter, 244, 245
McDonald, Robert, 83, 194, 197,
    211
McKinsey Solutions, 49
McNamara, Robert, 81
Medicaid, 82–83
Medicare, 82–83
MediSpend, 97
Meng, Xiao-Li, 192–193
mergers and acquisitions, 34
    analytics on, 105–106
meritocracy, 193
metadata repositories, 235

metrics, 261
  on analytical activity results,
    58–59
  exploitation and exploration of,
    49–51
  at Marriott, 71
  monitoring strategic, 163
  staffing, 125
Microsoft, 5
  analytical capabilities in software
    by, 35, 251
  crime statics analysis, 81–82
  energy cost management,
    101–103
  machine cognition at, 9
Milan Lab, 42
mining, 35
MIT Sloan Management Review, 77
MIT Sloan Sports Analytics
    Conference, 41, 42
MMIS, Inc., 35
mobile devices, 35, 132–133
Model Factory, 11–12
modeling
  predictive, 33, 110–111
  propensity, 11–12
  supply chains, 148–149
  uplift, 135
model management, 255–256
Modern Analytics, 11–12
Modular Category Assortment
    Planning System, 148
Moneyball (Lewis), 37, 80, 122
Monsanto, 7
Monte Carlo simulation, 93
Moore's Law, 8
Morey, Daryl, 42, 43
Morison, Robert F., 17, 46
Morris, Nigel, 67, 69–70
multiple regression analysis, 93–94,
    135
Mu Sigma, 208, 257

natural disaster preparedness, 83
natural language processing, 14, 241
needs assessment processes, 52
Netflix, Inc., 21–24
  analytical leadership at, 194
  experiments at, 73

senior management commitment
    at, 55, 56
  strategic, distinctive capability of,
    48, 51
neural networks, 8, 94, 245
New England Patriots, 41, 61,
    122–123, 194
NewVantage Partners, 14, 262–263
New York Police Department, 81–82
Nike, 190–191
Nucleus Research, 237
numeracy, 210–211

O2, 146
Oakland A's, 24, 37–38, 49
Oberhelman, Doug, 116
offshoring, 86, 208, 257–258
oil exploration, 35
OLAP (online analytical processing),
    31, 238–239
On Assignment, 125
open-source technologies
    analyst skills in, 13
    analytical tools, 35, 237
    for big data processing, 4–5
    distributed data frameworks,
      235–236
    machine learning, 9
    for machine learning, 9–11
    statistical programming, 26–27
operational analytics, 6, 106–117
    logistics, 114–117
    manufacturing, 106–111
    quality, 111–112
    safety, 112–114
operations, 99
Optum, 7
Oracle, 35
ORION. *See* UPS ORION project
Ormanidou, Elpida, 177
outcomes, managing for, 181–185
outsourcing, 86, 208, 257–258
override issues, 214–216
Owens & Minor, 51

Partners HealthCare, 215
Passerini, Filippo, 197
passion, 192

Patil, D. J., 5, 201
Perez, William, 191
performance, 67, 69–89
  analytics as competitive advantage
    and, 78–80
  commitment to analytics and,
    75–77
  drivers, improving, 162–163
  evidence assessment and, 73–78
  external reporting/scorecards and,
    96–98
  managing for outcomes and,
    181–185
  market for analytical products/
    services and, 84–87
  monitoring, 31
  predictions on, 97–98
  See also metrics
performance reporting. See
    descriptive analytics
personalization, 146–147
pharmaceutical industry, 80,
    118–120
Philips, 85
pickstreams, 35
Pig, 4
Pioli, Scott, 123
Planck, Max, 15
Podium Data, 236
point-of-sale (POS) systems, 30, 31
politics, 207
predictive analytics, 25, 254
  in Analytics 1.0, 2
  in customer life cycle management,
    145
  definition of, 26
  at Netflix, 22–23
  performance and embedded, 77,
    260
predictive lead scoring systems,
    143–144
predictive modeling, 33, 130
prescriptive analytics, 25, 254
  in Analytics 1.0, 2
  definition of, 26
Price, Mark, 108
Price, Paul, 106
price management and profit
    optimization (PMPO) solutions,
    140

price optimization, 135, 140–141
pricing trend analysis, 130
priorities, 177, 185
  technology investments and, 219
privacy, customer, 137–138
processes
  analytics integration in, 6
  deployment, 223, 246
  external, 129–153
  internal, 91–128
  managing for outcomes, 183
Procter & Gamble, 25, 34, 211
  analytical leadership at, 194
  data scientists at, 202
  experiments at, 73
  external processes analytics at,
    131
  mergers and acquisitions, 34, 106
  metrics at, 59
  outsourcing at, 258
  reporting relationships at, 197
productivity, 122
products
  constraint analysis for, 93
  development of, 5, 6–7
  extensions of existing, 117–118
  incorporating analytics in, 87
  managing for outcomes, 183–184
  research and development
    analytics, 117–121
Profit InSight, 107–108
programs, managing for outcomes,
    183
Progressive Insurance, 50–51, 72,
    80, 139, 219
  Snapshot, 229
propensity modeling, 11, 12
prove-it detour, 165–170
Python, 4

QlikView, 239, 243
quality analytics, 24, 106–107,
    111–112
quantitative algorithms, 239
quantitative analysis, 33
  assumptions in, 34
  at Netflix, 24
quantitative analysts, 5, 13–14
Quill, 98

R (programming language), 4, 237
radio frequency identification (RFID)
   sensors, 34–35
RapidMiner, 237
RBC Financial Group, 52
real-time analytics, 252–253
Recorded Future, 261
regulated industries, 80, 221–222
  external reporting in, 96–98
Reinhardt, Anders, 210–211
relational databases, 238–239
Renaissance Technologies, 85
renewable advantage, 80
Renwick, Glenn, 219
reporting, 96–98, 221–222
research and development (R&D)
  analytics, 117–121
resources
  allocation of, 163
  commitment of, 165
  nonfinancial/intangible, 99
retention agents, 145
return on investment (ROI), 74
revenue management, 71, 135
revenue opportunity, 71
revenue optimization, 82
Ricketts, Tom, 40, 194
right-time analytics, 252–253
risk management, 103–105, 121
Rocky Mountain Steel Mills,
   107–108, 110
Roland Rating, 42
routing, 149
Royal Bank of Canada, 52
rule engines, 239
RuneScape, 146
Ruthven, Graham, 42

sabermetrics, 38–39
safety analytics, 112–114
sales, converting customer
   interactions into, 143–145
Salesforce.com, 9, 35, 143, 251, 254
sales trend analysis, 130
San Antonio Spurs, 41–42
San Diego Padres, 38
San Francisco Giants, 141
SAP, 35, 239
Sara Lee Bakery Group, 55

Sarbanes-Oxley Act of 2002, 221–222
SAS Institute, 9, 31, 35, 242–243,
   245
  Enterprise Miner, 245
  High-Performance Analytics, 244
scenario planning, 142–143
scheduling, 149
Schmidt, Steve, 119–120, 243
Schneider National, 54, 56, 113, 197
scientific retailing, 140
scorecards, 98–100, 261
search engine optimization, 135
self-service analytics, 2–3
services, managing for outcomes,
   183–184
shareholders, external reporting to,
   96–98
Signet Bank, 58, 69
Silver, Nate, 39, 40–41
Simchi-Levi, David, 77
Simon, Herbert, 30–31
Simon, Rob, 107–108
simulation, 93, 94
  supply chain, 149
  tools for, 241
Singapore "Smart Nation" initiative,
   83
situational awareness systems, 261
Six Sigma, 106, 131
Skillsoft, 147
skimming the cream off the garbage,
   139
Smart Inventory Management
   System (SIMS), 110–111
Smith, Darrell, 101–102
soccer, 42
social media, 15, 228
social media analytics, 242
software, 223
  analytical, 26–27, 30, 35
  in Analytics 1.0, 3
  in Analytics 4.0, 8
  capability maturity model for, 61
  decision support systems, 30–31
  democratization of analytics,
   251–252
  humans replaced by, 187–190
  for pricing, 140–141
Sorrell, Martin, 136
Southwest, 88

Spacey, Kevin, 23
Spark, 4, 235
speech mining, 254–255
sponsors, 36
    in analytical aspirations stage, 170–174
    in analytical companies, 174
    in full-steam-ahead approach, 164–165
    in prove-it detour, 166
sports, analytics in, 37–43, 122–123
    pricing optimization, 141
    strategic, distinctive capability and, 48
spreadsheets, 3, 212–213, 238
    error rates in, 53
Sprint, 79, 145, 158
SPSS, 31
Stabell, Charles, 30
staffing metrics, 125
Stanley, Tim, 132
statistical algorithms, 239
statistical analysis, 33
Strata + Hadoop World conference, 146
strategy, 7
    analytical competitors and, 45
    change driven by, 259–261
    choosing focus or target in, 162
    cost management and, 100–103
    distinctive capabilities in, 48–51
    internal processes and, 91–92
    management skills for, 14–15
suppliers, sharing data with, 132–133
supply chain management, 129–133, 147–153
    analytical techniques in, 148–149
    connecting customers and suppliers in, 147–151
    logistics analytics in, 116–117
    logistics management in, 151–153
    optimization in, 6
support vector machine, 135
sustainable pipelines, 205–206
systems, analytics integration in, 6

Tableau, 239, 243
Talend, 233
talent management, 125–126
Tamr, 234

Target, 137–138
targets, 17, 46–47, 178, 179
    choosing strategic, 162
tax fraud, 82, 83
Taylor, David, 211
Tesco, 86, 138–139
Tesla, 118
"test and learn" approach, 23–24
text categorization, 241
text mining, 240, 254–255
textual analysis, 94
Thomas, Charles, 54
Thompson, Mike, 112
threat signatures, 104–105
time series experiments, 135
tools and technology, 236–245
    for analytical amateurs, 212–213
    for analytical competition, 32, 34–36
    in Analytics 1.0, 2–3
    in Analytics 2.0, 4–5
    architecture of, 217–224
    change driven by, 250–256
    in DELTTA model, 180
    machine learning, 8–11
    market for analytical, 84–87
    performance and spending on, 77
    returns from investments in, 74–75
    for self-service analytics, 2–3
    in sports data, 43
    visual analytics, 243
Toshiba Semiconductor Company, 111–112
Total Quality Management, 106
transaction data, 29
transformation tools, 222
transportation safety analytics, 112–113
Trifacta, 234
Trillium, 233
Troutwine Athletic Profile, 123
TrueCar, Inc., 236
trust, 203–204
Two Sigma, 85

uniqueness, 79
United Healthcare, 7
University of Utah Healthcare, 101
uplift modeling, 135

UPS ORION project, 7
  change management in, 13
  logistics analytics in, 114–116,
    151–152
  real-time analytics in, 252
  savings from, 59
  senior management commitment
    in, 57–58

Value Driven Outcomes (VDO), 101
value drivers, 99
VantageScore, 49–51
Vardi, Nathan, 85
Varian, Hal, 202
VELUX Group, 210–211
Verizon, 196–197
Verizon Wireless, 85
Vertex Pharmaceuticals, 65,
  118–120, 243
Veterans Affairs (VA) hospitals, 83
Visa, 47, 103
vision, 171
visual analytics approach, 112, 223,
  243

Walmart, 51
  human resources analytics, 122
  pricing, 140

strategic, distinctive capability of,
  48
supply chain management at,
  147–149, 260
talent management at, 125, 128
Wanamaker, John, 133, 136
Wayman, Bob, 97
Wealthfront, 172
wealth management, 171–174
web analytics, 242
welfare fraud detection, 82
Wells Fargo, 54, 205
Werner, Tom, 38
wine business, 30, 60–61
WPP plc, 136
Wynn, Steve, 79

Yahoo!, 9, 229
Yankee Group, 140
yield analysis, 94, 112
yield management, 59, 78, 135
YouTube, 255

Zillow, 5
Zimmer Biomet, 97

ACKNOWLEDGMENTS

SINCE WRITING THE FIRST EDITION OF THIS BOOK A DECADE ago, we've talked with hundreds of smart people about analytics. We view ourselves as synthesizers and organizers of all those great ideas, so our primary debt is to anyone who has shared their experiences with us since 2007.

Some people and organizations stand out, however. Here are those who made a big difference to this book, from Tom's perspective. At SAS, a great supporter of our research over the decade, they include Adele Sweetwood, Mike Bright, Scott van Valkenburgh (who kicked off the first edition by contacting Tom; he's now at Genpact), Randy Guard, Oliver Schabenberger, and many more. At Salesforce.com, Ben Pruden and Keri Brooke supported our research and discussed their approach to analytics with us. At FICO (and previously at Schneider National), Zahir Balaporia has been very helpful and insightful. Jack Levis at UPS was always genial and open about the company's analytics efforts. Gary Loveman provided tons of insight over the years about analytics at Harrah's/Caesars. Guy Peri and his then-colleagues at Procter & Gamble, Andy Walter and Filippo Passerini, gave Tom a lot of access to their pioneering work. Various folks at Deloitte, including Jane Griffin, Paul Roma, Alyssa Pharr, and Kelly Nelson, helped to expose Tom to the firm's extensive analytics work. At First Analytics, Mike Thompson and Rob Stevens faithfully reported to Tom every month on what they were up to. Tom also thanks Jack Phillips and John Ott (who first proposed this new edition) at the International Institute for Analytics, Colin Gounden at Via Science, Andy Palmer at Tamr, Christopher Ahlberg at Recorded Future, and Vikram Mahidhar at RAGE Frameworks for their frequent updates from the worlds of analytics and automation.

Both of us benefited from the fact that Harvard Business Review Press was wonderful the first time around, and even easier to work with the second time. We got considerable help from Hollis Heimbouch (now at Harper Business; she acquired and edited the first version), Melinda Merino (who acquired and edited this version), Julia Kirby (now at Harvard University Press), Walt Frick, Gardiner Morse, and Julie Devoll. Stephani Finks did her usual great job on the cover.

From Jeanne's perspective: I want to begin by thanking Tom Davenport, my longtime friend and coauthor, for first suggesting we write a book together on this topic. I especially want to thank the many executives, from every industry and around the world, who generously shared their experiences and insights. Thanks also to Professor Vijay Mehrotra at the University of San Francisco, who introduced me to many data scientists in Silicon Valley and coauthored our research on the distinctions between data scientists and analysts. Thanks to Jeremy Shapiro, Executive Director, Global Head of Talent Analytics, at Morgan Stanley, who coauthored "Competing on Talent Analytics" with us. A big thank you goes to Joan Powell of Leading Thoughts, for helping us share our message with a broader audience.

I also want to thank my former colleagues at Accenture who shared their enthusiastic support and encouragement along the way. Former CEO Bill Green said he thought the book was a great idea. Many smart, prominent senior executives willingly shared their firsthand experience and expertise working with clients to compete (and win) with analytics. Thanks especially go to our research sponsors for their support and honest feedback: Mike Sutcliff, Group CEO, Accenture Digital; Michael Svilar, Managing Director, Advanced Analytics; Royce Bell, former CEO of Accenture Information Management Solutions; and Dave Rich, formerly Global Managing Partner of Accenture Analytics (and later, CEO and president of Microsoft Advanced Analytics). Thank you also to the initial sponsors of the enterprise systems and analytics survey, where we first found a link between analytics and high-performance organizations: Dave Hill, Patrick Puechbroussou, Jim Hayes, and Mark Jones.

In addition to contributing their insights, many current and former Accenture executives helped me find some outstanding examples to showcase in the book, including Walt Shill, Brian McCarthy, Mark McDonald, Jeff Merrihue, Umesh Hari, Jane Linder, John Copeland, Glenn Gutwillig, Michael Bova, Ramin Mikhali, David Sheehy, Baiju

Shah, Andy Fano, Larry Lerner, Chris DiGiorgio, and John Ballow. Thanks also to the executives at Silicon Valley Data Science, including Sanjay Mathur (CEO), John Akred (CTO), and Scott Kurth (VP, Advisory Services), who always generously share their experiences and ideas. Kristi Kamykowski's insights are much appreciated. I am, as always, grateful to my friends at the Accenture Institute for High Performance (including Allan Alter, Dave Light, Bob Thomas, and Paul Nunes) for their generous assistance and willingness to contribute great ideas. Finally, I want to express special thanks to Pete Bott, Joel Friedman, Norm Rickeman, and Jean Davis, who many years ago set me on the path that eventually led to writing this book.

We'd also like to thank our families for their patience in dealing with us during the writing of this version. Jeanne especially thanks her husband, Carl, and her daughter, Lauren, for their love, encouragement, wit, and wisdom. They are the real analytical talent in her family. She could not have completed this book (twice!) without their understanding and support. She also thanks her mother, Rhoda Harris, and her sister, Susie, for their unwavering encouragement and enthusiasm. Tom thanks Jodi for predicting that the analytics topic would be a hot one back in 2005 (she still thinks it's hot) and for once again enthusiastically supporting his every venture. He's analyzed all his personal data and discovered that his wife's presence is highly correlated with his happiness. He thanks his sons Hayes and Chase for passionate discussions about sports analytics, particularly at the Red Sox, Celtics, and Patriots.

THOMAS H. DAVENPORT is the President's Distinguished Professor of IT and Management at Babson College and a research fellow at the MIT Initiative on the Digital Economy. He is also cofounder of the International Institute for Analytics and a senior adviser to Deloitte Analytics. Davenport has authored, coauthored, or edited nineteen books, including five on analytics and cognitive technology. His 2006 article "Competing on Analytics" was named one of the ten "must read" articles in *Harvard Business Review*'s ninety-year history. He has been named one of the top 25 consultants in the world by *Consulting* magazine, one of the 100 most influential people in the IT industry by Ziff Davis Publications, and one of the top 50 business school professors in the world by *Fortune* magazine.

JEANNE G. HARRIS is on the faculty at Columbia University, where she teaches Business Analytics Management. She is the coauthor of two books and over one hundred articles on analytics and information technology. Harris is executive research fellow emerita and was the global Managing Director of Information Technology and Analytics Research at the Accenture Institute for High Performance in Chicago. During her career at Accenture, she led various consulting practices, including business intelligence, analytics, and data warehousing. She also serves on the INFORMS Analytics Certification Board, which oversees the Certified Analytics Professional (CAP™) program. In 2009, she received *Consulting* magazine's Women Leaders in Consulting award for Lifetime Achievement.